T0259735

Database Development

FOR

DUMMIES®

Database Development FOR DUMMIES®

by Allen G. Taylor

Wiley Publishing, Inc.

Database Development For Dummies®

Published by
Wiley Publishing, Inc.
111 River Street
Hoboken, NJ 07030
www.wiley.com

Copyright © 2001 Wiley Publishing, Inc., Indianapolis, Indiana

Published simultaneously in Canada

For general information on our other products and services or to obtain technical support, please contact our Customer Care Department within the U.S. at 800-762-2974, outside the U.S. at 317-572-3993, or fax 317-572-4002.

Wiley also publishes its books in a variety of electronic formats. Some content that appears in print may not be available in electronic books.

Library of Congress Cataloging-in-Publication Data:

Library of Congress Control Number: 00-103400

ISBN: 0-7645-0752-4

10 9 8 7 6 5 4

10/TQ/RS/QV/IN

About the Author

Allen G. Taylor is a 28-year veteran of the computer industry and the author of 17 computer-related books, including *SQL For Dummies*. In addition to writing, he is a database consultant and seminar leader in database design and application development. Allen lives with his family on a small farm outside of Oregon City, Oregon. You can contact Allen at agt@transport.com.

Dedication

This book is dedicated to my wife, Joyce C. Taylor, who continues to encourage me, even though she believes I spend too much time staring into a computer monitor.

Acknowledgments

I have received help from many quarters in this book. I am especially indebted to Keith Taylor, Heath Schweitzer, Joshua McKinney, Sue Preston, and Ernest Argetsinger.

Thanks to my editor, John Pont, and all the folks at Wiley Publishing who helped make this book possible, including Debra Williams Cauley, Kristy Nash, Nancee Reeves, Angie Hunckler, and Constance Carlisle.

Thanks once again to my agent, Matt Wagner of Waterside Productions, who continues to help me advance my writing career.

Thanks to Patrick J. McGovern, who built a structure that gave me my first trip to China as well as the opportunity to write this book.

Thanks to Joyce, Jenny, Valerie, Melody, Neil, Rob, and Sam for sacrificing some of their time with me so that I could write.

Publisher's Acknowledgments

We're proud of this book; please send us your comments through our online registration form located at www.dummies.com/register/.

Some of the people who helped bring this book to market include the following:

Acquisitions, Editorial, and Media Development

Project Editor: John W. Pont

Acquisitions Editor: Debra Williams Cauley

Proof Editor: Teresa Artman

Technical Editor: Ernest Argetsinger

Editorial Manager: Constance Carlisle

Editorial Assistant: Sarah Shupert, Candace Nicholson, Amanda Foxworth

Production

Project Coordinator: Nancee Reeves

Layout and Graphics: Amy Adrian, Karl Brandt, John Greenough, LeAndra Johnson, Jill Piscitelli, Heather Pope, Brian Torwelle

Proofreaders: John Bitter, Nancy Price, Marianne Santy, York Production Services, Inc.

Indexer: York Production Services, Inc.

Publishing and Editorial for Technology Dummies
   Richard Swadley, Vice President and Executive Group Publisher
   Andy Cummings, Vice President and Publisher
   Mary C. Corder, Editorial Director

Publishing for Consumer Dummies
   Diane Graves Steele, Vice President and Publisher
   Joyce Pepple, Acquisitions Director

Composition Services
   Gerry Fahey, Vice President of Production Services
   Debbie Stailey, Director of Composition Services

◆

The publisher would like to give special thanks to Patrick J. McGovern, without whom this book would not have been possible.

◆

Contents at a Glance

Cartoons at a Glance

By Rich Tennant

page 103

page 39

page 281

page 7

page 229

page 159

page 257

Fax: 978-546-7747
E-mail: richtennant@the5thwave.com
World Wide Web: www.the5thwave.com

Table of Contents

Introduction

*B*ecause you are reading this, I assume that you have recently become interested in database. Perhaps you would like to impress your friends by casually tossing out some big words that they have never heard before — words such as semantic object model, denormalization, or maybe even tuple. Perhaps your boss at work has just informed you that your department will be computerizing its records and that you have been assigned to build the database. Whatever your motivation, this book will get you started down the path to becoming a true database guru. When you reach that exalted level, impressing your friends with big words will pale in significance compared to what you will be able to do with your organization's most important information.

Ever since computers became powerful enough to support them, databases have been at the core of both commercial and scientific data processing. The domain of database processing includes any problem or task that must deal with large amounts of data. Most database systems in existence today, and practically all new systems being implemented, make use of relational database technology, the subject of this book.

About This Book

This book takes you step by step through the conceptualization, design, development, and maintenance of relational database systems. It gives you a solid grounding in database theory and then shows how to reduce that theory to practice using two of the more popular database management systems in use today: Microsoft Access and Microsoft SQL Server. Major topics covered include

- ✔ Understanding database architecture and how it has evolved
- ✔ Recognizing how database technology affects everyday life
- ✔ Using a structured approach to database development
- ✔ Creating an appropriate data model
- ✔ Creating a reliable relational design
- ✔ Implementing a relational design
- ✔ Keeping a database secure
- ✔ Putting your database on the Internet

My objective with this book is to give you the information you need to build a robust database system that will do what you want it to do. When designed correctly, a database system will give you the performance, flexibility, and reliability to meet your needs, both now and in the future.

Who Should Read This Book?

Anyone tasked with the development of a software system that incorporates a database element, or anyone managing the people who do such development, should read this book. Any person in any organization that uses database technology (that should be just about anybody who works anywhere) can benefit from understanding the concepts I explain in this book.

Databases have penetrated every nook and cranny of our highly connected, information-intensive society. The more you understand about how they function and the differences between well-designed and poorly designed databases, the better you will be able to decide the best way to use your organization's database resources.

Foolish Assumptions

In order to write this book, I had to make some assumptions about who would be reading it and what their level of expertise would be. Based on feedback I have received from readers of *SQL For Dummies*, I know that accurately targeting readership is incredibly difficult. I expect that some readers will be gaining their first exposure to databases, while others will be professional database developers. I have tried to make the book understandable to the first group, while at the same time making it a useful guide to the second group.

How This Book Is Organized

This book contains seven major parts. Each part consists of several chapters. It makes sense to read the book from beginning to end because later material builds on an understanding of what has gone before. You may decide to skip either the Access chapter or the SQL Server chapter if they do not apply to you. However, the implementation details that I describe in those chapters will be similar to what you will encounter in other development environments, and thus will probably be valuable to you anyway.

Part I — Basic Concepts

Part I establishes the context for the rest of the book. It describes the position of data and databases in the world today and then describes how to systematically design and develop a database system incorporating a database and one or more applications that operate on that database. This part also describes challenges that often arise in the course of a database development project, and how you can best address them.

Part II — Data Modeling: What Should the Database Represent?

In any database development project, you must address a few key questions — for example: What exactly should the database represent, and to what level of detail? Answers to these questions come from finding out who will use the proposed system and how they will use it. Finding out the needs and expectations of the users, and then transforming those needs and expectations into a formal, structured data model forms the core of Part II. Getting this part right is absolutely critical to the successful completion of a development project.

Part III — Database Design

After you have a model of the proposed system that is satisfactory to everyone concerned, you need to convert that model into a database design. In order for your design to be reliable as well as functional, you need to decide how best to transform complex relationships among data items into simpler relationships that are not subject to the data corruption problems that often accompany complexity. Part III highlights the complexities you are likely to encounter, and in each case describes how best to transform them into a simpler form that eliminates the problems.

Part IV — Implementing a Database

Part IV starts with a database design, developed using the techniques that I explain in Part III, and shows step by step how to convert that design into a database using some of the more popular database development tools available today. First, I cover the process using Microsoft Access 2000. Then, I show you how to implement the same design using the SQL Server 2000 DBMS. Finally, I explain how to implement the design using straight SQL code, without the help of any fancy development tools. I clearly delineate the strengths and weaknesses of each approach as I describe each method.

Part V — Implementing a Database Application

The *application* is the part of a database system that the users see and interact with. It is the application that answers whatever questions the users pose to the database.

The implementation of a database application can differ greatly from one development environment to another. On the one hand, Access gives developers an integrated forms wizard and report writer and the ability to create a complete application without writing a single line of procedural code. On the other, a developer can write a database application using only procedural code with embedded SQL statements, without the aid of a DBMS such as Access. SQL Server falls somewhere in the middle. You can use external forms generator and report writer packages along with procedural code to operate on an SQL Server database. You can also employ a hybrid approach in which you use some or all of these facilities. The ability to use all these tools gives you the ultimate in flexibility, but also requires the highest level of expertise.

Part VI — Using Internet Technology with Database

Databases are most useful when resident on networks available to multiple people. That usefulness is multiplied when the number of users increases, as it does when the database is accessible over the Internet or a large organizational intranet. In Part VI, I discuss network architectures, the kinds of threats to data integrity that network operation causes, and the particular threats that are peculiar to the Internet. In general, good countermeasures to these threats exist, but developers and database administrators must be aware of the threats so they can apply the countermeasures effectively.

Part VII — The Part of Tens

Part VII distills the messages of the preceding six parts, providing concise summaries of the main things to keep in mind when designing and building systems based on relational database technology. If you keep these principles in mind, you can't go too far wrong.

Conventions Used in This Book

In this book, I use several typographical conventions. I use monofont type for code that appears within a regular paragraph of text — for example, to tell you about an `access denied` error message. I use command arrows (⇨) to present menu commands in the most concise manner possible. For example, if I didn't use command arrows, I would have to give you instructions like this: "In the menu bar, choose File. Then, in the resulting menu, choose Open." With the command arrow, all that verbiage boils down to this: "Choose File⇨Open."

Icons Used in This Book

Throughout the pages of this book, I use these icons to highlight particularly helpful information.

Tips save you time and keep you out of trouble.

You really should pay attention whenever you see this icon. A major danger is described, along with the best way to avoid it.

This material is not absolutely necessary for a good understanding of the concepts being presented, but is often interesting to know.

Generally, the text marked with this icon is material that you will need later. Make a mental note of it.

Where to Go From Here

Enough preliminaries! Dig into the real meat of this book — what databases are and how to build them. Understanding those two things is rapidly becoming a requisite for just about anyone involved in commerce, science, or anything else that involves the storage and processing of data. Start with Chapter 1. It gives you the perspective you need to understand where database technology came from and where it stands today.

Part I
Basic Concepts

The 5th Wave — By Rich Tennant

"DO YOU WANT ME TO CALL THE COMPANY AND HAVE THEM SEND ANOTHER REVIEW COPY OF THEIR DATABASE SOFTWARE SYSTEM, OR DO YOU KNOW WHAT YOU'RE GOING TO WRITE?"

In this part . . .

In Part I, I give you the background information you need in order to build high-quality databases and database applications. I describe the different classes of databases and what makes them different. I also describe the critical role that databases play in our data-saturated world, including the so-called "new economy." I offer a brief history of data processing and the advent of database systems, leading up to coverage of what databases and database applications are, followed by a structured approach to building them. I also describe some of the major pitfalls of database development, and explain how to avoid them.

Chapter 1

Database Processing

In This Chapter

▷ Sorting out the different classes of databases

▷ Discovering what databases can do for you

▷ Understanding database processing

Database processing is one of the more common operations performed on computers today. In fact, only word-processing and spreadsheet packages outrank database management systems among the most popular business tools. Everyone, from the largest corporate entities to private individuals, wants to keep track of something. Applications such as order entry, accounts receivable, accounts payable, and general ledger all incorporate databases. Companies keep track of their customers, product inventories, employees, and capital assets in databases. Businesses, governments, and organizations around the world would grind to a halt without databases.

The Different Classes of Databases

Large international corporations and national governments have substantially different data management needs from those of a private individual or even a small to medium-sized company. Large database users have demanding capacity and performance requirements and are willing to pay what it takes to meet those requirements. That kind of power would be serious overkill for an individual, local non-profit organization, or small business, and would be too expensive anyway. As a result, different database development tools are available for addressing different market segments. Some of these tools, called database management systems (DBMSs), are capable of supporting huge, high-performance databases, but require very powerful (and expensive) mainframe computers to do the job. Other tools run on personal computers, and are limited in the size and performance of databases they are able to support.

Enterprise databases

The first databases, back in the 1960s, although primitive by today's standards, were applied to large, enterprisewide problems, such as airline reservation systems, and maintaining bills of materials for NASA spacecraft. In those days, computers were big, expensive to buy, and expensive to run. Only large corporations or government agencies could afford to own the computers that could support a database. As a result, the first databases were enterprise class databases. The database management systems that were used to create databases were powerful, robust, and resource-hungry.

As computer power has steadily increased and become less expensive, enterprise class databases have become even more powerful and are capable of supporting much larger collections of data. The data on such systems is also accessible to thousands of simultaneous users. Today, large organizations get orders of magnitude larger and faster databases for much lower cost than was true in the early days of database, but costs of such systems are still out of reach for individual users. This is not a big problem, because few individuals need a database system that supports thousands of simultaneous users.

Personal databases

In 1975, the first, primitive personal computer kits arrived on the scene, and in 1976 you could buy one already assembled. (Pretty slick, eh?) These machines were not powerful enough to support even a very cut-down database management system, but performance improved steadily. With the advent of the IBM PC coupled with hard disk storage, database technology started to proliferate on personal computers in 1981.

Personal database products are much simpler than their enterprise class ancestors. For one thing, they have to support only one simultaneous user, rather than thousands. For another, typical single-user applications use much smaller databases than those needed to run an airline reservation system or something similarly huge. Furthermore, because there were soon millions of personal computers compared to a much smaller installed base of mainframe computers, the economies of scale kick in and it is possible to sell personal databases at a *much* lower price than mainframe databases and still make a profit. Development costs are spread over many more units.

Today, personal computers have become so powerful that the DBMS products available on them have much more capacity and much better performance than did the mainframe DBMS products of yesteryear.

The Y2K catastrophe

Remember the big Y2K scare? People were seriously concerned that on the stroke of midnight on December 31, 1999, the world as we knew it would come to an end. Well, maybe not come to an end, but terrible things would surely happen. Airliners would fall out of the sky. Elevators would drop down their shafts and crash into the building basement floor. Car engines would turn off while you were cruising at 60 mph on the freeway. Libraries would send fine money to patrons with overdue books, because the books were returned a hundred years before they were taken out. Who knows? Maybe even Pez® dispensers would cease functioning.

Billions of dollars were spent worldwide to exorcise the Y2K demon. Where did all that money go? Most of it went to modifying database files and the applications that accessed them. Some was spent on new equipment, because the threat of Y2K disaster made it easier for workers to convince management that, to be safe, they needed new Y2K-compliant computers or Pez dispensers.

Workgroup databases

After millions of personal computers had been sold and installed in companies large and small, people came to a fundamental realization. Millions of people, each with their own personal computer, now had far greater ability to do their work faster and with less effort than had been the case before. Productivity had taken a quantum leap forward. However, each one of those personal computers was an isolated island of compute power and data storage. Productivity would be boosted even more if somehow the data and compute power residing on those personal computers could be shared.

Networking connected the personal computers together, and a new class of database — the workgroup database — was invented to take advantage of the new connectivity. Workgroup databases, accessed by perhaps up to 50 or 100 simultaneous users, filled the gap between the enterprise database and the personal database. Today, in small to medium-sized organizations, workgroup databases are the most common of the three database classes.

So Much Data, So Little Time

Ever since electronic computers first came into use in the late 1940s, they have generated data of all types much faster that had ever been possible using adding machines along with paper and pencil. Since then, the power of computers has been increasing at an exponential rate. Moore's Law, named after Intel co-founder Gordon Moore, has held true for decades, stating that the power of computers doubles about every 18 months, as shown in Figure 1-1.

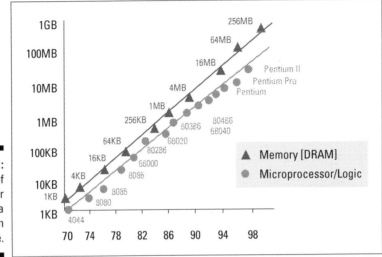

The amount of data that computers are able to process doubles at a comparable rate. As a result, we are being drowned in a veritable sea of data. Much of it is potentially valuable, but the situation has reached the point where data is being gathered so fast that much of it may never be put to use. Raw data has very little value. It gains value when it is organized in such a way that it conveys meaningful information to people who can use that information. Databases are our most powerful tool for organizing data into potentially valuable information.

Databases and privacy: We know who you are, and we know where you live

One of the unanticipated consequences of the tremendous growth in the amount of data that is generated every day is the erosion of personal privacy. A generation ago, as long as you were not a famous or notorious person, nobody knew much of anything about you. Your private life was just that, private. If you wanted to drop out of sight, move somewhere else and start a new life, it was not very difficult to do. Aside from a small number of people in your local community who had lived and worked with you, you were a complete unknown to the world at large. Those days are gone and will never return.

Now it is practically impossible to buy anything, sell anything, or travel anywhere by air, rail, or sea, without the fact being recorded in a database somewhere. Ever since the days of J. Edgar Hoover, the FBI has prided itself in its ability to know the whereabouts of and important facts about individuals it considers important. Nowadays, you don't have to be the FBI or the CIA to have that kind of knowledge about anyone you care to know about. Merchants, airlines, and travel agents have data on your living and buying habits. With the recent rash of mergers of all kinds of organizations into larger entities, this data is becoming centralized. Residing in databases that can be "mined" for useful information, companies can find out not only who you are and where you live, but also what you like to eat, what you like to read, who your favorite musicians and entertainers are. They know what your favorite sports teams are, and what sports you like to participate in yourself. They know where you shop and how often. They know when you are about to run out of something you buy regularly. They know when your kids are born, when they are about to enter kindergarten, when they will graduate from high school, and when they are engaged to be married.

All this data is stored in databases. The databases are growing larger, not only because more data is added to them on a daily basis, but because new kinds of data are being captured and stored, based on the activities and transactions that you participate in, in the course of your daily living. The amount of data being stored in databases every day, based on people's actions and transactions, is already huge, but will get even larger in the coming months and years.

Bottom Line: Although databases are constantly getting larger, even data stored in huge databases can be quickly and easily processed to give users exactly the information they want.

Amazon.com and the online merchants

The rise of e-commerce on the World Wide Web has accelerated the accumulation of data about people. Records are kept of people who visit Web sites, and even more elaborate records are kept about people who actually buy things at Web sites. Many Web sites require users to register before allowing access to their best content. By registering, the user reveals personal information that the site then uses to construct a user profile. The profile enables the site to display personalized content to visitors. For commercial sites, this means users are more likely to become buyers, because they are being presented with advertisements and other content that are tailored to their interests.

Amazon.com, the largest retailer on the Web, has perfected the technique of using databases to characterize its customers. By analyzing the kinds of products you have bought or expressed interest in, in the past, Amazon.com can present you with displays of similar products that you are likely to find interesting. This sales strategy requires not only massive, well structured databases, but also sophisticated data mining software that finds associations and relationships in customers' past behavior that allow predictions of what they are likely to do and want in the future.

Other online merchants are following Amazon's lead and using databases and data mining technology to offer visitors a customized experience. This is good in that people are not presented with content they are not interested in, or advertisements for products that do not interest them. It is potentially bad because merchants will know a lot about people, and that knowledge could be abused.

Bottom Line: Like it or not, unless you are a hermit living in a cave, people you don't know and have no reason to trust know many intimate details about your life. If you use checks or credit cards, your life is an open book. If you buy things from merchants such as Amazon.com on the Web, that book is an international bestseller.

Data deluge: It came from outer space

The United States has been launching rockets into earth orbit since 1958, and ever since, satellites have been radioing high-capacity streams of data back to Earth. Russia, Japan, China, and the European Space Agency do the same thing and are also receiving vast quantities of data from their space probes. All this data is being stored in the hope that someday it will be analyzed and human knowledge will be advanced as a result. The most promising data is analyzed fairly soon after it is received, but the large majority of data returned from space is not examined for years, if ever. The speed with which we collect data far exceeds the speed with which we can analyze it and draw useful conclusions.

In 1994, the Clementine spacecraft orbited the moon for several months, taking data on its entire surface. That data is stored on 88 CD-ROMs, each holding about 640MB, for a total of 56GB of data about the lunar surface. The data is in raw form, cataloged by orbit number. Only a small portion of the data has been examined in detail, particularly data about the areas around the North and South Poles. The spectral signature of water that appears in the data from the polar regions has caused excitement among scientists and advocates of space exploration. However, because the entire dataset is not organized into a database, it is difficult to search for specific features and make generalizations about them.

Another spacecraft, Galileo, has been studying the Jupiter system for several years. It also has sent back huge amounts of data. By studying a small fraction of that data, space scientists have inferred the existence of a global ocean under the ice covering the surface of Jupiter's moon Europa, and the probable existence of a similar ocean under the surface of Callisto. However, the large majority of Galileo's data remains unstudied, because in its unorganized state, it is very difficult to extract useful information from it, unless you already know what you are looking for. Organizing the data into a database would be of tremendous benefit, but NASA has no funding for such a massive effort.

Mars Global Observer, currently orbiting Mars, has returned huge quantities of data to Earth. Some of this, such as dramatic high-resolution photographs of the Martian landscape, has been analyzed and reported upon. Most, however, has merely been archived, against the day when resources will allow it to be studied. In its current raw form, it is practically impossible to discern patterns in the data that might lead to greater understanding.

Bottom Line: It is difficult to wring information from large datasets that are not organized into databases. As a result, much of this data sits in archives, unused. If the storage medium (magnetic tapes or disks, photographic film) is not maintained properly, the data could degrade to the point of being unusable. In that case, all the effort that went into collecting it is lost.

The fierce urgency of now

The data explosion is out of hand and getting worse every day. The only hope for making sense out of the floods of data that we are receiving is to organize it in a way that allows fast, efficient retrieval of just the information we want, regardless of how large the dataset is. The longer you wait to perform that organization, the harder it will be to do. If you are in business, your competitors are using databases to get a handle on their data. If you don't do the same, and soon, they will gain a huge competitive advantage. Whether you are just starting out, and as yet have not collected any data, or you are in an established organization that has been collecting data for years, there will never be a better time than right now to decide the best way to organize your data so that you can quickly receive answers to the questions you will want to ask both now and in the years to come. After you decide what kinds of information you are likely to want to extract from the data, you can design a database that will make it easy to do so.

Bottom Line: It is a good thing you are reading this book. Unless you have the cash to hire a highly paid database guru, you need to understand how to design a database, so you can do it yourself. Even if you *do* have the cash to hire a highly paid database guru, you still will be better off if you understand what that expert does for you. If you would like to *become* a highly paid database guru, this book will start you on your way, and serve as a valuable reference after you arrive.

What Is Database Processing?

By this time you are probably asking, "What makes database processing so wonderful?" You can understand the value of organized data compared to unorganized data, but there are many ways to organize data. What makes the database structure so superior to just plain old storing things in a consistent, logical order? That is a valid question. To answer it, I describe how computer scientists organized data before databases came into use, so you can see the advantages and disadvantages of that method. Then, I explain how the structure of an information system based on database technology differs, along with the advantages and disadvantages of the database method. On balance, the advantages of using database technology far outweigh the disadvantages.

File processing: The old way

As shown in Figure 1-2, computers consist of three principal subsystems: the processor, the memory, and the input/output subsystem, which includes such components as the keyboard and the monitor's screen. The processor performs all the computations and operations. The memory stores things when they are not being processed. The input/output subsystem conveys information back and forth between the computer and the user. You control computations and other operations with program code, which is stored in memory. The data that you operate on is also stored in memory.

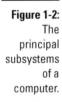
Figure 1-2:
The principal subsystems of a computer.

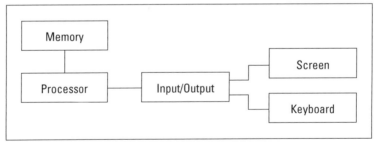

To early computer scientists, it made a lot of sense to rigidly separate the memory used to store program code from the memory used to store data, as shown in Figure 1-3. For most applications, data changes frequently while an application is processing it. On the other hand, it is very dangerous to allow program code to change while that very same program code is executing. More often than not, such self-modifying code causes what have come to be called computer crashes.

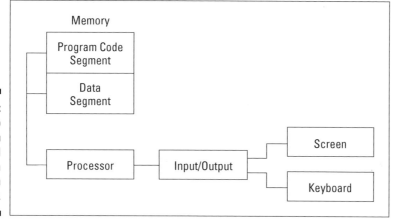

Without a doubt, it is good to keep program code separate from data. However, this thinking carried over into how computer files were structured. Early data files contained nothing but data, as shown in the following example:

```
Harold Percival26262 S. Howards Mill Rd Westminster CA92683
Jerry Appel     32323 S. River Lane Rd   Santa Ana   CA92705
Adrian Hansen   232   Glenwood Court      Anaheim     CA92640
John Baker      2222  Lafayette St        Garden GroveCA92643
Michael Pens    77730 S. New Era Rd       Irvine      CA92715
Bob Michimoto   25252 S. Kelmsley Dr      Stanton     CA92610
Linda Smith     444   S.E. Seventh St     Costa Mesa  CA92635
Robert Funnell  2424  Sheri Court         Anaheim     CA92640
Bill Checkal    9595  Curry Dr            Stanton     CA92610
Jed Style       3535  Randall St          Santa Ana   CA92705
```

Such files, often called *flat files*, are the kind used by early computer languages such as COBOL and Fortran. Application program files contained everything necessary to find a desired file on a storage device, and find specific desired items within the file. This architecture worked well for many years, but did cause some problems.

One big problem with the flat file architecture had to do with the fact that often multiple application programs dealt with the same data file. For instance, a business's CUSTOMER file might be used by several accounting applications, several applications used by the sales department, others used by marketing, and a few used by top management. If, for any reason, the data file needed to be changed, all the applications used by all the departments would have to be updated to run with the new data structure. For example, perhaps a field was added to show which salesperson had a particular account. This wouldn't matter to accounting, marketing, or top management, but all their applications would have to be updated anyway. Not only was this a lot of extra work, but it also made those applications subject to errors. The old adage, "If it ain't broke, don't fix it" applies in spades here. However, with the flat file structure, those unrelated applications *did* become "broke" and needed to be fixed.

Another problem with the flat file structure is not so obvious, but just as important. In today's rapidly changing computing environment, it is not wise to tie your applications to any specific hardware implementation. You can be sure that your hardware will become obsolete sooner or later, probably sooner. After a while, obsolete hardware is not supported any longer. Once you can't get replacement parts or operating system upgrades anymore, it is time to discard your old hardware. You don't want to discard your application programs along with it.

So, computer programs should be independent of the hardware they run on. That is not possible with flat file systems, because the information about the physical location of the data is included in the application programs. This fact caused major pain in the 1960s when IBM moved its customer base from the old transistor-based 709X architecture to the new integrated circuit-based System 360 architecture. IBM's customers were not happy about having to rewrite all their application code, but they had little choice.

Lesson Learned: Somehow, structure things so that application programs can access data without having to know its physical location.

Database processing: The new way

In 1945, even before the first electronic computer was built, Vannevar Bush described a structure that would solve the problem of application dependency on hardware configuration. He originated the concept of a database long before any hardware existed that could support one.

The main idea of a database is that a third structure lies between the application program and the data, as shown in Figure 1-4. This third structure is called the database management system (DBMS). The DBMS stores all the information about the physical location of data. The application refers to the data by logical address, and the DBMS converts the logical address to a physical address to access the data. Because the logical address of an item can be the same, regardless of what hardware is hosting the system, applications can migrate from one hardware platform to another without change. Changes made to the physical addresses of items in memory are transparent to the application as long as the logical address remains the same. The DBMS makes all necessary adjustments.

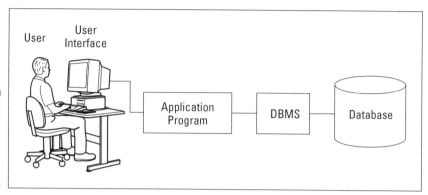

Figure 1-4:
A DBMS-
based
information
system.

Seems strange, doesn't it, that the idea of a database was known, but early computer pioneers went ahead and based their software on flat data files anyway? They had good reason, however, for this seemingly shortsighted choice. A DBMS requires a great deal of computer power, raw speed, in order to return results in a tolerable amount of time. The early computers did not have enough power to run a DBMS. As a result people designed around flat file systems. Without the overhead of a DBMS, these systems ran much faster, and meaningful work could be done on slow vacuum tube-based and later transistor-based hardware.

As computer performance improved, use of database architecture became more and more feasible. Finally, in the early 1960s, the first commercial database systems started to appear. Initially, they were used only on the largest computers, applied to the largest projects, such as keeping track of all the parts and documents associated with the Saturn V launch vehicle and Apollo moon landing spacecraft. At the time, the Saturn V/Apollo combination was the most complex machine that humanity had ever built. As computer power continued to increase, database technology trickled down to ever-smaller machines, until it became available on personal computers around 1980.

Today, robust database management systems are available on computers of all sizes and are used routinely by individuals and organizations to manage the data that is important to them.

Types of database systems

There are a number of ways that a DBMS could organize data, and there are advantages and disadvantages to each of those ways. A number of different structures have been tried, some with more success than others. IBM's DBMS for NASA's Saturn V/Apollo project, later dubbed IMS, had a hierarchical structure. Competing products of the same era had a network structure. The evolutionary descendants of these pioneering products are still in use today. The vendors that support them have maintained compatibility over the years so that their customers can continue to benefit from the massive investments they have made in applications that use those DBMS structures.

Hierarchical databases have a simple, hierarchical structure (no surprise there, I guess) that allows very fast data access. However, as Robert A. Heinlein once pointed out, "There Ain't No Such Thing As A Free Lunch (TANSTAAFL)." You pay for that fast access with structural rigidity. Once a hierarchical database has been implemented, it is very difficult to modify. In the real world that I live in, requirements change over time. Business models change, markets change, companies grow, companies shrink, companies enter new markets or exit old ones. They introduce new product lines and abandon others that are no longer popular. This situation caused early databases to be a major bottleneck and impaired many organizations' ability to react to change in a timely manner.

Network databases were not a significant improvement, although they had different problems. In contrast to the simple relationships characteristic of the hierarchical structure, network databases allowed any item in the database to be directly related to any other item. This allowed more flexibility than the hierarchical structure, but sacrificed some speed to do it. In addition, the added complexity made network databases more difficult to maintain.

In 1970, E.F. Codd, then at IBM, published a landmark paper that outlined the basic structure of a new type of database system: the relational database. Relational databases are much more flexible than either hierarchical or network, but at the same time have a simple structure. Nevertheless, TANSTAAFL is still in force. The advantages of the relational model are offset by the fact that it carries significantly more overhead than either of the other database models. This means that it runs significantly slower. However, as computer performance has improved over time, the use of relational databases has become progressively more feasible.

Over time, the relational model has displaced the earlier hierarchical and network models in practically all new installations and is the dominant type of database in use today. In some application areas, an even newer model, the object-oriented model, has gained adherents. A hybrid, the object-relational model, retains the advantages of relational DBMSs while gaining the benefits of the newer object model. However, the usage of object and object-relational DBMS products is still relatively small. In this book, I concentrate on relational database technology, with one chapter devoted to object-oriented and object-relational technology.

Chapter 2

Database Development

*I*n Chapter 1, I explain several important points about data and databases. Just in case you weren't paying attention, or you skipped Chapter 1 entirely, here are three key points that you need to consider:

✔ We all have lots of data.

✔ That data is much more valuable if it is organized.

✔ A relational database is probably the best way to organize most types of data.

So, what exactly is a database, specifically a relational database, and how does one go about building one? Those are two separate questions. The first can be answered rather simply. The answer to the second question could take a book. Fortunately, you have that book in your hands.

What Is a Database?

A database is a self-describing collection of integrated records. By *self-describing,* I mean that it contains a description of its own structure as part of the data that it stores. When I say that the records in a database are *integrated,* I mean that relationships exist among the records that bind them all together into a cohesive, logical system.

A relational database is a database that conforms to the relational model specified by E. F. Codd. I describe this model in detail in Chapter 7. For now, suffice it to say that relational databases are principally composed of two-dimensional tables with rows and columns. Of course, there's more to it than that, and Chapter 7 goes into it more deeply.

Developing a Database

Now that you know what a database is, how do you build one? This reminds me of the old riddle, "How do you eat an elephant?" Elephants are so huge and intimidating, it is bizarre to even think about eating one. However, there is a way. The answer to the riddle is, "One bite at a time." Databases can also be huge and intimidating, but there is a way to build one. The answer is, "One step at a time."

You can break the task of constructing a database into distinct phases, and then subdivide the phases into smaller, manageable tasks. Tackle the tasks one at a time until, by completing the last one, you have built a structure of great value to the organization that hired you.

The difference between a database and a database application

Sometimes when non-specialists talk about using a database to solve a particular business problem, they fail to make a distinction between two very different parts of the solution: the database and the database application. Databases do not solve business problems. A database is a collection of records that has some well-defined characteristics. It is a structured repository of data. It is not a kind of computer program.

To get a computer to perform some set of desired operations, you must give it a sequence of instructions. Such as sequence is usually in the form of a program. A *database application* is a program that is designed to operate on the data stored in a database. It is the database application that creates the screens the user looks at, the forms into which updates are made, and the reports that are printed out. So what the typical user is interfacing with is not the database itself, but rather the database application that lies between the user and the database, as shown in Figure 2-1.

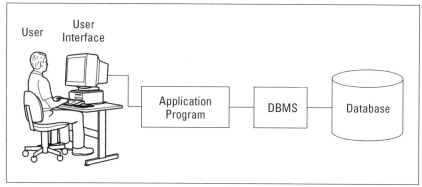

Figure 2-1:
The user interacts with the database through a database application.

It is possible for a user to operate directly on a database from the keyboard, using a data access language such as SQL. This is, however, uncommon. The usual mode of interaction with a database is through a database application program. This program may be written in a standard third-generation programming language such as Basic or C, in a more object-oriented language, such as Visual Basic or C++, or with a Rapid Application Development (RAD) tool such as Borland's InfoBuilder or C++ Builder.

The phases of system development

Building any software program with real utility — that is, one considerably more complex than the trivial examples often found in programming texts — is a challenging and often frustrating task. It is hard to build a program that does what you want it to do, avoids doing what you don't want it to do, and does so reliably and consistently. This is even more true for a database application than it is for just about any other kind of application.

To maximize the chances of creating a database and accompanying application that adhere to your specifications and give you the functionality and performance that you need, both reliably and consistently, you must divide the task up into manageable chunks, and then perform each one in sequence. The exact steps you go through may vary depending on the nature and scope of any particular development effort. Generally, however, your project should include the following major phases:

1. Definition

2. Requirements

3. Evaluation

4. Design

5. Implementation

6. Final documentation and testing

7. Maintenance

Each of these phases is critically important to a successful database project. Don't short-change any of these phases because of time pressure. Otherwise, you could end up with a buggy, unreliable product. Even worse, you could have an excellent and highly reliable solution to a problem that nobody has.

In the following sections, I look at each phase a little more closely and explain why it is important.

Definition phase

The definition phase is arguably the most important of all, although it is often not given the attention that it deserves. As the name implies, this is the phase in which you define the problem that your database application must solve.

Define the problem as concisely as possible, eliminating all ambiguity about what exactly is the desired result.

Following the problem definition, the next step is to determine project scope. How big is the project, and how much time and resource must be put into it in order to guarantee success?

Usually, any development effort has time and budget constraints. The final product must be delivered by a certain time, and the entire project must cost no more than some fixed budget. You may find that, considering the scope of the project, it will not be possible to complete it within the available time and budget, considering the resources at hand. This feasibility analysis may cause you to decide to turn down the project, rather than get involved in something that is doomed from the start. On the other hand, it may cause your client to grant you additional time and budget. Either way, you are better off than you would have been if you had just started working under the original time and budget constraints, then at some point hit a brick wall that you could not climb over or walk around.

After the problem definition, scoping, and feasibility analysis, you need to choose the development team that will tackle the project. Choose people whose combined talents and expertise satisfy all the requirements.

Finally, document everything you have done so far.

The definition phase involves the following tasks:

1. **Define the problem.**

2. **Determine project scope.**

3. **Perform feasibility analysis.**

4. **Form the project team.**

5. **Document problem definition, scope, feasibility analysis, and team membership.**

Requirements phase

During the definition phase, you receive a clear, but not necessarily detailed, picture of the desired outcome of the project. During the requirements phase, you find out, in detail, exactly what your final product will be expected to do. Getting the detailed picture you need could be a simple task, or it could be complex, difficult, and time-consuming. Which way it will be depends largely on the sophistication of your client.

Sophisticated clients have had database applications produced for them in the past, and they know what you will need to do your job. Such clients will give you very concise, complete specifications of exactly what they want the system to look like and be able to do. They can show you similar applications that they already have, which you can use as models. This is the type of client you will love to work with. There is no ambiguity or confusion about what you are to do. What is desired is clearly understood by all parties, and when you deliver it, the client is happy and you get paid. This type of client is, unfortunately, a database developer's fantasy. Any organization that knows this much about database development probably has its own in-house data-base developers and has no need to hire you. Occasionally, you might encounter this type of client, when its in-house staff is overbooked. Cherish such occasions.

A naive client is another situation altogether. Such clients do not really know what they want, except in vague terms. They have a general idea of what functions they want the application to perform, but have not thought out the details of what it should do or how it should interface with the user.

With this type of client, you need to spend time interviewing everyone who will touch the system. Who will actually be using it? Who is their supervisor and what will his involvement with the system be? Who is authorizing this development and signing your checks? What is her interest and involvement in this development effort? You need to talk to all these people.

You will find that as you talk to the different categories of people involved, you will hear different priorities, different expectations, different ideas of what features should be present, and different ideas about how the screens should look and how printed reports should be formatted. Somehow, you have to come up with a solution that is satisfactory to all the stakeholders. You may have to go back and talk to them repeatedly, and get them to communicate with each other, before you can get agreement on what is truly required, as opposed to what would be nice to have.

When you finally get the client stakeholders to agree among themselves on what is required, you can transform that into a model of the system you are to build. This model is called the *users' data model,* because it captures what the users of the system conceive the system to be. The users' data model incorporates all the types of items of interest and how they relate to each other. It also includes information on what specific items are included in each item type, as well as business rules that place restrictions on what can be done with those items. Chapter 3 gives specific pointers for developing the users' data model.

In order to get an accurate picture of all that the users want, you need to record what they tell you when you interview them. You can do this by taking very detailed notes, or by tape-recording your conversations with them and transcribing the tapes later. Transcriptions are better than notes, because they tend to be more complete. After you transcribe a conversation and read the transcript, you will frequently notice things that you failed to ask about, but that are potentially important. You can go back to those users on a follow-up call and fill in holes in your information or clarify any points that were not clearly expressed.

Part of the Statement of Requirements that is the main product of this phase is an explicit statement of the update, display, and control mechanisms that the application will include. Exactly what data items may need to be updated from time to time and how will that be done? How will the display work? Will there be multiple screens? How will navigation between screens be done? How will operations be controlled? By mouse? If so, what mouse operations will produce what results? By keyboard? If so, what key depressions will produce what results? If the user does not have a clear idea of the pros and cons of the various options, you can make suggestions.

What will the screens look like? How will information be arranged on each one? Is there a preferred color scheme? Should the screen contain dynamic elements? You should mock up prototype screens at this point for the client to look at. Sometimes they have an image in their mind that is not really feasible on the kinds of screens that they have. If they have 800x600 screens, build your prototype to those specifications. Let the client see what its idea will look like if you implement it in the way the client has asked for it.

The Statement of Requirements is essentially a contract. It describes exactly what is required to satisfactorily complete the project. It is based on what you have learned in your conversations with the client. Through those conversations, you have inferred the users' data model, and have gained agreement on the desired update, display, and control mechanisms, as well as the look and feel of the application's screens.

After you generate the Statement of Requirements, have the responsible party at the client organization sign and date it. You sign and date it too, indicating that you are both in agreement about what you will deliver.

To summarize, the requirements phase includes the following tasks:

1. **Interview representatives of all classes of client stakeholder.**
2. **Get all stakeholders to agree on what they want.**
3. **Create the users' data model of the proposed system.**
4. **Create the Statement of Requirements, describing in detail what functions will be provided, and what screens and reports will look like.**
5. **Get the responsible party at the client to sign and date the Statement of Requirements.**

Evaluation phase

After you know what you are supposed to do, you need to figure out how you are going to do it. Of course, you should already have a pretty good idea of how to do it, or you should not have signed the Statement of Requirements. Now is the time to fill in the details. How will you structure the system? The users' data model should be your guide here. What DBMS should you use to implement your design? Different DBMS products have different capabilities and limitations. Some will be appropriate for this particular job and others won't. At this time, you need to choose the one that fits the job best. A number of factors will figure into this decision besides the DBMS' capabilities and limitations. For example, your proficiency level and the amount of time available to come up to speed on a DBMS may be a factor. You may decide for strategic and career reasons to choose a platform that you are not experienced in, but would like to gain that experience. The client may specify the tool it wants you to use. This happens often when companies already have some database applications that were developed in one environment. They naturally want to keep new applications consistent with what they already have, so that they do not have to train for and support two different development environments in the maintenance phase.

In the definition phase, you determined who would be on the team that developed this project. Now is the time to create detailed job descriptions for these people so that everyone knows exactly what they will be called upon to do.

You can prevent a lot of conflict and frustration in the future if it is clear to all at an early stage, just who is responsible for what.

After you know the architecture you will use, the tools you will use to build it, and the people who will do the work, step back and reassess the feasibility of the whole project. You now know a lot more about the project than you did when you first assessed feasibility in the definition phase. It is entirely possible that knowing what you know now, it would be best not to proceed with the project. Considering the resources you have, and the deadlines and budgets you agreed to in the Statement of Requirements, you may find that a high probability exists that you will not be able to deliver what you promised. If you proceed anyway, the client will be angry, and you will have wasted a lot of effort and money. It is better to take the pain now, before you get in too deep. I am reminded of the old FRAM oil filter TV ads. They showed an auto mechanic replacing a car's oil filter with a new FRAM oil filter. He said, "You can either pay me now or pay me later." At that, the screen showed the mechanic replacing a blown engine. It is a lot cheaper to apply a little preventive maintenance early than to just keep driving until a much more expensive repair is required. By the same token, it is smart to pull the plug on a project that is likely to fail, rather than keep working in the hopes that through some miracle you will be able to pull it off.

When you reassess the feasibility of a project, and it looks bad, you don't always have to pull the plug. Perhaps you can change the requirements, still delivering the main functionality that the client wants. The client may be agreeable to deferring some features until later, and discarding others outright. These kinds of changes may turn what looked like a nightmare project into something quite doable. Be sure to explore all avenues with your client, and choose the one that is best for all concerned.

The final task in the evaluation phase, and an important component of every phase, is to document everything. What system architecture did you choose and why did you choose it? Include team member job descriptions in the documentation. Document the steps you went through in your feasibility analysis and the conclusion you came to. Document any changes to the Statement of Requirements based on the deferral or elimination of features. Put all these things into a single document that contains all the important information on the evaluation phase.

During the evaluation phase, you complete the following tasks:

1. **Select the best DBMS or development tool for the task at hand.**

2. **Create job descriptions for team members.**

3. **Reassess the feasibility of the project, based on what you know now.**

4. **Reduce the scope of the project if time and budget targets cannot be met.**

5. **Document all choices and decisions made in this phase.**

Design phase

You now have a refined and detailed representation of the users' data model. You know, from the Statement of Requirements, exactly what functionality you have agreed to deliver. You have examined those requirements and your capabilities with a critical eye, and have concluded that this is a job you can do, and do well. Now the task is to translate the users' data model into a relational database design that will run with the DBMS and on the hardware platform that you have chosen. After you design that database, you must design an application that runs on it and produces the agreed upon functionality.

Database design

There are a number of ways of representing the users' data model. In this book, I cover two of the more popular methods: the entity-relationship (E-R) model and the semantic object model (SOM). The first step in designing a database is to represent the users' data model in one of these paradigms. Both have been used over a number of years in every imaginable context. They have been refined and extended to cover just about any case that you might encounter. In Chapter 4, I discuss the entity-relationship (E-R) model, and in Chapter 5, I cover the semantic object model (SOM).

After you have your system modeled in terms of either the E-R model or the SOM, you need to transform that model into a relational model. The relational model consists of data items (called attributes), tables (called relations), relationships among tables, and constraints. Chapter 7 takes a general look at this conversion. Chapter 8 specifically addresses converting an E-R model to a relational database, and Chapter 9 discusses converting a SOM.

As is true in other phases, you need to document the conversion from the users' data model to the E-R model or the SOM. Record the reasoning behind any decisions that are not trivially obvious. Be aware that what may seem trivially obvious to you now might be a complete mystery to someone else who picks up this project six months from now, after you had moved on to something else. It might even seem mysterious to *you* six months from now, if you had been away from it for that long.

Database application design

Designing the database is only half the job. A database stores the data that interests you, but does not make it particularly accessible to the people who need to use it. For that you need a database application. The application mediates the interaction between the database and its users.

How will users access the various functions that they need to perform on the database. Will you supply them with a menu of choices? Will it be a pop-up, pull-down, or radio button menu? How will it look? Will it be centered on the screen? What font will you use? What labels should you apply to the menu choices? These are just a few examples of questions you must ask and answer. Of course, much of this has already been done in the requirements phase when you built your prototypes. However, now things are much more concrete and constrained than they were back in the requirements phase. You must design the actual user interface, based on the development tools available to you as well as on the client's expectations.

In addition to menus, you must design data entry and display screen forms, printed reports, and a method for making *ad hoc* queries of the database. The query capability needs to be there because it is impossible to anticipate all the possible questions that a user might want to ask of the database. Cover the ones you *can* anticipate with menu items. Provide an *ad hoc* query facility to cover the rest.

Now is the time to figure out exactly how you are going to implement the update, display, and control mechanisms that you defined during the requirements phase. It is also the time when you design the logical flow of control of your application. What functions are present and how are they related to each other? What are all the possible sequences of events that a user might possibly pass through in the course of using this application? What might go wrong, and what safeguards should you build into the application to assure that small user errors do not cause big problems in the database? These are the kinds of questions that must be asked and answered at this point in the development project.

Document the application design thoroughly — not only what the final design is, but also why you decided to do it this way as opposed to other ways that you considered.

The final task in this phase is to go to the responsible party at the client, explain your design in detail, backed up by your documentation, and get a sign-off, signifying client agreement with what you have presented. Signoff here is essential to prevent "feature creep." Feature creep is when the client comes to you in mid-project and says something like, "What you have here is very nice, but it would be a lot more valuable to our sales force if you could just add this one little feature that we forgot to tell you about at the beginning. It shouldn't be very difficult to add this one small thing." This sounds pretty harmless, and you might be inclined to go along and provide the extra feature for no extra charge. However, this could also be the first step down a path that will cause you much pain. The old adage "Give 'em an inch and they'll take a mile" comes to mind. Be aware of the dangers of feature creep, and protect yourself by obtaining client signoff at the end of the design phase.

Here are the key tasks in the design phase:

1. **Translate the users' data model into a standard database model, such as the E-R model or the SOM.**

2. **Transform the standard database model into a relational model.**

3. **Document the reasoning behind your translation from the users' data model to the standard database model.**

4. **Design the user interface of the database application.**

5. **Design the logical flow of control of the application.**

6. **Determine what might go wrong, and incorporate safeguards to prevent those potential problems.**

7. **Document the application design thoroughly.**

8. **Get the client to sign off your final design document, to head off any possibility of feature creep.**

Implementation phase

At last! The preliminaries are over! You have done all the planning that you can do, and you can finally apply fingers to keyboard and actually start building something. Believe it or not, sometimes developers, fueled either by over-confidence, naiveté, or schedule pressure, start here rather than going through the phases I describe in previous sections of this chapter. That is a dangerous thing to do.

Unless the project is extremely small and easy to understand (which would seem to be impossible for any project involving a database), starting the implementation without proper attention to planning often results in a product that does not meet the client's needs, even if it works the way you want it to.

The first implementation task is to build the database structure, using the tools provided by the DBMS you have chosen. Taking the relational model you build in the design phase, you can create tables that correspond to the relations, with columns that correspond to the table attributes. You can link the tables to each other using the relationships identified during the design phase. You can also add constraints to the tables, the relationships, and to the database as a whole, based on the business rules that you identified in the users' model and subsequently translated into constraints during the design phase.

Implementing the database application follows the implementation of the database itself, or you could do the two tasks in parallel. The database application depends heavily on the structure of the database, but you know what that structure is, because you established it during the design phase. Thus to save time, one member of the team could be working on implementation of the database while another could be working on the application. Often, tremendous amounts of money can be saved or earned by putting a critical database application online sooner rather than later. In such cases, tasks that can be performed in parallel, should be performed in parallel. It may make sense to assign a larger team to a project if the earlier completion that results from parallel development would bring a significant economic advantage.

Documentation of the implementation phase should be fairly easy. The DBMS you are using will provide printouts of the database structure that you build. You shouldn't need anything beyond that for the database. Regarding the database application, any program code that you write should be copiously commented so that the logic behind each functional block is clear. Where they might be helpful, comments on individual lines of code are also in order. Always ask yourself, "What if I win the lottery next week and decide to quit and live a life of luxury in Tahiti? Would a new developer be able to understand what I have done and why I did it the way I did?" If you cannot answer those questions with a resounding "Yes," you have not commented your code well enough yet.

During the implementation phase, you complete the following tasks:

1. **Build the database structure.**

2. **Build the database application.**

3. **Document what you have built, including detailed commenting of program code.**

Testing and final documentation phase

After your database is complete and the application does everything that the Statement of Requirements says it is supposed to do, it is time to subject the entire system to rigorous testing. Someone unconnected to the development team, who is completely independent and impartial, should do this testing.

The job of this tester is to confirm that the application does indeed do all the things it is supposed to do, that the user documentation is clear and complete, and that the system recovers gracefully when the user does something wrong. Another important chore is to find any latent bugs that may be lurking in the code. To find such bugs, it helps if the tester is an unconventional thinker, perhaps someone who "marches to the beat of a different drum." If everyone on the development team approaches the application in approximately the same way, it often takes someone with a very different perspective to uncover flaws that only show up under certain unusual conditions.

Really big projects may go through several stages of testing, each one finding subtler problems than the last one found. These stages are often called alpha, beta, and gamma testing. A product that is in gamma test should be almost of release quality, with only the most insignificant and obscure problems and deficiencies remaining. After the problems uncovered in the gamma test stage are corrected, the product goes "golden" and is ready for release, and if applicable, commercial production.

While testing is going on, documentation is being finalized in parallel by the development team. It should include all necessary user documentation, as well as all the documentation generated throughout the entire development process. User documentation may be in the form of online help files or printed manuals. In most cases, you should supply both. Online help is best for quickly giving short answers to common questions. Printed manuals are better for providing in-depth information that also covers a broader range of topics.

When testing and documentation is complete, the moment has finally arrived when you turn the system over to the client and you stand back, beaming, while she fires it up and runs it through its paces for the first time. If you have done your job right, everything works flawlessly, the client is pleased, and signifies her pleasure by signing the acceptance form that you provide. Add your copy of this to the rest of the documentation that you keep on the project. This is usually the time when the final payment for your work is released to you. You can now take your team out for a well-deserved celebration.

The testing and final documentation phase includes the following tasks:

1. **Turn the system over to an independent testing entity to test functionality and ease of use.**

   The tester should confirm that the application does everything it is supposed to do.

   The tester should confirm that the application does not do anything it is not supposed to do.

   For large projects, several stages of progressively more rigorous testing may be required.

2. **Produce final documentation.**

3. **Turn the system over to the client and receive signed acceptance and final payment for your work.**

4. **Celebrate success with your team!**

Maintenance phase

Just because you delivered your product and got paid for it, that does not mean that you are through with it. Even if you put a lot of thought into planning, design, implementation, and particularly testing, the product may still have bugs that do not come to the surface until after the client has accepted it and used it for a while. You may be obligated to correct any such problems or deficiencies, free of charge. Your responsibility for this class of task could continue indefinitely. You are never completely off the hook. This fact provides strong motivation for doing very thorough testing before your deliver to the client.

Even if the client never experiences problems, you still have a responsibility for the product. No matter how conscientious a client is in specifying to you everything that the application should do, sooner or later the client will want enhancements or updates to accommodate its changing business environment.

Because you and your team are the most knowledgeable people in the world on the application, it is natural for the client to come to you for any enhancements or updates. This is fine, because the client will pay you for this additional work, and maintenance work can provide a nice, steady, base revenue stream during times when new development jobs are not coming in. However, it is important to include the fact that this work will make demands on you when you are making staffing decisions and planning workloads.

The maintenance phase never really ends. It just slowly becomes less and less significant as the product ages. The classic case of this is the famous Y2K crisis. Applications written in the 1950s referred to data structures that would work just fine for over 40 years. No one ever dreamed that they would still be in use when the year 2000 rolled around, but they were. Hundreds of millions of dollars were spent in maintenance of those applications and the data files that they used, in order to make them Y2K-compliant.

During the maintenance phase, you perform the following tasks:

1. **Correct latent bugs that client finds after acceptance.**

2. **Provide enhancements and updates as required by the client, for an additional charge.**

Educating the client

A big part of success in database development is controlling client expectations. Typically, clients — the users of database technology — do not have an appreciation of what is doable and what is not doable with current technology. Even in the doable category, your client may not realize what is relatively easy to provide and what is extremely difficult.

Throughout the definition, requirements, and evaluation phases, you will be listening to client stakeholders, but also informing them on the costs, in terms of time and staffing, of the things they are asking for. This mutual sharing of information will help to ensure that the product that you ultimately deliver gives the client the best solution to its needs at the lowest cost. It also protects you from being trapped into promising to deliver functionality that neither the budget nor the schedule will support. It is in everyone's best interest that both client and developer know as much about the job as possible.

Resisting the Urge to Build a Database Right Now

It's awfully hard to predict the future. If I could do it, I would be living a life of luxury right now in Tahiti, rather than writing this book. It's no easier for managers of organizations large and small. As a result, they often don't realize that they will need a database application to handle their work until the need becomes painfully critical. All too often, they go into panic mode, so they call you in and task you with developing the database application they need.

The need becomes apparent

Things have been working just fine. The processes and procedures the organization has in place are handling the demands of daily operations and management feels good about the way things are working. However, change is inevitable. Perhaps the market for a firm's products suddenly explodes and much more volume must be produced and tracked than ever before. Maybe a new market opens up and must be addressed with a whole family of new products. Possibly the competitive landscape changes overnight as foreign competitors invade your traditional markets in force. Any number of things could happen, and in today's world, they can happen very quickly and change everything. Changes like these may suddenly make obsolete the processes and procedures that have served the firm so well in the past. The only way to stay abreast of things is to get a much better handle on relevant data. The firm needs a database and its associated applications, maybe several databases, and at last management knows it.

By the time the need for a database application becomes apparent to the decision-makers that can authorize the development of one, it is already late. The market is getting away. The competitors are gobbling market share. Something must be done, and it must be done right away.

The schedule is tight

Because the need for a database solution to a business problem is already acute by the time a developer is called in to discuss the project, you face significant pressure to deliver a finished product as soon as possible. The client wants to have it up and running the day after tomorrow. You know that doing the job right will take four months of intense effort by your full development team. Somehow, you have to bridge this gap. The only other option is to walk away from the job, and let somebody else crash and burn.

One way to bridge the gap is to make sure both you and your client have a clear understanding of the project scope. How big a job is the client asking for and how much effort will it require? This may cause the client to either relax the schedule somewhat or relinquish features that are not needed initially, but will take a lot of time and effort to develop.

Another way to bridge the gap is to get the client to agree to pay for additional team members, so that more of the work can be done in parallel, thus allowing faster completion. This only works to an extent, because much of the work is based on what has been done in previous phases. If the fraction of the total work that can be done in parallel is small, the speedup of the overall schedule will also be small.

Another thing that could help is to acquire and use more powerful development tools than the ones you are now using. The time gained will be offset somewhat as your team climbs the learning curve of a new unfamiliar tool. After the tool has been mastered however, it can be used on subsequent projects, causing productivity gains in the future.

Do not try to accelerate the schedule by skimping on any of the phases of development of database systems. Each phase is critical to the ultimate success of a development project, and should be executed in its entirety. Small projects do not need as careful adherence to each step of each phase as do larger projects. The amount of time and effort devoted to each phase should be commensurate with the size and complexity of the task at hand.

Standing your ground and preventing disaster

In the final analysis, *you* are the expert. You are the one who knows how to develop a solid, reliable, powerful database application. You know what is needed to do the job right and deliver a product that will satisfy the client and that you can be proud of. Don't let the client talk you into committing to deliver sooner than you believe is possible.

Perhaps you can speed things up somewhat by working your team harder. That route has its own dangers. If people burn out from excessive overtime, at best they become less efficient. At worst, they quit, and leave you with a much-diminished team, facing the same imminent deadline.

To avoid the problems caused by unrealistic schedules, be firm with the client about your schedule estimates. If you know what it will take to do the job and have developed your schedule accordingly, stick to it. Both you and the client will be better off in the long run.

Some Development Tools May Be Too User Friendly

Approximately 20 years ago, when the first relational database management systems were appearing on personal computers, creating databases was a fairly complex operation. Command-driven environments required you to enter a command to specify each column in a table. Command parameters specified keys and links between tables. Today, you can create databases, complete with tables, relationships and constraints, very easily. The vendors of database management systems and rapid application development (RAD) tools have done a good job of making database creation as painless as possible. This may not be an unalloyed blessing.

The ergonomically designed graphical user interfaces that characterize today's RAD tools make it easy for people to create database tables. This is particularly true for people who are more comfortable with pictures than with words. Because it is so easy to create database tables, there is a tremendous temptation to do so right away, rather than slog through tedious, time-consuming operations, such as the definition, requirements, evaluation, and design phases of database development. Inexperienced developers are most likely to fall prey to this temptation. They are also the ones who will suffer the most from skipping the early phases of development, because they lack the experience that might give them an intuitive understanding of what is required for success.

Not only do contemporary database development tools make it easy to create tables, they make connecting them together a snap. Generally, clicking a mouse button on the graphic object representing one table, and dragging to the object representing a second table is all that is needed to establish a relationship in the database.

To casual observers, it would seem that creating a database is not any more complicated than building a spreadsheet, and maybe less complex than creating a formatted word-processor document. What they may not see is all the conceptual work and client communication that must take place before the easy part with the RAD tool is begun.

Don't fall for the Siren Song: "Don't Waste Time Planning. Create the Database Now. It's Soooo Easy."

The DBMS or RAD tool calls out to you, imploring you to place your hands on the keyboard and start creating database tables. Resist the temptation until you are truly ready. Make sure that the definition, requirements, evaluation, and design phases have received their just due. Just as a house must be built on a strong foundation to resist being destroyed by stormy weather, a database must be built on the strong foundation of a good design, based on a clear understanding of what the client needs and what you can provide.

Part II
Data Modeling: What Should the Database Represent?

The 5th Wave   By Rich Tennant

"No, the solution to our system being down is NOT for us to work on our knees."

In this part . . .

A database and its associated applications constitute a model of some physical or conceptual reality. For that model to be accurate, it must be in close agreement with what the users conceive that reality to be. In Part II, I discuss the users' model, the people who have input into the users' model, and how to reconcile differing user inputs into a consensus that everyone can accept. After you have a users' model, you need to translate it into a formal structure. Part II provides details about two of the more popular formal modeling systems: the entity-relationship model and the semantic object model. Part II also offers some practical advice on how to conceptualize and scope the problem at hand based on what the client tells you and what you can infer based on your experience.

Chapter 3

The Users' Model

*A*ny successful database system must satisfy the needs of the people who are going to use it. This group includes the people who will actually be entering data or retrieving results. It also includes others, though. People in various levels of management may rely on reports generated by the system. People in other functional areas, such as sales or production, may use the products of the system, such as mailing lists or bar code labels. The information technology people who set overall data processing standards for an organization may also have a say in how the system is constructed and what its outputs will be. You must consider the needs of all these groups when designing your system. They all contribute to a consensus called the users' data model.

Who Are the Interested Parties, and What Are They Thinking?

When you are first called in to do a database development job, one of your first tasks is to determine who all the interested parties are, and what their involvement in the system will be after you have completed it. You also want to know who will be involved in decisions about the system while it is under development.

Human relations is an important part of your job here. When views in the client organization conflict with each other, as they often do, whom do you believe? You cannot simply take the word of the person with the most impressive title.

Often, the unofficial lines of authority in an organization (which are the ones that really count) differ significantly from what the official organization chart might show.

The manager who hired you

Generally, if you are dealing with a medium-sized to large organization, the person who contacts you about doing a development project is a middle manager of some sort. This person typically has the authority to find and recommend a developer for a needed application, but may not have the budget authority to approve the total development cost.

The person who hired you is probably your closest ally in the organization. She wants you to succeed because she will look bad if you don't. Be sure that you have a good understanding of what she wants and how important her stated desires are to her. It could be that she has merely been tasked with obtaining a developer and does not have strong opinions about what is to be developed. On the other hand, she may be directly responsible for what the application will deliver, and have a very specific idea of what is needed. In addition to hearing what she tells you, you must also be able to read between the lines and determine how much importance she ascribes to what she is saying.

The people who are scheduled to use your application

After the manager who hires you, the next group of people you will probably meet are the ones who will actually use the system you will build. These are the people who will enter the data that will populate your database tables. They are the ones who will run queries to answer questions that they and others in the organization may have. They are the ones who will print reports that will be read by co-workers and various levels of management. They are the ones that will come into closest contact with what you have built.

Generally, these people are already accustomed to dealing with the data that will be in your system, or data much like it. They are either using a manual system, based on paper records, or a computer-based system that your system will replace. In either case, they have become comfortable with a certain look and feel for forms and reports.

To ease the transition from their old system to the new one you are building, you will probably want to make your forms and reports look as much like the old ones as possible. Your system may present them with new information, but if it is presented in a familiar way, the users will accept it more readily and start making effective use of it sooner.

The people who will actually be using your system probably have very definite ideas about what they like and what they don't like about the system they are currently using. It is important that your system eliminate the things they don't like, and retain the things they do like. The acceptance of these people is critical to your overall success. Even if your system does everything that the Statement of Requirements specifies, it will be an utter failure if this group of people does not embrace it. Aside from providing them with what they want, you should be careful to build up rapport with these people during the development effort. Make sure they are in agreement with what you are doing, every step along the way.

The data processing standards people

Larger organizations, with existing software applications, may have standardized on a particular hardware platform and operating system. This choice may well constrain which DBMS you use, because not all database management systems are available on all platforms. The standards organization may even have a preferred DBMS. This is almost certain to be true if the organization already supports other databases.

Supporting database applications on an ongoing basis requires a significant infrastructure. That infrastructure includes DBMS software, periodic DBMS software upgrades, training of users, and training of support personnel. If the organization already supports applications based on one DBMS, it makes sense to leverage that investment by mandating that all future database applications use the same DBMS. If the application you have been brought in to create would best be built upon a foundation of another DBMS, you will have to justify the increased support burden. Often, this can only be done if the already supported DBMS just cannot do the job that is needed.

Aside from your choice of DBMS, the standards people might also have something to say about your coding practices. They might have standards requiring structured programming and modular development, as well as very specific documentation guidelines. You will have to make sure that you are in compliance with all these standards.

Smaller organizations probably will not have any data processing standards people enforcing data processing standards guidelines. In those cases, you must act as if *you* were the data processing standards people. Try to understand what would be best for the client organization in the long term. Make your selections of DBMS, coding style, and documentation with those long-term considerations in mind, as well as what might be most expedient for the current project. Be sure to make the clients aware of why you make the choices you do. They may want to participate in the decision, and at any rate will appreciate the fact that you have their interests at heart.

The big boss

Unless you are dealing with a very small organization indeed, the manager who hired you for this project is not the highest-ranking person who has an interest in what you will be producing. It is quite likely that the manager with whom you have direct dealings must carry your proposals to a higher level for approval, and must also get approval for your payment. You may negotiate a schedule in which you get paid at the completion of specific milestones along the way, or you may receive a lump sum at the completion of the entire project. Either way, someone higher than your direct contact probably must accept your work and approve payment.

It is important that you find out who the big boss is, and get a sense of what that person wants your application to accomplish for the organization. Once again, this person may or may not carry the most prestigious title in the organization. Generally, the troops on the front line, the people who will be using your system, will be able to tell you where the real power resides. If possible, find out what is most important to this person. After you find out, make sure you provide it in your final product.

The big boss's relatives

I shouldn't have to say this. It should never be an issue, but alas, sometimes it is, so I will alert you to it. Sometimes a person with a very minor position in the organization will have an inordinate amount of influence on whether a system is accepted or rejected. I call this person "the big boss's girlfriend," but actually it could be a person of either gender.

Particularly in smaller organizations (mainly because larger organizations have rules against it), relatives or close friends of managers will be given jobs. If they don't have other skills, they might have a position as an administrative assistant or data entry operator. Such people, who may be less qualified than others who were selected on an impartial basis, may be the ones entering data into your database application or running queries on it. If this is the case, be sure you spend time with them and make sure that your application runs in a way that is satisfactory to them. This may actually be good in that it will force you to make sure that the user interface of your application is as easy to understand and use as possible.

What Should the System Be?

After you have talked to all the interested parties in the client organization, you are likely to be confused. Some people will want one feature and not care about a second. Others will insist upon the second and not even mention the first. Some will want it to look and operate one way, and others will want an entirely different look and feel. Some people will consider one particular report to be the most important thing about the application, and other people will not care about reports at all, but only be interested in the *ad hoc* query capability. It would be a rare situation indeed if everyone in the client organization wanted the same things and assigned the same levels of importance to them.

In order to create a users' data model, you are going to have to transform all these diverse messages into a compromise that everyone can agree upon. It is not enough just to satisfy the big boss. The rank-and-file users can torpedo the entire project just by refusing to use it. By the same token, it is not enough to satisfy the rank-and-file users. If the big boss doesn't like the results that the system provides, you may never get final acceptance and payment. To be successful in the database development game, you have to be a good negotiator and somewhat of a politician to boot.

Politics: Whose opinions really count?

If different people or groups in a client organization express differing views on what an application should do or how it should interact with the user, it is not always easy to tell whom to believe. It should not be your job to arbitrate disagreements within the client organization, but sometimes you must in order for the work to move forward. There are various categories of stakeholders, and those categories will vary from one organization to the next. In one case, the big boss will have a lot to say about your system's look and feel, and in another case, that person may care only about the reports the system produces. One class of users might want one thing, and another class that uses it in a different way, may want another.

You are going to have to spend time in the client organization, both with individuals and groups, to get a sense of who cares most passionately about how the system will work and what it will produce, and whose opinions carry the most weight. There is no one right answer to these questions. Each organization will be different. The judgements you make regarding whose opinions carry the most weight will probably affect the way you design your system. This in turn will affect how long it takes to develop, and how much the development effort will cost.

Reconciling differences

Somehow, the conflicting input you receive from all the stakeholders you interview about your project must be combined into a uniform vision of what the proposed system should be and do. You may need to ask the disagreeing groups or people to sit down together and arrive at a compromise that is at least satisfactory to all, if not everything that they had wished for. To arrive at a system that can be built within the time and budget constraints that have been set out for the project, some people may have to give up on features that they would like to have, but that are not absolutely necessary. As an interested but impartial outsider, you may be able to serve as a facilitator in the discussion about what absolutely must be included and what could be left out without seriously inconveniencing anyone.

Arriving at a consensus users' model

After you help all the stakeholders to agree on what they want the new database system to do for them, you need to transform this consensus into a model that represents their thinking. The model should include all the items that are of interest. It should describe how these items relate to each other. It should describe in detail the attributes of each of the items of interest. This users' model will be the basis for either an entity-relationship model or a semantic object model that you will then convert into a relational database model.

If it seems as if I am talking about lots of models all of a sudden, I am. Subsequent chapters clarify the role that these various models play in the development process. In this chapter, I describe the importance of finding out how the system's stakeholders view it. Their views are the basis for the users' model. However, you cannot build a database directly from the users' model. It is neither definite enough nor detailed enough. You can, however, derive either an entity-relationship model or a semantic object model from it. In Chapter 4, I show how to derive the E-R model, and in Chapter 5, the SOM. Chapter 8 shows how to convert an E-R model into a relational model, and from there into a database. Chapter 9 does the same thing for a SOM.

The key point here is that your database model is *not* based on the organization's business. Rather, it is based on the users' *perception* of that business. Many database development projects have failed because the developers based the system on *their* perception of the organization and how it worked. Any database/database application combination that you build will be used by people. It must be consistent with the way those people view reality rather than with reality itself.

After you identify all the items that the users deem important, their attributes, and the relationships among them, you are ready to move on to the next step: transforming that users' model into either an entity-relationship model or a semantic object model. Either of those can be directly translated into a relational model, from which you can build a database.

So, what is the users' model, anyway? It is a conceptual structure on which all stakeholders agree. The structure includes all items that are deemed to be important parts of the system. It also includes the attributes of those items, and the relationships among the items. As a developer, you must generate a complete list of items, identify the significant attributes of each item, and recognize and document any relationships among items.

Chapter 4

The Entity-Relationship Model

*A*fter you have a users' data model that all stakeholders can support, you need to put that model into a formal structure that you can map directly into a relational model and then implement as a database. This chapter describes the most popular such formal structure, the entity-relationship model.

In 1976, six years after E. F. Codd's seminal paper on relational database theory appeared, Peter Chen published a paper in the *ACM Transactions on Database Systems* that described the entity-relationship (E-R) model. The E-R model was significant because it could be directly translated into a relational model that met Codd's criteria for a true relational design. At that time, relational database was still a theoretical discipline. The first commercial relational database management system had not yet reached the market. The practical applicability of the E-R model gave added incentive to software companies to take the financial risk inherent in developing the first relational DBMS products.

Exploring the Structure of the E-R Model

The E-R model can be used to represent a wide variety of systems that people want to track in some detailed manner. The system could be physical, such as the space shuttle or the human genome, or it could be conceptual, such as the financial records of a large corporation. One of the strengths of the E-R model is that even the largest and most complex systems can be modeled using just four elements:

- ✔ Entities
- ✔ Attributes
- ✔ Identifiers
- ✔ Relationships

Entities

Although you might at first think that an entity is a highly advanced intelligence from another galaxy, or perhaps a creature from a higher dimension, it is actually a pretty mundane concept. In the context of the E-R model, an *entity* is merely something that the user can identify and wants to keep track of. Examples might be EMPLOYEE Santos McKinney, SALESPERSON Joshua Flores, CUSTOMER 1732, and SALES_ORDER 314159.

Entities of a given type are grouped together into *entity classes*. Thus, EMPLOYEE is an entity class, and Santos McKinney is an *instance* of the EMPLOYEE entity class, as shown in Figures 4-1 and 4-2.

Figure 4-1: EMPLOYEE, an example of an entity class.

```
EMPLOYEE
    EmpID
    FirstName
    LastName
    JobTitle
    Exempt/Non exempt
    HireDate
    Extension
    Email
    Department
```

Figure 4-2: Santos McKinney, an example of an entity instance.

```
97209
Santos
McKinney
Database Developer
E
01/03/2000
267
smckinney@acme.com
Molecular Biology
```

Attributes

There are some things about an entity instance that an organization wants to track and others that it probably does not. For instance, the company that employs Santos McKinney will doubtless want to record his first and last names, and perhaps his hire date, but not his shoe size.

The *attributes* of an entity are the characteristics of that entity that are of interest to the user. Thus, FirstName, LastName, and HireDate would likely be attributes of the EMPLOYEE entity class, but ShoeSize would not. In most organizations, management does not care about the shoe size of its employees.

Identifiers

In a database, it is pretty important that you be able to distinguish one entity instance from another. For example, it is bad form to send a bill to a CUSTOMER for an item that the customer did not order. It is even worse to fail to bill a CUSTOMER who did order, and then took delivery on your company's top-of-the-line luxury yacht.

So, you must have some way to identify the individual instances of an entity class. Logically enough, the E-R model does this with attributes or combinations of attributes called *identifiers*:

- A *unique identifier* will identify one and only one instance of an entity class.
- A *non-unique identifier* will identify a set of instances that share some common characteristic or group of characteristics.
- An identifier that is composed of two or more attributes is called a *composite identifier*.

Often, a single attribute will serve as a unique identifier for an entity class. At other times, however, no single attribute will narrow things down to that extent. In such cases, other attributes, making up a composite identifier, can be added until the combination of attributes is enough to uniquely identify every instance in the class. For example, a Social Security Number is a unique identifier of a resident of the United States. A person's last name is probably a non-unique identifier of a resident of the United States, particularly if that last name happens to be Smith, Rodriguez, Lee, or Nguyen. A composite identifier, such as the combination of a person's first name, last name, street, city, and state is probably enough to uniquely identify a person, unless perhaps a father and son have the same name and live at the same address.

Relationships

Entities are associated with other entities through *relationships*. *Relationship classes* are associations among entity classes. *Relationship instances* are associations among entity instances.

Relationships can exist in varying *degrees*. A degree 2 relationship is one between two entity classes or two entity instances. A degree 3 relationship relates three entity classes or entity instances to each other. An example of a degree 2 relationship would be that between a basketball team and its players. Each team has a set of associated players, none of whom are associated with any other team. Figure 4-3 shows a diagrammatic representation of the relationship.

Figure 4-3:
Degree 2
relationship.

An example of a degree 3 relationship would be that among a composer, a lyricist, and the songs they jointly create. Each song is created by the combined efforts of a composer and a lyricist. Figure 4-4 shows a diagrammatic representation of the relationship.

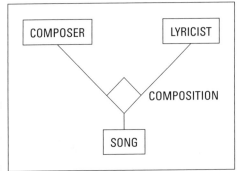

Figure 4-4:
Degree 3
relationship.

Degree 2 relationships, also called *binary relationships*, are very common and are simpler than relationships of higher degree. Happily, most problems of practical significance to businesses and other organizations can be modeled using binary relationships. Degree 3 relationships can often be reduced multiple degree 2 relationships, which can then be handled more easily.

Three kinds of binary relationships exist:

- **A one-to-one (1:1) relationship** relates one instance of one entity class to one instance of a second entity class.
- **A one-to-many (1:N) relationship** relates one instance of one entity class to multiple instances of a second entity class.
- **A many-to-many (N:M) relationship** relates multiple instances of one entity class to multiple instances of a second entity class.

Figure 4-5 shows a diagrammatic representation of an example of a 1:1 relationship between a driver and a driver's license. Every driver has one and only one license, and every license belongs to one and only one driver.

Figure 4-5:
One-to-one
relationship
between
DRIVER and
LICENSE.

Figure 4-6 shows an example of a 1:N relationship between a driver and the traffic tickets he has received. A driver may receive multiple traffic tickets for multiple infractions of the traffic laws, but each ticket is written for one and only one driver.

Figure 4-6:
One-to-
many
relationship
between
DRIVER and
TICKET.

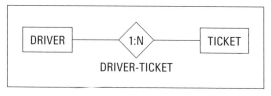

Figure 4-7 shows an example of a N:M relationship between a driver and the routes that she might take to get to work. A driver may take any one of several routes to get to work. Similarly, each route may be taken by multiple drivers.

Figure 4-7:
Many-to-
many
relationship
between
DRIVER and
ROUTE.

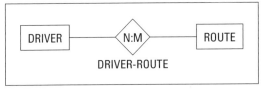

Creating Entity-Relationship Diagrams

Figures 4-5, 4-6, and 4-7 are examples of entity-relationship diagrams. Entities are represented as named rectangular boxes, and relationships as lines connecting the boxes. The relationship lines contain symbols that represent the maximum and minimum cardinality of the relationship. Cardinality? What's that? Read on to find out.

Maximum cardinality

The diamond at the center of the relationship lines in Figures 4-5, 4-6, and 4-7 shows the *maximum cardinality* — that is, the maximum number of instances of an entity on each side of a relationship. For example, the 1:1 in the diamond in Figure 4-5 means that a single instance of the entity on the left is related to a single instance of the entity on the right. Similarly, the 1:N in the diamond in Figure 4-6 means that a single instance of the entity on the left is related to multiple instances of the entity on the right. The N:M in the diamond in Figure 4-7 means that multiple instances of the entity on the left are related to multiple instances of the entity on the right, and the maximum number of instances on the left is not necessarily equal to the maximum number of instances on the right.

Minimum cardinality

Just as maximum cardinality is the maximum number of instances of an entity on each side of a relationship, *minimum cardinality* is the minimum number of instances of an entity on each side of a relationship. In some cases, the minimum number of instances of an entity might be zero. For example, in the DRIVER-LICENSE example shown in Figure 4-5, it is possible that a DRIVER might have his LICENSE revoked. If so, it would be possible for an instance of the DRIVER entity class to have no corresponding instance in the LICENSE entity class. In such a case, the minimum cardinality of LICENSE would be zero. On the other hand, every instance of the LICENSE entity class corresponds to an instance of the DRIVER entity class. So the minimum cardinality of DRIVER would be one.

Figure 4-8 shows the same relationship as Figure 4-5 but with minimum cardinality denoted. The oval on the LICENSE side of the relationship means that the minimum cardinality of LICENSE is zero. The slash on the DRIVER side means that the minimum cardinality of DRIVER is one.

Figure 4-8:
E-R diagram
showing
minimum
cardinality.

No general rules exist for determining minimum cardinality. Cardinality is strictly determined by how the users view the system of interest. In other words, the users' data model determines cardinality. Consider the case where a DRIVER moves to a small island near Tahiti, where there are no cars. He is no longer a DRIVER, but his license remains in the LICENSE entity class until it expires. In this case, the minimum cardinality of DRIVER would be zero.

Make sure that your model reflects nuances such as this. The only way to get it right is to question the users carefully on how they view their reality. Figure 4-9 shows the same relationship as Figure 4-8, but with a different minimum cardinality value, based on a different users' data model.

Figure 4-9:
The
minimum
cardinality
depends on
the users'
data model.

In most cases, the minimum cardinality of an entity will be either zero or one. It is zero if the existence of at least one instance of the entity is *not* required, and it is one if the existence of at least one instance *is* required. In some cases, however, the minimum cardinality for an entity may be more than one. For example, a baseball team must have at least nine players to engage in a game of baseball. Any group of athletes that consists of less than nine players, is thus not a baseball team. You could argue that the minimum cardinality of a baseball team is nine. You could also argue otherwise. It all depends on the users' data model.

The difference between a minimum cardinality of one and a minimum cardinality of zero is the difference between "must exist" and "need not exist." This is a pretty big difference. On the other hand, the difference between a minimum cardinality of one and a minimum cardinality of nine is merely a matter of degree. In both cases, something exists. In most systems that you model, you only need to distinguish between those things that must exist and those that need not. The exact value of the minimum number that exists is usually not of major concern as long as that minimum number is not zero.

Refining the E-R Model

Many real world systems can be modeled using entities, attributes, identifiers, and relationships, incorporating the notions of maximum and minimum cardinality. However, for many other systems, those elements alone cannot be combined in such a way as to adequately match the users' model of the system. For those cases, the E-R model must be extended in any of several ways to provide a better match. A major extension is the recognition that not all entities are alike. There can be different kinds of entities.

Strong entities and weak entities

In previous sections of this chapter, I talk about entities as if they were roughly equivalent to each other, at least conceptually. For example, a retail database might have a CUSTOMER entity class, a SALESPERSON entity class, and a PRODUCT entity class. These three classes might all be related to each other through a SALES_ORDER entity class. Figure 4-10 shows one possible E-R diagram for such a system.

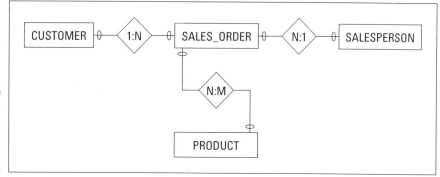

Business rules may vary from one company to another, but one reasonable set might comprise the following rules:

- A CUSTOMER can exist who has not yet bought anything.
- A SALESPERSON can exist who has not yet sold anything.
- A PRODUCT can exist which has not yet been sold.
- A SALES_ORDER can exist without a CUSTOMER, SALESPERSON, or PRODUCT.

The first three rules seem reasonable, based on how the user views the business. You might consider anyone on your mailing list to be a customer, whether or not they have bought anything yet. You would certainly consider a newly hired salesperson to be a salesperson, even if she had not sold anything yet. Products sitting on your shelves, but as yet unsold, are still products.

However, the fourth rule might require some explaining. Perhaps someone walks into the business, buys a special service for cash, and then walks out. There is no opportunity to enter this person into the CUSTOMER table, the special service is not listed in the PRODUCT table, and the technician who performed the service is not listed in the SALESPERSON table. Nevertheless, a SALES_ORDER is generated to record the sale. So, in this four-entity E-R model, none of the four entities depend on any of the others for its existence. They all can exist independently of the other entities.

Now consider the DRIVER-LICENSE relationship that I mention in previous sections of this chapter. A driver can exist without a driver's license, but a driver's license cannot exist without a driver. A driver's license is existence-dependent on a driver. An entity that is existence-dependent on another entity is called a *weak entity*. Any entity that is not a weak entity is called a *strong entity*. Thus, LICENSE is a weak entity, and DRIVER is a strong entity.

You denote weak entities by rectangles with rounded corners. The diamond showing the maximum cardinality of a relationship between a weak entity and its associated strong entity also has rounded corners. Figure 4-11 shows the DRIVER-LICENSE relationship, with LICENSE displayed as a weak entity.

Figure 4-11:
DRIVER-
LICENSE
relationship,
showing
LICENSE
as a weak
entity.

ID-dependent entities

A special class of weak entity depends on a strong entity not only for its existence, but also for its very identity. Consider the case of a seat on an airline flight. A seat cannot exist unless it is installed in an airliner. Thus, the identifier 10-B by itself does not specify a seat. However, seat 10-B on today's flight 1372 from San Jose to San Diego does specify a seat adequately. In this case, seat 10-B is a weak entity that depends on the strong entity flight 1372 for its existence. It also depends on flight 1372 for its identity, because the identifier for the flight is part of the identifier for the seat. SEAT is *ID-dependent* on FLIGHT. Figure 4-12 shows the SEAT-FLIGHT relationship.

Figure 4-12:
FLIGHT-
SEAT
relationship,
in which
SEAT is ID-
dependent
on FLIGHT.

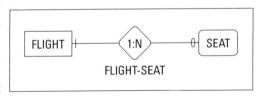

Supertype and subtype entities

An entity class might include instances that share some characteristics with all other instances, but have other characteristics that they do not share with all other instances. Consider a college community. It will have students, faculty members, and staff. Students are working toward a degree. Faculty members teach classes and do research. Staff employees, such as the president and the janitors, provide other services besides teaching and research.

All members of the community have some common characteristics, such as name, home address, telephone number, and e-mail address. Other characteristics are unique to each group. Students would have a grade point average, but faculty and staff would not. Faculty would have an academic rank, but students and staff would not. Staff would have a job category, but students and faculty would not.

In this example, STUDENT, FACULTY, and STAFF are all subtypes of the supertype COMMUNITY.

An important feature of supertype/subtype relationships is the notion of *inheritance*. The subtypes in such a relationship inherit all the attributes of the supertype entity. The inherited attributes combine with the attributes that are exclusively held by the subtype to provide a total description of the subtype entity. Thus, all members of the COMMUNITY have the attributes Name, HomeAddress, TelephoneNumber, and EmailAddress. Only members of the STUDENT subtype would also have the GradePointAverage attribute. Only members of the FACULTY subtype would have the AcademicRank attribute, and only members of the STAFF subtype would have the JobCategory attribute. Figure 4-13 is an E-R diagram of a supertype-subtype relationship.

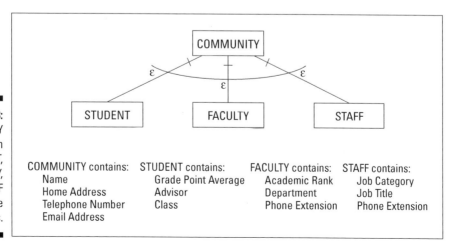

Figure 4-13: COMMUNITY entity with STUDENT, FACULTY, and STAFF subtype entities.

COMMUNITY contains:
Name
Home Address
Telephone Number
Email Address

STUDENT contains:
Grade Point Average
Advisor
Class

FACULTY contains:
Academic Rank
Department
Phone Extension

STAFF contains:
Job Category
Job Title
Phone Extension

In Figure 4-13, the ε next to the relationship lines shows that STUDENT, FACULTY, and STAFF are subtypes of COMMUNITY. The curved line indicates that every member of COMMUNITY must be a member of one of the three subtypes, and cannot be a member of more than one subtype.

A supertype member does not necessarily have to belong to a subtype, nor must subtypes be mutually exclusive. Consider American League baseball players. They all share certain characteristics, including name, height, weight, position played, as well as such offensive statistics as at-bats, hits, runs, stolen bases, and runs batted in. Every player could at least potentially be called upon to go to the plate and try to get a hit, although weak-hitting pitchers and pinch runners may never be called upon to do so.

Weak-hitting pitchers are rarely called upon to hit because in the American League a manager may use a designated hitter to hit for any player in the lineup. This is usually the pitcher. Pitchers in general are notoriously weak hitters because they must spend so much time concentrating on pitching, they are not able to practice hitting as much as the other players.

Players who are not pitchers, but play other defensive positions, such as first base, shortstop, or center field, are called position players. Position players have defensive statistics, including putouts, assists, and errors. Pitchers share those characteristics but have additional ones such as innings pitched, strikeouts, walks, wins, losses, and saves.

All players have offensive statistics, but designated hitters, pinch hitters, and pinch runners that never play the field would not have defensive statistics. Position players do have defensive statistics. Pitchers have defensive statistics and also have pitching statistics. Pitchers and position players are subtypes of the supertype baseball player.

Figure 4-14 shows an E-R diagram for baseball players. PLAYER is the supertype that includes the PITCHER and POSITION-PLAYER subtypes. Designated hitters do not fall into either of these categories, but are still members of the PLAYER supertype. Also, it is possible that a player who is normally a position player might be called upon to pitch in an extra-innings game after all the regular pitchers have been used. In this case, the subtypes are not mutually exclusive.

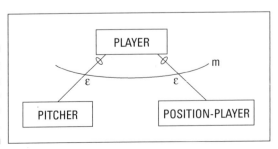

Figure 4-14:
E-R diagram
of non-
exclusive
subtypes.

The *m* next to the curved line means that a member of PLAYER may belong to from zero to many subtypes. A designated hitter would belong to zero. A position player who also occasionally pitched would belong to multiple subtypes.

Capturing business rules

In previous sections of this chapter, I make occasional references to business rules. Business rules are formal statements about how an organization does business. For example, one university may have a rule that a person may not simultaneously be a student and a member of the faculty. Another university may allow faculty to take classes for credit, thus making them students.

Business rules vary from one organization to the next, even though the organizations seem otherwise to be virtually identical. Even two branch offices of the same company may differ in their employee relations policies, for example. You must interview the actual users at the location where your program will be used and ask them detailed questions about the way they conduct their business. From their responses, you can infer the appropriate business rules.

To ensure that your database application accurately reflects the way your clients conduct their business, you must capture all the important business rules. You should interview people representing every group that has a stake in the application, and ask every question you can think of, to maximize the accuracy of your user's model.

It s Time to Look at Some E-R Examples

One of the better ways to understand a fairly complex concept is to carefully examine one or two examples, so that you can relate theory to actual practice. In this section, I show you two examples of usage of the E-R model — one fairly simple, and the second more complex. After you understand these examples, you should be able to construct E-R models of your own.

A fairly simple example

Consider a small dot-com business named Mistress Treasure that sells women's intimate apparel from its Web site. The business displays its products and takes credit card orders on the site. There is no "brick and mortar" store. Fulfillment is outsourced to a fulfillment house, which receives and warehouses products from vendors, and then, upon receiving orders from Mistress Treasure, ships orders to customers.

The Web site front end consists of HTML pages that include text descriptions and graphic images of products, as well as a virtual shopping cart and forms for capturing customer and payment information. The Web site back end contains a database that stores customer, payment, inventory, and shipment status information. Figure 4-15 shows an E-R diagram of the Mistress Treasure system. It is a very small system for a very small "boutique" business.

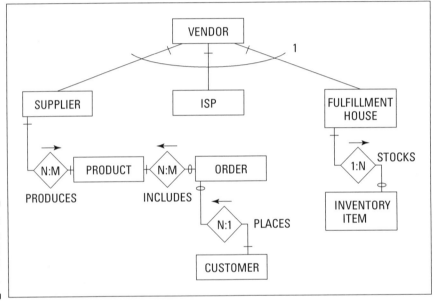

Figure 4-15:
E-R diagram
of small
Web-based
business.

Note that VENDOR is a supertype of the SUPPLIER, ISP, and FULFILLMENT_HOUSE subtypes. Shared attributes of all vendors belong to the VENDOR entity, while attributes that are unique to each subtype belong to either the SUPPLIER, ISP, or FULFILLMENT_HOUSE entities. The 1 at the end of the curved line means that the subtypes are mutually exclusive. An entity can be a member of one and only one subtype.

A many-to-many relationship exists between SUPPLIER and PRODUCT, as well as between PRODUCT and ORDER. Chapter 7 explores the problems that such relationships can cause, as well as techniques for overcoming those problems. For now, you just want to create an E-R model that matches the users' data model as closely as possible.

Other relationships in the model are one-to-many. The model has no one-to-one relationships. Often, a one-to-one relationship between two entities means they are actually two aspects of the same entity. In such cases, you should combine the attributes of both into a single entity. In other cases, however, keeping the two entities separate makes sense. For example, if some attributes are public information and others are confidential, assign the public attributes to one entity and the confidential attributes to the second entity.

A more complex example

Most real-life applications are more complex than the Mistress Treasure example that I describe in the preceding section. Consider the Sawbones Placebo Clinic, which treats hypochondriacs with a variety of therapies. By interviewing the clinic manager, Pat Answer, you find that she wants to keep records on all employees, and also track the treatment of patients by clinic staff. She tells you what her mental model of the clinic is, and what information she wants to capture for later review and analysis. You listen carefully to her description, either writing it down or recording it for later transcription.

Sawbones employs doctors, nurses, medical technologists, and medical assistants. The company extends certain benefits to employees and to their dependents. Doctors, nurses, and medical technologists all must be licensed by a recognized licensing authority. Medical assistants may be certified, but need not be, to be employed in a hospital or clinic.

Typically, a patient will see a doctor, who will examine the patient and then order one or more tests. A medical assistant or nurse will take samples of the patient's blood, urine, and so on, and take the samples to the laboratory. In the lab, a medical technologist will perform the tests that the doctor ordered on these samples, usually called specimens. The medical technologist then sends the test results to the primary care physician who ordered the tests, as well as perhaps one or more consulting physicians. Based on the test results, the doctor, in consultation with the consulting physicians, makes a diagnosis of the patient's condition and prescribes a course of treatment. One or more nurses then administer the prescribed treatment to the patient.

To build a database that meets the client's needs, using the tool of the Entity-Relationship diagram, the first step is to identify those important items that should be considered entities. By carefully listening to Ms. Answer and asking for clarification frequently, you come up with the following list of candidate entities:

Employee	Medical assistant
Manager	Benefits
Doctor (physician)	Dependents
Nurse	Patients
Medical technologist	Doctor's license

Nurse's license

Medical technologist's license

Medical assistant's certificate

Examination

Test order

Test

Test result

Consultation

Diagnosis

Prescription

Treatment

This list is a first cut at an entity list. You build the list by extracting the major nouns that Pat Answer used in her description of the business. Some of these nouns definitely represent entities and others do not. After listing them all, go over the list carefully and eliminate those items that are perhaps attributes of entities, as well as those that are not relevant to the client's goals for your database solution.

Pat has told you that she wants to keep track of employees, and mentioned several different types of employees. She also made a point of mentioning benefits and the fact that employee dependents receive some of those benefits. From this information, you conclude that EMPLOYEE, MANAGER, DOCTOR, NURSE, MEDTECH, and MEDASSIST are entities, while MANAGER, DOCTOR, NURSE, MEDTECH, and MEDASSIST are subtypes of the supertype EMPLOYEE. You also assume that DEPENDENT is an entity that you will be concerned about. You find upon asking, that the company provides only one benefit plan that applies to all employees equally. You conclude that BENE-FITPLAN should also be an entity.

Because doctors, nurses, and medical technologists must possess current licenses in order to legally practice their professions, it is important to keep track of license status for these professionals. However, because each professional can have one and only one license for its job category, you assume that these licenses are attributes of their respective professional's entity. The same would be true for medical assistant certification.

PATIENT clearly deserves to be an entity, as does EXAMINATION. These are things that questions might arise about later. The examination is the first step in a chain of events, each represented by an entity. The TESTORDER is an entity, as are TEST and TESTRESULT. You may want to record the physicians that took part in the CONSULTATION that arrived at a DIAGNOSIS and issued a PRESCRIPTION. Finally, the results of the TREATMENT should be recorded.

Knowing the entities, you can start thinking about how they relate to each other and what the minimum and maximum cardinalities of those relationships should be. Figure 4-16 shows one possible E-R diagram that represents my understanding of the users' model. Other interpretations are possible, and could be equally valid.

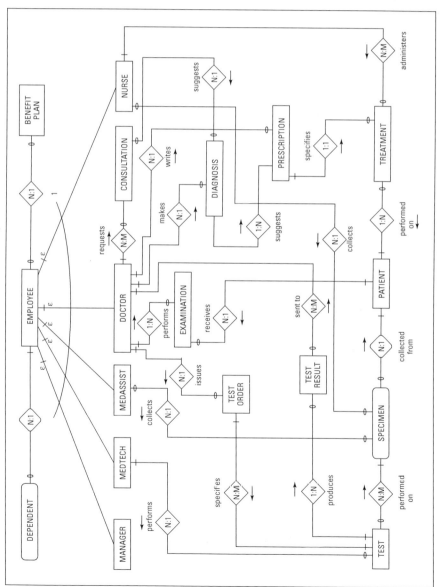

Figure 4-16:
E-R diagram
for
Sawbones
Placebo
Clinic.

This diagram reflects certain things you know about the system. You can state these things in a series of sentences:

- An EMPLOYEE can have from zero to many DEPENDENTs, but a DEPENDENT must be associated with one and only one EMPLOYEE.

- An EMPLOYEE could be a MANAGER, MEDTECH, MEDASSIST, DOCTOR, or NURSE.

- A DOCTOR can perform many EXAMINATIONs, but each EXAMINATION is performed on one and only one PATIENT.

- A DOCTOR can issue many TESTORDERs, and each TESTORDER can specify multiple TESTs.

- A MEDASSIST or a NURSE can collect multiple SPECIMENs from a PATIENT, but each SPECIMEN is from one and only one PATIENT.

- A MEDTECH can perform multiple TESTs on a SPECIMEN, and each TEST might be performed on many SPECIMENs.

- A TEST can produce multiple TESTRESULTs, but each TESTRESULT is associated with one and only one TEST.

- A TESTRESULT is sent to one or more DOCTORs.

- A DOCTOR may request a CONSULTATION with one or more other DOCTORs.

- A CONSULTATION may suggest a DIAGNOSIS.

- A DOCTOR may make a DIAGNOSIS of a PATIENT, based on one or more TESTRESULTs and possibly one or more CONSULTATIONs.

- A DIAGNOSIS could suggest multiple possible PRESCRIPTIONs.

- A DOCTOR writes many PRESCRIPTIONs for the TREATMENT of PATIENTs.

- Each PRESCRIPTION specifies one and only one TREATMENT for each PATIENT.

- One or more NURSEs administer a TREATMENT to a PATIENT.

Chapter 5

The Semantic Object Model

*T*he semantic object model (SOM) is an alternative to the E-R model, and in many situations may be preferable to it. (I describe the E-R model in Chapter 4.) The SOM is particularly well suited to projects that use the bottom-up design methodology. It also has the advantage of being easier to translate into a relational database design.

Examining the SOM Structure

The semantic object model is similar to the entity-relationship model at the highest level of structure, but differs when you take a more detailed look:

▶ Where the E-R model has entities, the SOM has semantic objects.

▶ Where the E-R model has attributes, the SOM has attributes, although they are defined slightly differently from E-R model attributes.

▶ Where the E-R model has identifiers, the SOM has object identifiers.

▶ Where the E-R model has relationships, the SOM also has relationships.

▶ Both models also have the concepts of domains and view. The discussion of domains and views, in this chapter, also applies to the E-R model.

Semantic objects

A *semantic object* is a representation of some identifiable thing that the user cares about. Formally, a semantic object is a collection of attributes that sufficiently describes a distinct identity. This is similar to the definition of an entity.

Top-down versus bottom-up

You can take two approaches to a complex problem: top-down or bottom-up. These approaches are, in many ways, the opposite of each other. The top-down approach, which is often taken by people who use E-R models, has a global perspective. Designers look not just at the immediate task at hand, but also at how that task fits in with other elements of the system that already exist or that may be needed in the future. Design decisions are made based on "the long view." The rationale for this approach is that if possible future needs are considered now, there will be less need for rework of the current task when additional elements of the total system are eventually added.

The bottom-up approach uses the opposite logic. The developers narrow their focus to the task immediately at hand and implement the quickest, best solution for that specific task, without worrying about what may or may not be added later. The rationale is that if significant time is spent speculating on what future needs might affect the current design decision, an entire market window might be lost. The delay in completing the project and starting its use may severely reduce its value. If future expansion requires rework of the current design, so be it. It will have paid for itself by then, thanks to its early availability.

So, which approach is better? That depends on each project's requirements. Sometimes, when immediate availability is not critical, and future expansion is inevitable, the top-down approach is better. Other times, getting the application operational as soon as possible, regardless of other considerations, dictates the bottom-up approach.

There are additional similarities. For example, semantic objects are grouped together into classes. A Web site development company might have a semantic object class PROGRAMMER, and an instance of that class might be Glenn Cooper. The fact that semantic objects represent distinct identities means that each instance of a semantic object class is unique and identifiable.

Semantic objects can represent physical identities, such as a PROGRAMMER, or things that do not physically exist, such as an INVOICE. An INVOICE is a representation or model of a business transaction. So something does not need to be physical in order to be considered a semantic object. It does need to be identifiable by the users as separate and distinct.

Attributes

Semantic objects have attributes in the same way that entities have attributes, but differences exist between the attributes in the semantic object model and the attributes in the entity-relationship model.

The semantic object model has three types of attributes:

✔ *Simple attributes* correspond to the ordinary attributes in the E-R model. (See Chapter 4 for more information about the E-R model.)

✔ *Group attributes* correspond to composite attributes in the E-R model.

✔ *Semantic object attributes* have no parallel in the E-R model. They are a distinguishing feature of the SOM. To understand semantic object attributes, study Figure 5-1, a *semantic object diagram.*

Figure 5-1:
Semantic
object
diagram
of the
PROGRAM-
MER object.

PROGRAMMER
ID ProgrammerID
    FirstName
    LastName
    JobTitle
    Phone

DEPARTMENT

MANAGER

The diagram in Figure 5-1 shows the attributes of the PROGRAMMER object. Two of those attributes — DEPARTMENT and MANAGER — are semantic object attributes. They indicate that the PROGRAMMER object is linked to the DEPARTMENT and MANAGER objects.

The semantic object diagram in Figure 5-1 is incomplete in a couple of ways. Most obvious is the fact that it refers to the DEPARTMENT and MANAGER objects, but does not show them. A subtler deficiency is the fact that the diagram does not show maximum and minimum cardinalities of the attributes.

In the entity-relationship model, cardinalities are applied to the relationships between entities. The SOM features a finer granularity of cardinality, in that maximum and minimum cardinalities are assigned to each attribute, as shown in Figure 5-2.

Here is an opportunity for you to impress your friends at cocktail parties or down at the Midway Pub and Restaurant. Casually work into your conversation something like this: "I believe the finer granularity of cardinality of the semantic object model makes it more useful that the entity-relationship model in many applications." This statement will probably leave your listeners in slack-jawed awe of your sophistication and technical knowledge. Offers of employment and requests for dates cannot be far behind.

A brief history of the SOM

David Kroenke developed the semantic object model, based on earlier work by E. F. Codd, Michael Hammer, and Dennis McLeod. He first published the SOM in 1988 in his widely used textbook, *Database Processing — Fundamentals,* *Design, & Implementation.* Since that time, the model has gained widespread use because it is relatively easy to understand and because many developers prefer the bottom-up approach to database development.

Figure 5-2:
Semantic object diagram of the PROGRAM-MER object, showing maximum and minimum cardinalities.

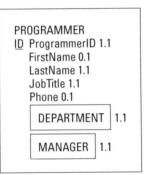

Of course, it helps if you know what all this means. You already know what *cardinality* means; it is the minimum possible or maximum possible number of instances that one side of a relationship may have. *Granularity* has to do with the level of detail of something. In the E-R model, cardinality is defined at the entity level rather than the attribute level. In the SOM, granularity is finer, at the attribute level rather than the semantic object level. This allows a more accurate modeling of the users' conception of the real world system that your database will capture data about.

The SOM shows the cardinality of each attribute as a subscript in the format $N.M$, where N represents the minimum cardinality and M represents the maximum cardinality. In most cases, minimum cardinality is either 0 or 1. If minimum cardinality of an attribute is 0, that means the attribute need not exist. If minimum cardinality of an attribute is 1, the attribute must exist. If the minimum cardinality of an attribute is 9, the attribute must exist, and at least nine instances of that attribute must exist. For example, the object BASE-BALLTEAM would have an attribute Player. A baseball team must have at least nine players in order to be a valid team.

The maximum cardinality of an attribute is the largest number of instances allowed for that attribute. For example, a baseball league might impose a limit on the number of players that a team may have, such as 27. In such a case, the Player attribute of the BASEBALLTEAM semantic object would have a minimum cardinality of 9 and a maximum cardinality of 27, denoted Player$_{9.27}$. For most systems of interest, the exact value of the maximum cardinality of an attribute is not known. In such cases, the variable N is used to represent a value greater than 1.

Object identifiers

In the E-R model (see Chapter 4), you need a way to identify individual instances of an entity class. To do this, you use identifiers, consisting of one attribute, or composite identifiers, consisting of multiple attributes. Similarly, in the SOM, you need to be able to identify individual instances of a semantic object class. *Object identifiers* perform this job.

If an object identifier consists of a single attribute, it is called a *simple-value identifier*. If an object identifier consists of more than one attribute, it is called a *group identifier*. In semantic object diagrams, the letters *ID* to the left of the attribute name denote object identifiers. If the object identifier is unique, the letters ID are underlined.

Generally, if an attribute is an identifier, it must have a value, meaning that the minimum cardinality may not be 0. Similarly, an identifier should not have more than one value, so the cardinality of an identifier is almost always 1.1.

Other simple-value attributes that are not identifiers usually are not required, and thus may have a minimum cardinality of 0. They may also have a maximum cardinality of more than one, so their overall cardinality in some cases is 0.N. However, in most cases, non-identifier simple-value attributes need not exist, but have a cardinality of one if they do exist. So, to reduce clutter in semantic object diagrams in the remainder of this book, I do not show cardinality for simple-value identifier attributes if cardinality is 1.1, and I do not show cardinality for simple-value non-identifier attributes if cardinality is 0.1.

Relationships

Relationships in the semantic object model are denoted differently from the way relationships are denoted in the entity-relationship model. Consider Figure 5-3, which shows two related semantic objects: CUSTOMER and ORDER.

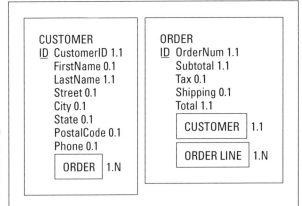

Figure 5-3: CUSTOMER and ORDER objects.

Note that the CUSTOMER object has a semantic object attribute named ORDER, and the ORDER object has a semantic object attribute named CUS-TOMER. This is an example of *paired attributes*. It is a way of showing the rather obvious fact that if CUSTOMER is related to ORDER, then ORDER must be related to CUSTOMER.

The respective cardinalities of the semantic object attributes show that a one-to-many relationship exists between the CUSTOMER and ORDER seman-tic objects. One CUSTOMER may make many ORDERs, but each ORDER is made by one and only one CUSTOMER. The ORDER object is also paired with the ORDER LINE object (not shown).

Attribute domains

The *domain* of an attribute is the set of all possible values that the attribute may assume. This set may be described in several ways. One way is an *enu-merated list*, which merely lists each value that the attribute may take. If, for instance, the attribute in question were North American countries, the domain would be (Canada, United States, Mexico).

Another way to describe a domain is to give a combination of a physical description and a semantic description. The physical description might be an alphanumeric string no more than 30 characters in length. The semantic description conveys meaning, and might be the street address of a customer. However you specify a domain of an object attribute, it should contain all possible instances of the attribute.

Semantic object views

If you think of a semantic object as being a house, then a semantic object view is a window in one of the walls of that house. When you look through a window into a house, you see some of the things in the house but you don't see other things. If you look through another window, you might see some of the same things you saw through the first window plus some things that were not visible through the first window. Semantic object views are similar. One semantic object view will contain some, but not all, of the attributes of a semantic object. A second semantic object view might contain some attributes that were in the first view plus others that were not. It might contain a set of attributes, none of which were included in the first view.

Figure 5-4 shows a semantic object for a company's EMPLOYEEs. This object contains information that is public and other information that is confidential. The public information may be viewed by anyone, but the confidential information should be seen only by human resources employees and an employee's direct supervisor. To ensure that the appropriate information is available to those who should see it and to no one else, you can create two views. PUBLIC_ VIEW can be viewed by anyone who has access to the system. CONFIDENTIAL_ VIEW can be viewed only by people with the appropriate permissions.

Figure 5-4:
EMPLOYEE
semantic
object
with two
different
views of its
contents:
PUBLIC_
VIEW and
CONFIDEN-
TIAL_VIEW.

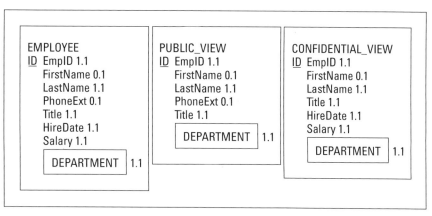

Confidential information, such as an employee's hire date and salary, appears only in the CONFIDENTIAL_VIEW. Information that is appropriate for both views, such as FirstName and LastName, appears in both views. Information that should be public, but has no human resources significance, such as PhoneExtension, is only in the PUBLIC_VIEW.

Different Types of Objects Model Different Situations

Some objects represent very simple ideas. Others represent complex concepts, and concepts can be complex in different ways. As a result, various object types have been defined. I discuss the most common of these, and give typical examples of their usage. First, though, I define some terms that I use throughout the following sections:

✔ A *single-value attribute* is an attribute whose maximum cardinality is 1.

✔ A *multi-value attribute* is an attribute whose maximum cardinality is greater than 1.

✔ A *nonobject attribute* is a simple or group attribute.

Simple objects

A *simple object* is a semantic object that contains only single-value, nonobject attributes. Figure 5-5 shows an example of a simple object VEHICLE that models the vehicles on a used car lot.

Figure 5-5:
Example of
a simple
object:
VEHICLE.

```
VEHICLE
ID  VehicleID 1.1
ID  LicenseNo
ID  LicenseState
    Make
    Model
    Engine
    Color
```

In Figure 5-5 and subsequent figures, cardinalities have been omitted from simple attributes having a value of 0.1.

Composite objects

A composite object is a semantic object that contains one or more multi-value, nonobject attributes. For example, the invoice shown in Figure 5-6 requires a composite object, in order to be modeled accurately.

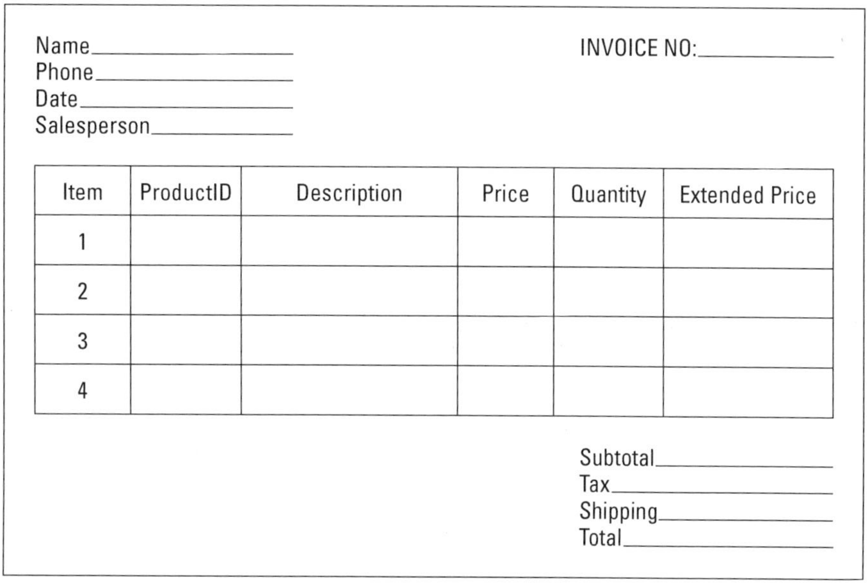
Name__________ INVOICE NO:__________
Phone__________
Date__________
Salesperson__________

Item	ProductID	Description	Price	Quantity	Extended Price
1					
2					
3					
4					

Subtotal__________
Tax__________
Shipping__________
Total__________

Figure 5-6: Modeling this invoice requires a composite object.

Figure 5-7 shows an object diagram for the INVOICE object. The attribute Item is a group attribute having a maximum cardinality of N. The attributes that make up Item (ProductID, Description, Price, and so on) can occur multiple times in an instance of the INVOICE semantic object. The minimum cardinality of the Item attribute is 1, meaning that an INVOICE cannot exist unless it has at least one Item. Some businesses may allow an invoice to be started before any item is specified for purchase; in such cases, the minimum cardinality would be 0. You must interview the users to find out which specification for minimum cardinality is appropriate for a given case.

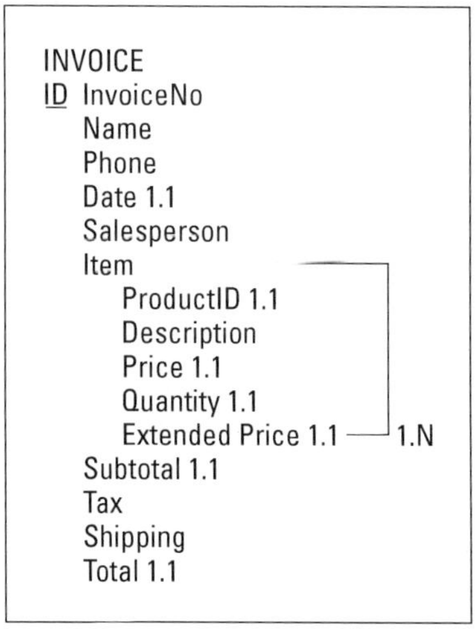

Figure 5-7: Object diagram for the INVOICE composite object.

Compound objects

A compound object contains at least one object attribute. In other words, it is directly related to at least one other object. Figure 5-8 shows two data entry forms: one for basketball teams and the other for athletes that play on those teams. Figure 5-9 shows the TEAM and PLAYER compound objects that you infer must exist, from examining the forms in Figure 5-8. You deduce maximum cardinality by observing that a team can have multiple players, but each player plays for one and only one team. By questioning the users, you determine that a player must be on a team to be considered a player, and that a team must have at least five players to be considered a team. This gives you the minimum cardinalities for the TEAM and PLAYER semantic objects.

As shown in Figure 5-9, the object attributes always occur in pairs, indicating a relationship between the TEAM and the PLAYER objects.

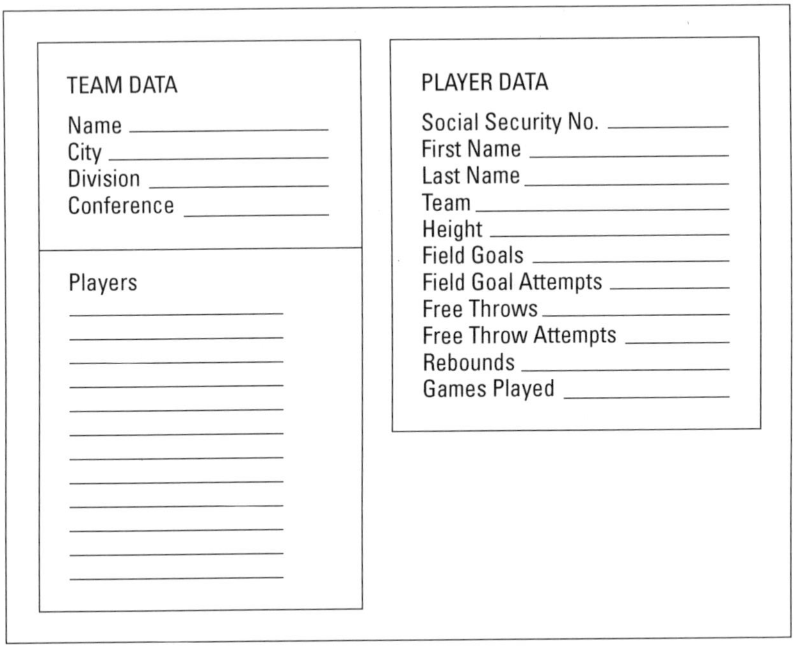

Figure 5-8:
Example
data entry
forms for
compound
objects with
1:N paired
attributes.

TEAM DATA

Name _____
City _____
Division _____
Conference _____

Players
_____
_____
_____
_____
_____
_____
_____
_____
_____
_____
_____

PLAYER DATA

Social Security No. _____
First Name _____
Last Name _____
Team _____
Height _____
Field Goals _____
Field Goal Attempts _____
Free Throws _____
Free Throw Attempts _____
Rebounds _____
Games Played _____

Hybrid objects

A *hybrid object* contains at least one multivalued group attribute that includes a semantic object attribute. For example, Figure 5-10 shows a Locker Assignment Report for the Sun City Legends basketball team. It displays the names and phone numbers of the general manager and coach, as well as listing each player, the player's uniform number, and the number of the locker currently assigned to that player. A player need not have a locker assigned, and a locker need not be assigned to any player. A player may be assigned no more than one locker. Figure 5-11 shows the semantic objects that you can deduce from the report. LockerAssignment is a multivalued group attribute that includes the PLAYER semantic object attribute.

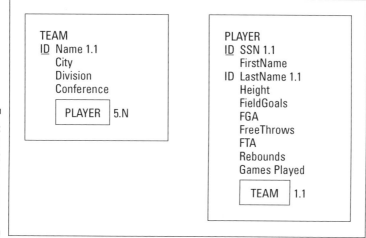

Figure 5-9:
TEAM and
PLAYER
compound
objects with
1:N paired
attributes.

```
TEAM
ID  Name 1.1
    City
    Division
    Conference
    ┌─────────────┬──────┐
    │  PLAYER     │ 5.N  │
    └─────────────┴──────┘
```

```
PLAYER
ID  SSN 1.1
    FirstName
ID  LastName 1.1
    Height
    FieldGoals
    FGA
    FreeThrows
    FTA
    Rebounds
    Games Played
    ┌─────────┬──────┐
    │  TEAM   │ 1.1  │
    └─────────┴──────┘
```

Figure 5-10:
Report
suggests
a hybrid
object
TEAM,
which
contains a
multivalued
attribute
that
includes the
PLAYER
semantic
object.

Sun City Legends   General Manager: R. Cousy (555) 555-5555
                      Coach: W. Chamberlain (555) 555-5100

Locker Assignment Report

Player	Uniform No.	Locker
D. Schayes	34	101
W. Reed	54	102
E. Johnson	33	103
M. Jordan	23	104
M. Lemon	15	105
R. Parrish	00	106
L. Bird	15	107
E. Baylor	12	108
G. Petrie	44	109
B. Walton	22	110
B. Russell	51	111

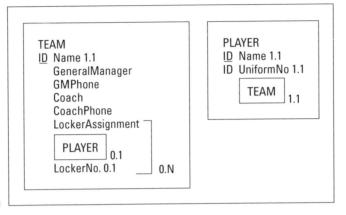

Figure 5-11:
Semantic
objects
deduced
from the
sample
report in
Figure 5-10.

An alternative representation would put the LockerNo attribute into the PLAYER semantic object rather than the TEAM semantic object. This would eliminate the need for a LockerAssignment attribute. In general, there is usually more than one valid way to model a system.

Association objects

An association object relates two or more objects and stores data about the relationship. Figures 5-12, 5-13, and 5-14 show a report and two data entry forms that refer to freight train scheduling on the Great Eastern & Nutley Railroad.

Figure 5-12:
Source
document
used to infer
relevant
semantic
objects: a
railroad's
schedule for
the morning
of a typical
day of
operation.

> ### Great Eastern & Nutley Railroad
>
> ---
>
> #### 09-16-2000 Morning Schedule
>
> Run: OIBU1
> Scheduled Departure Time: 6:20
> Engineer: C. Jones
> Engine: BALDWIN382
>
> Run: OIBU2
> Scheduled Departure Time: 8:45
> Engineer: J. Dockerty
> Engine: GE3544
>
> Run: OIBU3
> Scheduled Departure Time: 11:09
> Engineer: K. Herbert
> Engine: GE6624

Great Eastern & Nutley Railroad

Engineer Data Form

Name:	
Social Security Number:	
Street:	
City:	
State:	
Phone:	

Freight service on the Great Eastern & Nutley Railroad runs East to West and West to East. Runs are identified by their points of origination and destination. Run OIBU3 refers to the third train from Oak Island to Buffalo on the current day. Engineers are identified by their employee ID number, and engines are identified by engine number. GE6624, for example, refers to Great Eastern & Nutley engine 6624, which was manufactured by General Electric.

Figure 5-15 shows three semantic objects that you can infer based on the report and forms. The RUN object associates the ENGINEER object with the ENGINE object.

Great Eastern & Nutley Railroad

Engine Data Form

Engine Number:	
Manufacturer:	
Model:	
Date of Last Overhaul:	

Parent/subtype objects

In many cases, a category of items contains some attributes that are shared by some but not all of the instances of the category. For example, on a baseball team, all players share such defensive statistics as put outs, errors, and assists. Pitchers have additional defensive statistics that do not apply to other players, such as wins, losses, walks, balks, wild pitches, saves, and earned run average.

You could include pitchers along with other players in a single semantic object named PLAYER. In that case, semantic object instances for non-pitchers would have null values for those attributes that pertain only to pitchers, as shown in Figure 5-16.

Figure 5-15:
The association object named RUN forms an association between a railroad ENGINEER and the ENGINE that person drives.

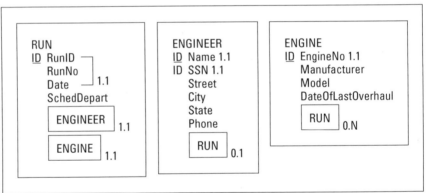

Figure 5-17 shows the same information modeled differently. In this case, a *parent object* PLAYER contains the attributes that apply to all players and a PITCHER semantic object attribute that forms a link to the *subtype object* PITCHER. PITCHER holds only the attributes that apply exclusively to pitchers and a semantic object attribute PLAYER that links back to the PLAYER parent object.

Subtype objects have the property of inheritance. A subtype object inherits all the attributes of its parent (or supertype) object. It is possible for a semantic object to have multiple subtypes, or even nested subtype objects. Happily, these more complicated models are beyond the scope of this book. There is quite enough complication here for your eyes to glaze over and your attention to drift off, as it is.

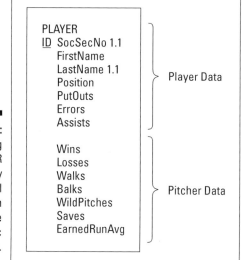

Figure 5-16:
Representing
PLAYER
data by
including all
players in
a single
semantic
object.

Figure 5-17:
Separating
out pitchers
into the
PITCHER
object as a
subtype of
the parent
object
PLAYER.

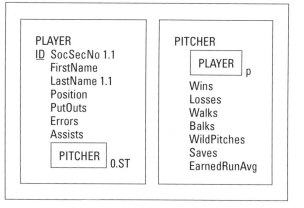

Archetype/version objects

An *archetype object* is one that encompasses multiple versions, releases, or editions. The archetype object contains those attributes that are common to all versions. The *version object* contains those attributes that distinguish one version from another. Figure 5-18 shows the archetype and version semantic objects that model a software product that goes through multiple revisions after its initial release.

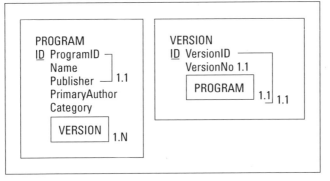

Figure 5-18:
Example of
archetype/
version
semantic
object.

Building a Semantic Object Model, an Example

The best way to figure out how a modeling system works is to see it in action. In this section, I describe a users' data model, and then show you how to translate it into a semantic object model.

You can use several methods to obtain a users' conceptual model of a system that you have been asked to move to a database system. One valuable method is to talk to the users and record what they say. This probably should be a supplemental method rather than the primary method of finding out about the system, however.

In all probability, your clients already have a system of some sort, either computerized or manual. They no doubt have printed reports and data entry forms. These printed documents can reveal much about the underlying structure of the users' model. From the reports and forms, you can infer much about the semantic objects that you will need to accurately represent the users' model as a semantic object model.

The Zetetic Institute is a fictitious interdisciplinary research institute located in Champaign, Illinois. It was founded by the unrecognized genius and visionary who first invented and demonstrated sound motion pictures, Joseph T. Tykociner. The Institute is divided into 12 departments, each one dedicated to a major area of human knowledge. One of the basic ideas of the Institute is to place top scholars from each of the 12 areas in close proximity to each other. This facilitates the discovery of new knowledge through the interaction of world-class researchers who would not normally interact with peers from other disciplines. Membership in the Institute includes both permanent and visiting staff. Permanent staff provide continuity, and visiting staff periodically infuse fresh ideas and perspectives into the conceptual mix.

One way to model the Zetetic Institute is to examine reports and forms that are generated there, and infer what the important objects at the Institute must be. After you develop a semantic object model based on these documents, you can talk to users to refine the inferences you have made. Start your analysis by looking at the Institute's top-level organizational report, as shown in Figure 5-19.

This report shows information that applies to the entire Zetetic Institute, such as its name, street address, director, phone, and e-mail address. It also shows a repeating group that lists the departments that make up the Institute. From this report, you can infer that in addition to an INSTITUTE semantic object, the model should also include a DEPARTMENT semantic object.

In general, when you see a repeating group such as this in a report, it usually (but not always) means that another semantic object exists in the system, and that it bears a many-to-one relationship to the first object.

The report lists the names of the 12 departments that make up the Institute, along with their managers and each department's main telephone number. These will all translate to attributes of the DEPARTMENT semantic object. Figure 5-20 shows the INSTITUTE and DEPARTMENT objects that you infer from your inspection of the organizational report.

Zetetic Institute
401 E. Green Street
Champaign, IL 61822
Paul Doering, Director
(217) 555-8642
www.zeteticinstitute.org

Department	Manager	Phone
The Arts	W. A. Mozart	555-1357
Symbolics of Information	C. Shannon	555-1010
Hylenergetics	A. Einstein	555-8888
Biological Area	G. Mendel	555-0880
Psychological Area	S. Freud	555-0000
Sociological Area	M. L. King, Jr.	555-4386
Exeligmology	C. Darwin	555-1234
Pronoetics	R. A. Heinlein	555-2120
Regulative Area	A. Smith	555-3003
Disseminative Area	A. Carnegie	555-5555
Zetetics	W. Rose	555-9182
Integrative Area	L. daVinci	555-1504

Figure 5-19:
Organizational
report for
the Zetetic
Institute.

Within the INSTITUTE semantic object, the Institute address has a cardinality of 1.1, indicating that the Institute must have an address, but can have
no more than one. Street has a minimum cardinality of zero because the
Institute is so well known in Champaign that the letter carrier can find it
easily, even without street information. City and State have a minimum cardinality of zero, because PostalCode is sufficient by itself to direct mail to
Champaign. By the same token, PostalCode has a minimum cardinality of
zero, because it duplicates City and State information. The DEPARTMENT
semantic object attribute has a cardinality of 1.N, which makes sense,
because the INSTITUTE does indeed have multiple departments.

Now that you see that the Institute has departments, if your client has not
already volunteered the information, you can ask to see the documents that
specifically pertain to departments. Figure 5-21 shows a report similar to the
Institute's organizational report, but for the Symbolics of Information
Department instead.

This report shows information that is specific to this department. Some of
this information you have already seen in the Institute's organizational
report, but some is new. You already knew the name of the department, the
name of the manager, and the department phone number. New information
includes the department e-mail address, physical address, and information
about the department's staff. The staff information is in the form of a repeating group, suggesting that you should add another semantic object to your
model: the STAFFMEMBER object. This report specifically does *not* reveal
whether a staff member is a member of the permanent staff or a visiting
scholar. This is intentional on the part of the Institute to emphasize that all
members are on an equal footing. There are no 'second-class' citizens. Figure
5-22 shows a revised semantic object diagram reflecting the addition of the
STAFFMEMBER object.

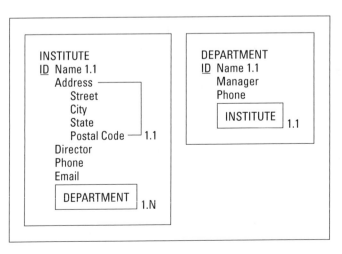

Figure 5-20:
SOM
derived
from the
organizational
report of the
Zetetic
Institute.

Zetetic Institute
Symbolics of Information Department

Manager: Claude Shannon
Dept. Phone: 555-1010
Dept. Email: symbol@zeteticinstitute.org
Office: Boole Hall 101

Staff	Office	Phone	E-mail
C. Babbage	BH 103	555-0001	cbabbage@zeteticinstitute.org
A. Augusta	BH 105	555-0010	aaugusta@zeteticinstitute.org
R. Descartes	BH 104	555-0011	rdescartes@zeteticinstitute.org
A. Turing	BH 211	555-0100	aturing@zeteticinstitute.org
J. Bell	BH 51	555-0101	jbell@zeteticinstitute.org

Figure 5-21: Organizational report for the Symbolics of Information Department.

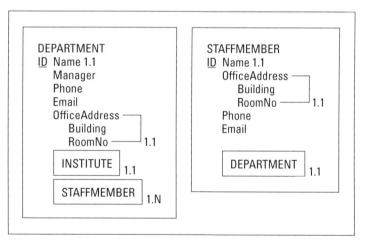

Figure 5-22: SOM derived from the organizational report of the Symbolics of Information Department.

The DEPARTMENT object now contains semantic object attributes for both the INSTITUTE object and the STAFFMEMBER object. Cardinality of the INSTI-TUTE semantic object attribute is 1.1 because this department must belong to an INSTITUTE, and can belong to only one. Cardinality of the STAFFMEM-BER object is 1.N, because a department must have at least one staff member, but may have many. Cardinalities of the STAFFMEMBER object follow a similar logic. A staff member might not have an office, but may have no more than one.

A second document provided by your contact in the Symbolics of Information Department is an example of the organizational report for one of the Department's several research laboratories. Figure 5-23 shows that report.

Zetetic Institute
Symbolics of Information Department
Quantum Computation Lab

Lab Director: John Bell
Lab Phone: 555-7777
Location: Boole Hall 51

Principal Investigator	**Project**
A. Turing	Graph Coloring
R. Descartes	Knapsack
C. Babbage	Traveling Salesman

In this report, you can see additional information about some of the staff members that you encountered earlier. You also see what these people are working on. Another thing you may notice is that people are working on *projects* in the lab. In fact, the list of projects is a repeating group. This indicates that in addition to a LAB semantic object, there may be a PROJECT semantic object, too.

Whether or not to consider projects as semantic objects depends on the nature of the projects and the way the users view them. If they are relatively long-term endeavors that will need to be reported on repeatedly, they probably should be considered semantic objects. If they are transient, quick-turn jobs that are referred to once and then filed away, they probably do not deserve to be considered semantic objects. However, if that were the case, they probably would not show up on an organizational report such as the one shown in Figure 5-23. For that reason, in this example, consider PROJECT to be a semantic object. Figure 5-24 shows a semantic object diagram, based on the new information you obtained from the Quantum Computation Lab.

You could continue "drilling down" forever, creating an ever more detailed semantic object model of the Zetetic Institute's structure. However, you must exercise judgment about when to stop that process. If the model is detailed enough to produce a database design that gives the client what they want, then it is detailed enough. At this point, you have taken the process as far as you need to go.

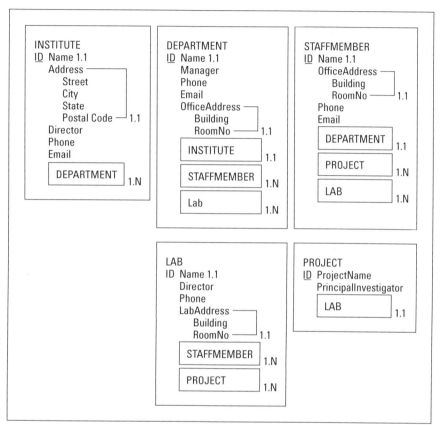

Figure 5-24: SOM for the Zetetic Institute.

Comparing the E-R Model to the SOM

The entity-relationship (E-R) model and the semantic object model (SOM) are two different types of representation of a physical or conceptual system. These representations can be converted into a relational database. Some people find it easier to think of the users' model of a system in terms of the E-R Model and others find the SOM more congenial. You should study both at least to the extent that you are able to tell which one you like best.

The SOM does have some advantages. Semantic objects are generally a closer match to what users think of as important elements in their system than entities are. Also, semantic objects explicitly differentiate between unique and non-unique identifiers. Semantic object group attributes tell you something about the relationships among SOM attributes that is not a part of the description of an E-R entity's attributes.

You can design excellent database systems using either modeling system. Pick one, learn it thoroughly, and then use it consistently.

Chapter 6

Determining What You Are Going to Do

*T*hroughout the previous chapters in this book, I emphasize that database developers should not try to build a model that accurately represents an existing reality. That would be impossible anyway, because a real system potentially has an infinite level of detail. Instead, you try to build a model of the users' model of the system. This model includes only those aspects of the real system that are important to the user — a much more manageable task.

Development projects come in two major varieties: those that replace an existing paper-based or computerized system, and those that implement a new function that the client organization does not have. The two varieties of tasks call for two different approaches to design and development. In this chapter, I consider both types.

Upgrading an Existing System

Assume that a system already exists, but your client deems it to be inadequate for some reason, and calls you in to build its replacement. To replicate the users' model in a database, you need to find out what is important to the users. That involves several tasks.

Identify the stakeholders

Different categories of people will have a stake in the system you build. Not all those stakeholders will be immediately evident, but you can easily identify some of them. For example, the regular users of the system definitely have an interest in what you produce. They are already accustomed to doing things in a specific way, and probably would not be comfortable with radical changes to the way they do their job. Another interested party is the users' immediate supervisor, who probably also has definite ideas about how the system should work and what it should look like.

Other interested parties may not be so easy to identify. You might have to ask some probing questions to find them. For example, you might ask for a list of all people or job functions that will look at reports generated by the system. You might ask, "Aside from the regular users, who might use the system on an infrequent basis?" Check to see if the organization has any ergonomic or usability standards for software. You need to know what is important to all possible interested parties before you make a serious attempt to define the requirements of the system you are to build.

Examine existing documents

You can discover the structure of the system that your client wants you to build by examining documents that your client already uses. (The Zetetic Institute example in Chapter 5 uses this method.) In all likelihood, if something appears in documents that are being actively used, the client considers it to be important.

Interview stakeholders

You can verify the importance of documents in use by questioning the people who use them. Some of the information in the documents may be carried along for historical reasons and no longer serve any useful purpose. If none of the stakeholders care about this "fossil" information any more, leaving it out will simplify your job and will make your final product easier to understand and use.

Some things in the existing documents will be important to some stakeholders but not others. It is important that you hear from all interested parties, so that you do not eliminate something that turns out to be important to someone who you failed to interview.

In some cases, the people you talk to will agree that certain information is very important, even critical, and other information is less important but still needed. This kind of feedback can guide how you will present information on screen and in printed reports. You want the most important information to be very easy to find and very easy to identify. Those functions that will be used most often should be the easiest to access and perform.

Which parts of the old system should you retain?

Clearly, the existing system is not ideal. If it were, you would not have been called in to replace it. On the other hand, because people are accustomed to using it, and because it was originally designed to fill the need, it probably has aspects that you should retain.

What you should keep will vary from one project to another. You will probably want to keep some of the old system, throw some of it away, and add new functions that the old system lacked. The decisions you make here will affect the complexity of your model.

Replacing a paper-based system

If you are replacing a paper-based system, you may want to retain the printed reports, the data entry forms, and the procedures used to process entered data into printed reports. If people are satisfied with the existing reports and data entry forms, duplicate them as closely as possible with your computer-based database system. The procedures that are currently used to process data can be reduced to algorithms that you can implement in your database application. Taking this approach shortens the learning curve for users of your new system, and makes them more comfortable with it from the start.

Even if you can think of a more efficient or logical way of presenting the information, it is often better to stick with what the users are accustomed to seeing. You will have to use your judgment in each case, as to whether it is better to make improvements or leave the user interface as similar to the old system as possible.

You can reverse engineer existing reports and forms to arrive at a semantic object model of the system you are going to rebuild. (See the Zetetic Institute example in Chapter 5.) If you are going to add new functionality to an existing system, you will need to prototype new reports and screen forms, get user concurrence, reverse engineer them, and then combine the result with the model you obtained from reverse engineering the existing forms and reports, to arrive at a complete model of the proposed new system.

Replacing an old computer-based system

If you are replacing a record-keeping system that is already computerized, all the considerations that I mention for a paper-based system still apply. People are already familiar with reports in a certain format. They are accustomed to entering data into screen forms that are laid out in a certain way. Unless you find general agreement that the forms and reports should look or work differently, you will probably want to retain the format of the existing forms and reports. If additional functions are desired, construct prototype forms and reports for those new functions, and then reverse engineer a semantic object model from the complete set of both old and new reports and forms.

Which parts of the old system should you discard?

If the existing system has been in use for any period of time, the needs of the organization it serves have probably changed. Features and capabilities that once were needed are no longer relevant. Other capabilities may still be needed, but it is now clear that they were not implemented in the best possible manner. In those cases, you may want to discard what exists and replace it.

If you are replacing a paper-based system, this means redesigning the existing forms and reports to more accurately meet current requirements. If you are replacing a computer-based system, it means discarding the designs of the obsolete program modules, and replacing them with new designs that meet the new requirements.

If you are considering the removal of any part of an existing system, make sure you identify all the stakeholders in the system. Make sure they are all aware of your plan to remove an existing function and that they all concur with that removal. You don't want clients coming to you after you finish the project and complaining that you have eliminated a function that is critical to them. Adding it back will be much more difficult than keeping it in the first place.

What new features should you add?

At the start of a project to upgrade an existing system, stakeholders typically come up with wish lists of all kinds of things they would like the new system to do, that it does not do now. In many cases, the features that they have been dreaming about are either beyond the capability of current technology or at the very least budget busters that the organization cannot afford. You need to discover the true priorities. Which new features are truly critical, which are important, and which are "nice to have?" You may get different answers to these questions, depending on whom you ask. Human relations skills and business savvy are just as important here as are the technical skills involved in designing a good database model.

After you get all the input from all the stakeholders, you will have to perform "feature triage." In hospitals after a major disaster such as an earthquake or volcanic eruption, when the doctors are confronted with an overwhelming number of injured people, they divide the patients up into three groups: those that are not badly hurt, those that are badly hurt and in need of immediate attention, and those that are so badly hurt that they will die, even if they receive immediate attention. The best use of the doctors' time is to concentrate immediately on the second group. The third group is going to die anyway, so the best you can do is ease their pain. The first group can afford to wait. It is the second group where the doctors' efforts can make a lifesaving difference. After those are taken care of, the doctors can go back to the first group of people who are not badly hurt and attend to their needs.

Similarly, when modeling a database design, divide the proposed new features into three categories:

- ✔ Features that are feasible to include, considering time and budget constraints, but are not of critical importance.
- ✔ Features that are both feasible to include and critically important.
- ✔ Features that are either technically or financially infeasible.

Concentrate on the second group of features — those that are both technically and financially feasible and also critically important. After you include those features, if you have any time and budget left, go back and implement as many of the noncritical features from the first group as you can. You can exclude the third group completely.

Building a New System from Scratch

Building a new system entirely from scratch has both positive and negative aspects, when compared to upgrading an existing system. The positive side is due to the fact that you can design the system based on what it best today, without having to worry about maintaining compatibility with some existing legacy system. Such compatibility considerations could force you to use a DBMS or application development language that would not be your first choice. Another advantage you gain when you implement a brand new function for the client organization is that users will not have to "unlearn" any established habits before they can start becoming effective with the new system.

Identify the stakeholders, and find out what they want

When you are building a new system, implementing a function that the organization has not previously had, it is just as important to identify and talk to all the potential stakeholders as it was in the case of replacing an existing system. Who will input data into the system? Who will make online queries? Who will ask someone else to make online queries for them? Who will read the reports?

Besides the obvious users, multiple levels of management may be involved, as well as outside auditors and accountants. You need to find out who all these people are and what they all need. After you identify the stakeholders, talk to them about their needs and expectations for the system you have been called upon to develop.

Notwithstanding the foregoing, it shouldn't be your job as a database developer to also be a stakeholder detective. You usually can't afford to spend a lot of non-billable time tracking down and interviewing possible stakeholders. This is where the formal requirements document comes in.

Insist on a formal requirements document

Sometimes, in fact often, a communications breakdown occurs between the client and the developer when it comes to exactly what the system under development will do and when it will be delivered. Such breakdowns usually work to the disadvantage of the developer, because payment for services is normally contingent on client acceptance of the finished system.

Feature creep is that insidious process by which the client continues to ask for additional functionality that you did not originally understand to be part of the system. You could be on the hook forever, providing free development services, if it is not clearly understood right from the beginning, exactly what is to be delivered. The formal requirements document is your best defense against feature creep.

A formal requirements document is generated by the client, hopefully after extensive dialog with the developer, that spells out specifically what the proposed system will do. It may also specify a required delivery date.

Often, a client's first attempt at a requirements document will be so vague that leaves too much room for varying interpretations. You may have to meet with the client and clarify in detail what is actually required. The revised requirements document that results from this process should give a very clear description of exactly what the client wants and expects.

Create a solutions document

The requirements document is the clients' statement of what they want. The *solutions document* is the developers' statement of what they will deliver, how it will be implemented, and when they will deliver it.

In an ideal world, the requirements document and the solutions document would agree completely on the deliverables. The developer would commit to providing the client with exactly what the requirements document called for in terms of functionality, delivery time, and cost. However, in the world where I live, things are rarely ideal:

- ✔ It may not be possible to provide all the functionality specified in the requirements document.

- ✔ It may be possible to provide the required functionality, but not within the time constraints specified.

- ✔ It may be possible to meet both functionality and time requirements, but not for the specified cost.

The solutions document is the developers' statement of what they can do. If all functionality, time, and cost requirements cannot simultaneously be met, the solutions document should describe what *can* be done. It may be appropriate to include several alternative solutions. Sometimes the client is willing to sacrifice some functionality in order to obtain delivery by the stated deadline. Sometimes delivering on time is more important than cost, and at other times the opposite is true. If your solutions document offers choices, the clients can select the one option that best meets their goals for the project.

If you respond to a requirements document with a solutions document that does not promise to simultaneously meet all the clients' functionality, time, and cost criteria, you may not get the job. That may be disheartening, but it is better than the alternative. If you commit to doing more than you are really capable of, you could lose far more than the opportunity to do a job. You could lose staff members who burn out trying to do something they don't have the time or expertise to do. You could lose money by having to put more resources onto the project than you can afford to commit. Worst of all, you could lose your hard-earned reputation by failing to deliver what you have promised. You might even be sued for nonperformance on a contract. Give the solutions document your best estimate, and if the clients don't agree to it, or show some flexibility in their requirements, thank them for their time and move on.

Obtain client signoff on the solutions document

The solutions document is effectively a contract. In it, you state what you will do, when you will do it, and what your fee will be. If your clients agree to what you are proposing, they signify that acceptance by signing the document in the space you have provided at the end. Getting a formal signoff is important. After you have that signature, there can be no dispute at a later date as to what you committed to deliver. After you deliver everything that you promised in the solutions document, you have upheld your part of the deal. Feature creep should never become an issue.

If during the course of development your clients should ask you to do something additional, refer them to the signed solutions document. If what they are asking for is not mentioned in the document, you are not obligated to provide it. You may offer to provide the new feature, but for an additional cost, and with a new delivery deadline. Don't commit to any additional work if it will jeopardize your chance to complete the original job in the time originally allotted.

What Will Matter Five Years from Now?

Remember back in 1999, when everyone was worried that our computer-addicted society would come to a screeching halt when the clock struck 12 midnight on December 31? Most of those fears were exaggerated, but some concerns were well founded.

- ✔ Many of the data files that dealt with dates used the last two digits of a four-digit year to represent the year.

- ✔ Many of the programs that dealt with those data files assumed that the missing first two digits were 19.

- ✔ When computers incremented the date from 12-31-99 to 01-01-00, many programs would assume that the current year was 1900 rather than 2000. This could have caused confusion at the very least, and might have caused many other problems that were hard to anticipate.

- ✔ A massive, multimillion dollar effort went into making existing computer hardware and software Y2K compliant. This effort was largely successful, as evidenced by the fact that there was very little disruption on New Years Day 2000 or during the succeeding months.

Lessons learned from the Y2K bug

Although the multimillion-dollar effort to squash the Y2K bug was successful, it still cost organizations hundreds of millions of dollars worldwide. Could that expense have been avoided? Yes. Much of it could have been avoided with the application of a little foresight.

The idea of representing years with only two digits and assuming the other two were 19 occurred to people early in the history of electronic computers when memory was very expensive. Each decimal digit takes one byte of memory, so if a database contained one date per record, developers could save two bytes for every record by using a two-digit year rather than a four-digit year. In the 1950s, that amounted to a significant savings. By the 1980s the cost of memory had decreased substantially, and to an even greater extent by the 1990s. However, the habit of using two-digit year codes had become so ingrained in programmers' minds that they kept on using them even as the year 2000 bore down on them relentlessly like a gigantic tidal wave.

It was not until the latter half of the 1990s before anybody took any serious action to address what became known as the Y2K problem. If the problem had been recognized and addressed sooner, Y2K compliance could have been merged into existing software as it underwent normal upgrades and maintenance. That would have been a lot cheaper than the panicked effort that many organizations had to exert to beat the December 31 deadline.

What can we learn from this? We can learn that it is wise to think ahead. Of course, you must meet the requirements of the present, but it is wise to think of what the future might bring also. What kind of business will your clients have five years from now? What will their business be like one year from now? Some industries are changing so rapidly that the only sure answer to that question is that things will be very different from what they are now.

Perhaps you or your client can anticipate some changes with a degree of confidence. It would be wise to build your system in such a way that those changes will not cause disruption or require a major reworking of the system. There will probably be other changes that you cannot anticipate. With that in mind, can you design things in such a way that flexibility is built in? That way, whatever the future holds, your system will be adaptable to the new reality. This kind of adaptability has real value to your client, and is a strong selling point if you are able to bring it out at the beginning.

How will the organization grow or evolve?

One change that you can anticipate for a client organization is that it might be successful. Certainly your client will be working to make that happen. Success usually implies growth. If the business grows bigger, what impact will that have on its database system? It will probably impact the database in several ways.

Greater volume of business

Success can be measured several ways. One might be to have one of your products favorably reviewed by *Consumer Reports* magazine. Another might be for your mother, after all these years, to finally say she is proud of you. In the fast moving world of dot com businesses, the most widely recognized measure of success is that you are doing three times as much business this year as you did last year. Even if you are not in a hot e-business, your sales volume might still increase significantly. One can always hope.

If your sales do increase, that probably means you have more customers, who are buying more products. You have more different products, and are keeping more of them in stock in your warehouse. You have more vendors supplying you with the raw materials for your wider range of products. You probably have to think more about taxes, and all the record keeping that goes along with them. All these things mean that you must have greater capacity in your database. You need more storage and faster processing speed to give you performance comparable to what you enjoyed when your database was smaller. The database engine you use to implement your database must be robust enough to take advantage of the increased capacity of your upgraded hardware.

Bottom Line: Buy increased capacity before you need it. Anticipate success. Build your system on top of a platform that will grow with the business.

More people

If you are successful and doing a larger volume of business, you will doubtless need more people to handle the increased load. More people means more people trying to access the database at the same time. How many simultaneous users can your system handle? This is something that you should consider at the beginning, when you are choosing a DBMS. Some have a lot more capacity in this area than others.

Bottom Line: Choose to build your database system on the foundation of a DBMS that will be able to support as many simultaneous users as you are likely to have if your business is wildly successful in the next few years.

Greater need for structure

As a business grows, the informal management style that worked so well at the beginning becomes less effective. The CEO no longer knows everyone by name. The all-company meetings become less frequent, and eventually cease altogether. The organization becomes harder for one person to understand and harder to control. It is time to add some structure to the way things are run. More structure means that additional functions must be added to the company database system.

Bottom Line: Structure your database and the application that uses it in such a way that new tables can be added to the database and new functional modules can be added easily and seamlessly to the application. Keep in mind that the system you create now might have to be expanded in the future.

Higher level of security

As an organization grows and more people have access to the database system, it becomes clear that access to some of the data in the database should be restricted. In the early days of a small business, everyone is an owner or a highly trusted employee and has access to everything in the database. As the business grows, confidential information must be more tightly controlled.

Bottom Line: Different database management platforms offer different levels of security for data. Choose a DBMS that has security facilities that will meet your future needs as well as those you have now.

More concern for data integrity

Whether your business is large or small, you want the data stored in your database to be accurate and complete. Nobody wants to lose data or have it corrupted. However, larger systems are more susceptible to data corruption and loss than are small ones. Large systems, with large numbers of users are more likely to encounter conflicts in which two users try to access the same data at the same time. Such conflicts can cause incorrect values to be written into database records.

Bottom Line: With an eye toward possible future expansion, build your database application on top of a platform that offers robust data integrity features.

Determining the Project's Scope

One of the more critical determinants of whether a database development project will be successful for both the developer and the client is that the scope of the project be accurately determined at the very beginning:

- ✔ How big a project is it?
- ✔ What will it require in terms of expertise?
- ✔ What will it require in terms of time?
- ✔ What will it require in terms of development tools?
- ✔ What will it require in terms of workspace?
- ✔ What will all these things cost?

If you underscope a project, at best you will lose money. At worst, you will not be able to deliver as promised. If you overscope a project, your costs will be too high and the client will hire a different developer to do the job.

Bottom Line: Put a lot of thought, time, and effort into scoping any development project that you pursue. The investment you make in scoping will be well worth whatever it costs.

A number of factors enter into the scope of a development project. The first of those factors is what the client wants the new system to do.

What the client wants

The dialog between developer and client that occurs between the writing of the requirements document and the final signing of the solutions document should put what the client wants and is willing to accept, into concrete form. After you know what the client wants the system to do, you can determine the best way to implement it. You will be able to come up with answers to such questions as

- ✔ What DBMS would be best for this system?
- ✔ What development tools (both hardware and software) will I need?
- ✔ What expertise will I need?
- ✔ Do I already have the needed expertise, or will I need to either learn it or hire it?

What the client wants to pay

After you have scoped and costed out the project, based on what the client wants, as specified in the signed solutions document, you should have a good idea of what it will cost you to do the project. Does your projected cost, along with some profit, match the price that the client is willing to pay for the job? If your scoping exercise shows that you will lose money, it is best to cut your losses and decline to take the job rather than go ahead with it and suffer a much larger loss. A compromise might be to go back to the client and negotiate either a larger payment or a less ambitious project.

When the client wants it

Often, delivery time is much more critical for a client than cost. A system may be worth a great deal to the client if it can be put into use before some particular critical date, such as the start of the fall semester at a college or the beginning of the fiscal year for a business. When you are scoping a job, scope the time it will take to complete it as well as what it will cost. Before you take a job with a hard and fast deadline, make sure you can meet the required delivery date. You may be able to get the client to pay for additional developers or other resources to help assure that you deliver on time.

Part III
Database Design

"I STARTED DESIGNING DATABASE SOFTWARE SYSTEMS AFTER SEEING HOW EASY IT WAS TO DESIGN OFFICE FURNITURE."

In this part . . .

*P*art III is the heart of the book. It describes the relational model, covers the importance of normalization, and then tells you how to design a database based on the transformation of an entity-relationship model or a semantic object model into a relational model. You can apply the material in this part to any problem that requires a database management system.

Chapter 7

The Relational Model

As I explain in Chapters 4 and 5, you can capture what the users want for a proposed database system in the form of either an entity-relationship (E-R) model or a semantic object model (SOM). These two modeling systems correspond well with how the users think of their system. They do not, however, translate directly into a database design.

After you create either an E-R model or a SOM of your target system, you must convert the model to a relational model consisting of tables and relationships. A relational model translates directly to a database design. After you have a relational model, you will probably need to refine it in order to ensure data integrity, system reliability, and acceptable performance. In this chapter, I explain how to convert a model (either E-R or SOM) to a relational model, and then optimize that model to meet your clients' needs.

Relations, Attributes, and Tuples

Relational database theory traces back to a paper published in 1970 by E. F. Codd, then of IBM. In that paper, Dr. Codd gave names to the major constituents of a relational model. Definite parallels exist between the elements that make up a relational model and the corresponding elements of the E-R and semantic object models.

Items that people can identify and that they consider important enough to track are called *relations*. Relations in the relational model are similar to entities in the E-R model and to semantic objects in the SOM. Relations have certain properties, called *attributes*. Attributes in the relational model correspond to the attributes in the E-R model and the SOM.

Relations can be represented in the form of two-dimensional tables. Each column in the table holds the information about a single attribute. The rows of the table are called *tuples* in theoretical database journals. Each tuple corresponds to an individual instance of a relation. Figure 7-1 shows an example of a relation, consisting of a set of attributes and a few tuples.

	Column 1 Name	Column 2 Instrument	Column 3 Style
Tuple 1	Mel Taylor	Drums	Ventures
Tuple 2	Al Hirt	Trumpet	Jazz
Tuple 3	Pablo Casals	Cello	Classical
Tuple 4	Carlos Montoya	Guitar	Spanish
Tuple 5	Frederick Chopin	Piano	Classical

Figure 7-1:
MUSICIAN
relation.

Nomenclature confusion

One thing that can be confusing to database newbies is the fact that different database veterans often use different words to mean the same things. In fact, often the same database veterans will use different words to mean the same thing. They might even do it within the same sentence. This bizarre situation has come about because three distinct groups of people have made important contributions to the development of database systems. Coming from different backgrounds, each of these groups had its own names for things.

I have already mentioned the database theorists, such as Dr. Codd, and their use of the terms *relation, attribute,* and *tuple.* A second group consists of the flat-file folks. They were the ones doing database processing before the relational model was proposed. Their terms *file, field,* and *record* correspond with what the relational theoreticians call relations, attributes, and tuples. Finally, the PC community, which came to database after mastering the spreadsheet paradigm, calls the same three items *table, column,* and *row.* Table 7-1 shows the correspondences.

Table 7-1	Three Ways of Saying the Same Thing		
Theoreticians say	Relation	Attribute	Tuple
Flat-file folk say	File	Field	Record
PC community says	Table	Column	Row

It is not uncommon for database veterans to mix these terms in the course of explaining or describing something. Don't let that throw you. Use this handy table to keep things straight in your mind.

Formal definition of a relation

Actually, a relation is not exactly the same thing as a file or a table, although those terms are often used interchangeably. Because relations were defined by theoreticians, they have a very precise definition. The words *file* and *table,* on the other hand, are in general use and are often much more loosely defined. When I use those terms in this book, I use them in the more restricted sense, as being alternate terms for *relation*.

So, what's a relation? Formally, a relation is a two-dimensional table that has the following characteristics:

- ✔ Each cell in the table must contain a single value, if it contains any value at all. Repeating groups and arrays are not allowed as values.

- ✔ All the entries in any column must be of the same kind. For example, if a column contains an employee name in one row, it must contain employee names in all rows that contain values.

- ✔ Each column has a unique name.

- ✔ The order of the columns doesn't matter.

- ✔ The order of the rows doesn't matter.

- ✔ No two rows may be identical.

If and only if a table meets all these criteria, it is a relation. You might have tables that fail to meet one or more of these criteria. For example, a table might have two identical rows. It is still a table in the loose sense, but it is not a relation.

Functional dependencies

Functional dependencies are relationships between or among attributes. Consider the example of two attributes of the CUSTOMER relation: Zipcode and State. If you know the customer's zip code, you can obtain the state by a simple lookup, because each zip code resides in one and only one state. In relational terms, you say that State is *functionally dependent* on Zipcode or that Zipcode *determines* State. Zipcode is called a *determinant*. The reverse is not true. State does not determine Zipcode, because states can contain multiple zip codes.

The following example shows how you denote functional dependencies:

Zipcode → State

A group of attributes may act as a determinant. Consider the relation INVOICE (Inv#, CustID, W/R, ProdID, Quantity, Price, Extprice). Assuming products have both a wholesale and a retail price, the W/R attribute tells whether this is a wholesale or a retail transaction. ProdID identifies the product. Extprice is extended price, derived by multiplying Quantity by Price.

ProdID tells us which product we are considering. W/R tells us whether we are charging the wholesale price or the retail price. Thus, the combination of W/R and ProdID determines Price. Similarly, the combination of Quantity and Price determines Extprice:

(W/R, ProdID) → Price

(Quantity, Price) → Extprice

Neither W/R nor ProdID by itself determines Price; they are both needed to determine Price. Both Quantity and Price are needed to determine Extprice.

Keys

Keys are groups of one or more attributes that uniquely identify a tuple in a relation. One of the characteristics of a relation is that no two rows (tuples) are identical. You can guarantee that no two rows are identical if at least one field (attribute) is guaranteed to have a unique value in each row, or if some combination of fields is guaranteed to be unique for each row.

Figure 7-2 shows an example of the PROJECT relation. It lists researchers affiliated with the Zetetic Institute's Quantum Computation Lab, the project they are working on, and the room in which they are conducting their research.

ResearcherID	Project	Location
aturing	Graph Coloring	QC-103
rdescartes	Knapsack	QC-121
cbabbage	Traveling Salesman	QC-201
bowen	Knapsack	QC-121

Figure 7-2: PROJECT relation.

In this table, each researcher is assigned to only one project. Is this a rule? Must a researcher be assigned to only one project or is it possible for a researcher to be assigned to more than one project? If a researcher can be assigned to only one project, then ResearcherID is a key. It guarantees that every row in the PROJECT table is unique. What if no such rule exists? What if a researcher may work on several projects at the same time? Figure 7-3 shows this situation.

ResearcherID	Project	Location
aturing	Graph Coloring	QC-103
aturing	Traveling Salesman	QC-201
rdescartes	Knapsack	QC-121
cbabbage	Traveling Salesman	QC-201
cbabbage	Knapsack	QC-121
bowen	Knapsack	QC-121

Figure 7-3: PROJECTS relation.

In this scenario, Dr. Turing works on both the Graph Coloring and the Traveling Salesman projects, while Professor Babbage works on both the Traveling Salesman and the Knapsack projects. Clearly, ResearcherID cannot be used as a key. However, the combination of ResearcherID and Project is unique and is thus a key.

You are probably wondering how you can reliably tell what is a key and what is not at key. Looking at the relation in Figure 7-2, it looks like ResearcherID is a key because every entry in that column is unique. However this could be due to the fact that you are looking at a limited sample, and any minute now someone could add a new row that duplicates the value of ResearcherID in one of the existing rows. How can you be sure that won't happen? Ask the users.

The relations you build are models of the mental images that the users have of the system they are dealing with. You want your relational model to correspond as closely as possible to the model the users have in their minds. If they tell you that in their organization researchers never work on more than one project at a time, you can use ResearcherID as a key. On the other hand, if it is even remotely possible that a researcher might be assigned to two projects simultaneously, you will have to revert to a composite key made up of both ResearcherID and Project.

A question that might arise in your mind is, "Is it possible for a relation to exist that has no key?" By the definition of a relation the answer is "no." Every relation *must* have a key. One of the characteristics of a relation is that no two rows may be exactly the same. That means you can always distinguish any two rows from each other, although you may have to include all the relation's attributes in the key to do it.

Problems with Your Relations

Most people have trouble with their relations at one time or another. Quite often, the relation in question is the mother-in-law. She never really believed that you were worthy of marrying her pride-and-joy. Now she knows for sure that you are no good because you spend way too much time with your computer and not nearly enough with your spouse. Personally, I have a very good relationship with my mother-in-law. Of course, the fact that she lives about 3,000 miles away from me may have something to do with that. She wouldn't see me very much even if I didn't spend too much time with my computer.

Like humans, databases are also subject to problem relations. The fact that a table meets the minimum requirements to be called a relation does not mean that it is structured appropriately for the entity it is modeling. If the structure of a relation is inappropriate, problems can arise when you make changes to the data. A database wouldn't be much use if you couldn't add to or delete from the data in it, so these problems, called *modification anomalies*, are pretty important.

Take another look at Figure 7-2. Suppose Dr. Babbage was taken off the Traveling Salesman project and his row was deleted from the PROJECT table. This causes a problem because not only do you lose the fact that Babbage is working on the Traveling Salesman project, you also lose the fact that this project is located in room QC-201. This problem is called a *deletion anomaly*. In general, a deletion anomaly occurs when, in the process of deleting information you no longer want, you also delete information that you want to retain. The fact that Babbage is no longer working on the Traveling Salesman project should not cause you to lose the fact that the project is being investigated in lab QC-201.

Suppose the director of the Quantum Computation Lab decides to begin an investigation of the Clique problem, and puts the quantum computational equipment for that project into lab QC-203. However, he has not yet assigned a researcher to that project. He cannot add a new row to the relation in Figure 7-2 until a researcher has been assigned. This problem is called an *insertion anomaly*. You should be able to record the fact that the new Clique project is located in lab QC-203 whether or not a researcher has been assigned to the project.

Clearly, the relation in Figure 7-2 has value, and can be used for some things. However, the fact that it is subject to deletion and insertion anomalies seriously compromises its value. You can eliminate the anomalies by breaking the PROJECT (ResearcherID, Project, Location) relation into two relations: RES-PROJ (ResearcherID, Project) and PROJ-LOC (Project, Location). Figure 7-4 shows these two relations.

Figure 7-4:
RES-PROJ
and
PROJ-LOC
relations.

ResearcherID	Project
aturing	Graph Coloring
rdescartes	Knapsack
cbabbage	Traveling Salesman
bowen	Knapsack

Project	Location
Graph Coloring	QC-103
Knapsack	QC-121
Traveling Salesman	QC-201

Now, if Babbage is removed from the RES-PROJ relation, the fact that the Traveling Salesman project is located in lab QC-201 is preserved in the PROJ-LOC relation. Also, you can add the fact that the new Clique project is located in lab QC-203 to the PROJ-LOC relation, even though a researcher has not yet been assigned to that project.

The problem with the PROJECT relation in Figure 7-2 is brought about by the fact that the relation deals with two distinct ideas. First, it records which researchers are assigned to which projects. Second, it tells you where on campus each project is located. Although these two ideas are related, they are clearly distinct. You eliminated the modification anomalies in PROJECT by splitting it into two relations: one that dealt only with the researcher assignment idea, and another that dealt only with the project location idea.

Generally, if a relation deals with more than one idea, it is probably subject to modification anomalies. You may want to seriously consider breaking it up into two or more relations, each of which deals with only one idea.

Remember TANSTAAFL? (There ain't no such thing as a free lunch.) Breaking one relation into two has some associated costs. First, you have the obvious cost of having to deal with more relations. Another cost is the fact that you have introduced some redundancy into the model. In the PROJECT relation, the Project attribute appears only once. However, after you break the relation into two, the Project attribute appears in both the RES-PROJ and the PROJ-LOC relation. A third cost is that you may have created a referential integrity constraint.

I talk about referential integrity in a moment, but for now, look at the current example and see what the possible effects of breaking PROJECT in two might be. I indicated earlier that the director of the Quantum Computing Lab wanted to be able to assign a project to a location even if a researcher had not yet been assigned to the project. Suppose the Zetetic Institute also has a business rule that a researcher may not be assigned to a project unless the project has a location. Perhaps the Institute does not want to pay a researcher's salary unless the researcher is doing productive work, and productive work cannot be done in the absence of a properly equipped lab. You must incorporate this rule into the database model in the form of a constraint, which you might state like this:

> A row may not be added to the RES-PROJ relation unless the value of its Project attribute matches the value of the Project attribute in one of the rows of the PROJ-LOC relation.

This is a *referential integrity constraint,* which restricts what can be done to one relation, based on what is contained in a second relation. Referential integrity constraints may be needed when two relations share one or more columns. Whenever you break a relation incorporating two ideas into two relations, they are going to share at least one column, and so referential integrity may become an issue. On the other hand, it may not become an issue.

For example, suppose the business rules of the Zetetic Institute say that a researcher can be assigned to a project whether or not a location for the project has been assigned, and that a project can be given a location whether or not a researcher has yet been assigned. In this case, you can add and delete rows from either the RES-PROJ or the PROJ-LOC relations without worrying about referential integrity.

The way the users view their system is critical to the creation of a correct model. You must ask them about their business rules so that you can apply all the needed constraints to your model. Without those constraints, your system will not match the system it is modeling.

Fixing Problems through Normalization

When Dr. Codd described the relational model, he recognized that modification anomalies could cause problems. He identified certain problems with the structure of the relations that caused those problems. To eliminate the problems, he described additional restrictions on relations beyond those that I describe in the formal definition of a relation, earlier in this chapter. Each of these additional restrictions was designed to prevent a specific type of modification anomaly. Codd called these restricted structures *normal forms.*

In Codd's definition of a relational database, any table that qualifies as a relation is said to be in *first normal form* (1NF). Relations in 1NF are immune to some kinds of modification anomalies but susceptible to others. By adding a restriction, you eliminate some of those anomalies and put the relation in second normal form (2NF). Successively adding restrictions puts a relation in third normal form (3NF), Boyce-Codd normal form (BCNF), fourth normal form (4NF), and fifth normal form (5NF).

By the time you get to 5NF, a relation is pretty well protected from anomalies, but it cannot be proven that a relation in 5NF is *guaranteed* to be free of modification anomalies. Domain/key normal form (DKNF), which was described by Rob Fagin in 1981, does give such a guarantee.

The normal forms have a nested structure. First normal form is the least restrictive, so all the relations that are in 2NF are, by definition, also in 1NF. All relations in 3NF are also in 2NF, and so on. Figure 7-5 shows a schematic representation of the relationships among the normal forms.

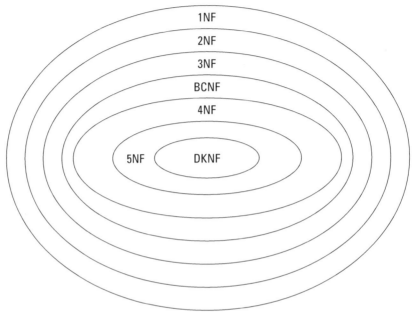

Figure 7-5:
The normal
forms
hierarchy.

Relations in DKNF are guaranteed to be free of anomalies and thus are automatically in 5NF, 4NF, BCNF, 3NF, 2NF, and 1NF. The reverse is also true. A relation that is free of all possible anomalies must be in DKNF.

First normal form

The definition of first normal form is the same as the definition of a relation. *If a table qualifies as a relation, it is in 1NF.* The criteria are

- Each cell in the table must contain a single value, if it contains any value at all. Repeating groups and arrays are not allowed as values.
- All the entries in any column must be of the same kind. For example, if a column contains an employee name in one row, it must contain employee names in all rows that contain values.
- Each column has a unique name.
- The order of the columns doesn't matter.
- The order of the rows doesn't matter.
- No two rows may be identical.

These "restrictions" are pretty loose. If, for example, each column did not have a unique name, you could not distinguish between two columns that had the same name. If two rows could be identical, you could not distinguish between those two rows. In either case, the ambiguity would be a source of problems. The result is that practically any table that a reasonable person might construct is probably in 1NF. The PROJECT relation in Figure 7-2 is in 1NF. It satisfies all the criteria in the preceding bulleted list.

Second normal form

To understand 2NF, take a look at the PROJECTS relation in Figure 7-6.

ResearcherID	Project	Location
aturing	Graph Coloring	QC-103
aturing	Traveling Salesman	QC-201
rdescartes	Knapsack	QC-121
cbabbage	Traveling Salesman	QC-201
cbabbage	Knapsack	QC-121
bowen	Knapsack	QC-121

Figure 7-6: PROJECTS relation.

This relation differs from the PROJECT relation in Figure 7-2 in that a researcher may be involved with more than one project. The PROJECTS relation is in 1NF, but is nonetheless subject to modification anomalies. Say Dr. Turing decides to remove himself from the Graph Coloring project so that he can concentrate his full energies on the Traveling Salesman project. If the appropriate row is removed from the PROJECTS relation, you lose the fact that the Graph Coloring project is located in room QC-103. This is a deletion anomaly. Furthermore, if you decide to start a new project to investigate the Clique problem, you cannot do so until a researcher is assigned to that project. This is an insertion anomaly.

Why is there a problem here? The problem has to do with keys and dependencies. In the PROJECTS relation, because a researcher can be assigned to more than one project, ResearcherID might be repeated and thus cannot be a key. The combination of ResearcherID and Project can be a key, however. The fact that PROJECTS has a composite key does not necessarily cause a problem, but in this case the Location attribute depends only on Project:

Project → Location

Project is a determinant, but it is only part of a key. To avoid anomalies, every non-key attribute must be dependent on the entire key.

A relation is in second formal form if it is in first normal form, and every non-key attribute is dependent on the entire key.

To eliminate the anomalies in the PROJECTS relation, you need to transform it into a structure in which every determinant is a key. You can do this by breaking it up into two relations, each of which has a single-attribute key. Figure 7-7 shows the result.

Figure 7-7:
RES-PROJ
and
PROJ-LOC
relations.

ResearcherID	Project
aturing	Graph Coloring
rdescartes	Knapsack
cbabbage	Traveling Salesman
bowen	Knapsack

Project	Location
Graph Coloring	QC-103
Knapsack	QC-121
Traveling Salesman	QC-201

The two relations RES-PROJ and PROJ-LOC each have a single-attribute key, so all the non-key attributes depend on all the keys, by default.

Third normal form

A relation in 2NF can still have anomalies. Consider the SALARYRANGE relation shown in Figure 7-8.

Figure 7-8:
SALARY-
RANGE
relation.

ResearcherID	AcademicRank	RangeCode
eschroedinger	Full professor	4
pdirac	Associate professor	3
wheisenberg	Full professor	4
hbethe	Assistant professor	2
jwheeler	Adjunct professor	1

The attributes are ResearcherID, AcademicRank, and RangeCode. ResearcherID is unique and is a single-attribute key, so the relation is in 2NF. However, anomalies are possible. What if Professor Dirac is lured away by MIT and his row is removed from the SALARYRANGE relation? Not only do you lose the fact that he was an associate professor; you also lose the fact that associate professors are paid according to salary range 3. This is a deletion anomaly. What if you want to add the rank of a visiting scientist at salary range 4? You cannot do so until you actually hire a visiting scientist. This is an insertion anomaly.

What causes this problem? Again, the problem has to do with keys and dependencies. AcademicRank depends on ResearcherID. RangeCode depends on AcademicRank, and through AcademicRank it depends on ResearcherID. This is a *transitive dependency*:

$$\text{ResearcherID} \rightarrow \text{AcademicRank} \rightarrow \text{RangeCode}$$

You can eliminate the anomalies by breaking SALARYRANGE into two relations, RES_RANK(ResearcherID, AcademicRank) and RANK_RANGE(AcademicRank, RangeCode). This eliminates the transitive dependency and serves as an example of third normal form.

A relation is in third normal form if it is in second normal form and has no transitive dependencies.

Boyce-Codd normal form

A relation in 3NF can still harbor anomalies, due to considerations of keys and dependencies. Consider the case in which a Zetetic Institute associate may be affiliated with multiple departments within the Institute. The cross-disciplinary nature of the Institute's founding philosophy encourages such relationships. However, within each department, a researcher will be assigned to a team whose leader is affiliated with only that department. In every case, team leaders work exclusively in their major area of study, and may lead only one team in that area, but team members may cross disciplinary lines. Figure 7-9 illustrates this scenario.

ResearcherID	Department	TeamLeader
eschroedinger	Hylenergetics	I. Newton
eschroedinger	Pronoetics	A. Clarke
bskinner	Psychological Area	C. Jung
bskinner	Biological Area	L. Pasteur
aturing	Symbolics of Information	G. Boole
aturing	Disseminative Area	B. Franklin
aturing	Zetetics	A. von Vogt
santhony	Sociological Area	F. Douglass
jsalk	Biological Area	E. Jenner

Figure 7-9:
AFFILIATION
relation.

Because a researcher can be affiliated with more than one department, ResearcherID does not determine Department, and thus cannot by itself be a key. For the same reason, Department does not determine ResearcherID, and so it cannot by itself be a key either. However, because a researcher can be assigned to only one team within a department, the combination of ResearcherID and Department does determine TeamLeader, so (ResearcherID, Department) is a composite key.

Similarly, because a team leader can be affiliated with only one department, the combination of ResearcherID and TeamLeader determines department. Either (ResearcherID, Department) or (ResearcherID, TeamLeader) could serve as primary key for this relation. Both are considered to be *candidate keys* until you select one to be the primary key. You have the functional dependencies:

(ResearcherID, Department) → TeamLeader

(ResearcherID, TeamLeader) → Department

One additional functional dependency exists, because a team leader must be associated with one and only one department:

TeamLeader → Department

This can lead to problems. Suppose Susan Anthony leaves the Institute. When you remove her tuple from the relation, you lose the fact that Douglas is a team leader in the Sociological Area. This is a deletion anomaly. What if the Institute has just hired Richard Feynman to be a team leader in the Nanotechnology Area? You cannot show that fact until a researcher signs on in that area. This is an insertion anomaly.

The problem is due to the fact that the relation contains a determinant that is not a candidate key. To eliminate this problem, you can put this relation into Boyce-Codd normal form.

A relation is in Boyce-Codd normal form if every determinant is a candidate key.

To achieve that condition, you can break the relation into two in which all determinants are candidate keys. Figure 7-10 shows how this is done.

ResearcherID	Department
eschroedinger	Hylenergetics
eschroedinger	Pronoetics
bskinner	Psychological Area
bskinner	Biological Area
aturing	Symbolics of Information
aturing	Disseminative Area
aturing	Zetetics
santhony	Sociological Area
jsalk	Biological Area

ResearcherID	TeamLeader
eschroedinger	I. Newton
eschroedinger	A. Clarke
bskinner	C. Jung
bskinner	L. Pasteur
aturing	G. Boole
aturing	B. Franklin
aturing	A. von Vogt
santhony	F. Douglass
jsalk	E. Jenner

Figure 7-10: RES-DEPT relation and RES-LEADER relation.

In the RES-DEPT relation, (ResearcherID, Department) is the primary key, and includes every attribute in the relation. Thus, there are no non-key determinants. Similarly, in the RES-LEADER relation, (ResearcherID, TeamLeader) is the primary key, and includes every attribute in the relation. There are no non-key determinants here, either. These two relations are in Boyce-Codd normal form.

Fourth normal form

Boyce-Codd normal form does a fine job of protecting you from modification anomalies caused by problems with functional dependencies and keys. However, other types of anomalies are possible. Suppose the management of the Zetetic Institute encourages physical fitness among its staff members by sponsoring a number of intramural sports leagues. Researchers can represent their departments in a competitive context. A variety of different sports are supported so that all researchers can participate in activities that they enjoy. Suppose that Schroedinger participates in jogging and weightlifting, while Skinner prefers swimming and handball. Figure 7-11 shows how this information might be represented in a relation that shows the researchers, their departments, and the sports they play.

ResearcherID	Department	Sport
eschroedinger	Hylenergetics	jogging
eschroedinger	Pronoetics	jogging
eschroedinger	Hylenergetics	weight lifting
eschroedinger	Pronoetics	weight lifting
bskinner	Psychological Area	swimming
bskinner	Biological Area	swimming
bskinner	Psychological Area	handball
bskinner	Biological Area	handball

Figure 7-11:
SPORTS
relation.

Something must be wrong here because this table has a tremendous amount of redundancy. It takes four rows to show the two activities Schroedinger does and the two departments he represents. If he were to decide to engage in a third activity, you would need to add two more rows, one for each of his two departments. You can only hope that he would not then decide to affiliate himself with another department. If he did, you would need nine rows to show all the relationships.

The SPORTS relation is clearly in 1NF. No single attribute uniquely identifies a row, nor does any pair of attributes. All three attributes (ResearcherID, Department, Sport) must be used to define the key. There are no non-key attributes, so by default SPORTS is also in 2NF. There are no transitive dependencies for the same reason, so SPORTS is in 3NF. (ResearcherID, Department, Sport) is the only potential determinant in the relation, and is a key, so every determinant is a candidate key (in fact, a primary key). Thus, SPORTS is in BCNF. However, even though SPORTS is in BCNF, as I've already noted, *something* is wrong. A design incorporating this much redundancy can't be the best. If Schroedinger were to add or drop a department or an activity, multiple rows would have to be updated. This is an open invitation to error.

The problem arises because of unrelated multivalued dependencies. ResearcherID is not a determinant of Department because a researcher may be affiliated with multiple departments. It is also not a determinant of Sport because a researcher may be engaged in multiple sports. Because Department and Sport are not related to each other, you must use multiple rows to capture all the meaning. Multivalued dependencies are denoted as follows:

ResearcherID $\rightarrow \rightarrow$ Department

ResearcherID $\rightarrow \rightarrow$ Sport

ResearcherID multi-determines Department, and ResearcherID multi-determines Sport. Department and Sport are unrelated except through ResearcherID. This is the source of the problem and also a hint at its solution. The PROJECT relation discussed earlier in this chapter harbors anomalies because it has attributes that embody two distinct ideas. Department and Sport are two distinct and unrelated ideas, and should not both be in the same relation. You can overcome the problem with the SPORTS relation by breaking it into two relations, one containing the Department attribute and the other containing the Sport attribute. Figure 7-12 illustrates this normalization.

Figure 7-12:
RES-DEPT relation and RES-SPORT relation eliminate the multivalued dependency.

ResearcherID	Department
eschroedinger	Hylenergetics
eschroedinger	Pronoetics
bskinner	Psychological Area
bskinner	Biological Area

ResearcherID	Sport
eschroedinger	jogging
eschroedinger	weight lifting
bskinner	swimming
bskinner	handball

RES-DEPT and RES-SPORT are in 4NF.

A relation is in fourth normal form if it is in BCNF and does not contain two or more unrelated multivalued dependencies.

Both RES-DEPT and RES-SPORT qualify as being in BCNF, and because each has only one multivalued dependency, they are both in 4NF.

Fifth normal form

The problems that lead to the definition of 4NF are not nearly as clear-cut as are those that lead to 1NF, 2NF, 3NF, and BCNF. You can have considerable redundancy in relations that are not in 4NF, but you can also have redundancy in tables that are in 4NF, as shown in Figure 7-12. How much redundancy is too much? It is not an easy call.

You put a relation containing multiple unrelated multivalued dependencies into 4NF by breaking the relation into multiple relations that separate the unrelated attributes. What about a relation that contains multiple *related* multivalued dependencies? Sometimes, you can reduce redundancy by breaking such relations into multiple relations, each of which contains only one multivalued dependency. Doing this creates relations that are in 5NF.

Fifth normal form is even harder to comprehend than 4NF, and doing so is probably not worth the effort. Even if you could put a relation into 5NF, you do not guarantee that it will be free of all anomalies. You only guarantee that it will be free of all anomalies that have been identified so far. To be sure a relation is anomaly-free, you must put it into domain/key normal form (DKNF). In his 1981 paper in the *ACM Transactions on Database Systems*, Rob Fagin defined DKNF and proved that it eliminates all modification anomalies.

Domain/key normal form

Although the definitions of the normal forms become progressively more complex as you proceed from 1NF to 5NF, the definition of DKNF is refreshingly simple.

A relation is in domain/key normal form if every constraint on the relation is a logical consequence of the definition of keys and domains.

The only things you need to understand are constraints, keys, and domains:

- A *constraint* is a rule that governs the static values of attributes. The constraint must be precise enough for you to tell whether it is true or not. Static values are those that do not vary with time.
- As you have already seen, a *key* is a unique identifier of a tuple.
- A *domain* is a description of an attribute's values.

If enforcing key and domain restrictions causes all constraints to be met, then the relation is in DKNF. This also ensures that the relation has no modification anomalies.

Because relations in DKNF are guaranteed to be anomaly-free, you may wonder why anyone would want to fool around with 1NF through 5NF. Why not just go for DKNF from the outset? Good question. You might want to do just that. However, a couple of good reasons exist for putting relations into lesser normal forms. Often, one of the lesser normal forms is good enough. 3NF is sufficient for many cases, and BCNF covers most that you are likely to encounter.

An advantage of using one of these lesser normal forms is that the process of normalization can be automated. Algorithms exist for checking for the presence of dependencies that could cause anomalies, and for splitting such relations so that the anomalies are eliminated. No such algorithm exists for putting a relation into DKNF. Human intuition is required. Normalizing a relation into DKNF requires the time and effort of a person who is knowledgeable about the problem domain and about database theory. The problem domain knowledge will address the constraints and attribute domains. The database theory will make sure keys are correctly identified.

Look at an example of the process of putting a relation into DKNF. Consider the SALARYRANGE relation first shown in Figure 7-8. Figure 7-13 shows the specification of this relation.

Figure 7-13:
Specification
of SALARY-
RANGE
relation.

SALARYRANGE (ResearcherID, AcademicRank, RangeCode)

Key: ResearcherID

Constraints: AcademicRank $\longrightarrow$ RangeCode
               RangeCode in ('1', '2', '3', '4')

This relation is not currently in DKNF, but you can put it into DKNF by making all constraints a logical consequence of domains and keys. You can make the constraint "RangeCode in ('1', '2', '3', '4')" a logical consequence of domains by declaring the domain of RangeCode to be ('1', '2', '3', '4'). That is easy. What about the other constraint?

You can make the functional dependency AcademicRank → RangeCode a logical consequence of keys by making AcademicRank a key. AcademicRank is not a key of SALARYRANGE, but you can break that relation into the two relations: RES-RANK (ResearcherID, AcademicRank) and RANK-CODE (AcademicRank, RangeCode). ResearcherID is the key of RES-RANK, and AcademicRank is the key of RANK-CODE. Thus, the functional dependency AcademicRank → RangeCode is a logical consequence of a key. The relations RANK-CODE and RES-RANK are in DKNF. Figure 7-14 shows the definition of these new relations derived from SALARYRANGE.

```
Domain Definitions:

ResearcherID in CHAR (30)

Academic Rank in ('full professor', 'associate professor', 'assistant professor',
'adjunct professor')
RangeCode in ('1', '2', '3', '4')


Relation and Key Definitions:

RES-RANK (ResearcherID, AcademicRank)
       Key: ResearcherID

RANK-CODE (AcademicRank, RangeCode)
       Key: AcademicRank
```

Figure 7-14:
Definition of
RES-RANK
and RANK-
CODE
relations.

Because these relations are in DKNF, you can be sure that they are free of modification anomalies.

Using Functional Dependencies to Build Relations

If the system you are studying has a number of attributes, it may not be clear how best to aggregate those attributes into relations. Some ways of dividing up the attributes will yield better performance than others. Some ways will yield a more robust and reliable structure than others will. You can use the relationships between and among attributes as determined by functional dependencies, to decide how best to synthesize relations.

Three classes of relationships exist between two attributes:

- ✔ One-to-one: One instance of the first attribute corresponds to one and only one instance of the second attribute.

- ✔ One-to-many: One instance of the first attribute corresponds to multiple instances of the second attribute, but each instance of the second attribute corresponds to one and only one instance of the first attribute.

- ✔ Many-to-many: One instance of the first attribute corresponds to multiple instances of the second attribute, and one instance of the second attribute corresponds to multiple instances of the first attribute.

One-to-one attribute relationships

A relation can contain two attributes that bear a one-to-one relationship with each other. For example, consider the STAFF relation maintained by the Zetetic Institute's Human Relations Department: STAFF (ResearcherID, SSN, Fname, Lname, Street, City, State, Zipcode). The ResearcherID attribute bears a one-to-one relationship with the SSN attribute, because each researcher has a unique ResearcherID and a unique Social Security Number. The following dependencies hold:

ResearcherID → SSN

SSN → ResearcherID

If one attribute determines a second attribute, and the second attribute determines the first attribute, the two attributes have a one-to-one relationship with each other.

ResearcherID and SSN are both candidate keys of the relation STAFF. All the other attributes of STAFF must be functionally determined by either ResearcherID or SSN in order for STAFF to be in DKNF. By the same reasoning, you cannot add a new attribute to STAFF unless that new attribute is functionally determined by either ResearcherID or SSN.

One-to-many attribute relationships

A relation may also contain two attributes that bear a one-to-many relationship with each other. The SALARYRANGE relation illustrated in Figure 7-8 is an example of such a relation. Every researcher, identified by ResearcherID, has one and only one value of AcademicRank. If Dr. Schroedinger holds the rank of full professor, he cannot also be an associate professor. However, each academic rank may correspond to many researchers. Multiple researchers may hold the rank of full professor, and several others may be assistant professors. In this case, the following dependencies hold:

ResearcherID → AcademicRank

AcademicRank → ResearcherID

ResearcherID determines AcademicRank, but AcademicRank does not determine ResearcherID. Because ResearcherID determines AcademicRank, ResearcherID must be a key. Any additional attributes that you might want to add to the SALARYRANGE relation must also be determined by ResearcherID in order for SALARYRANGE to be in DKNF.

Many-to-many attribute relationships

A relation may contain two attributes that bear a many-to-many relationship to each other. In a many-to-many relationship between two attributes, the first attribute does not determine the second attribute, and the second attribute does not determine the first attribute.

The RES-DEPT relation in Figure 7-12 contains a many-to-many relationship. A researcher, identified by ResearcherID, may belong to multiple departments, identified by Department. Similarly, a Department may employ multiple researchers. This relation has the following nondependencies:

> ResearcherID $\not\to$ Department
>
> Department $\not\to$ ResearcherID

Because ResearcherID does not determine Department, and Department does not determine ResearcherID, neither one by itself can be a key. Together, ResearcherID and Department form a composite key. Any new attribute that you might want to add to the relation must be dependent on the entire key in order to be in DKNF. Such a new attribute cannot be dependent on either ResearcherID or Department alone.

Can a Database be too Normalized?

In previous sections of this chapter, I go to great lengths to demonstrate the evils of unnormalized relations and, in contrast, the virtues of normalized relations. I portray DKNF as the ultimate in both virtue and normalization. Now I put forward the heretical notion that, in some cases, you may not want to fully normalize the relations in your database.

Although normalization can protect you from modification anomalies, it comes at a price. TANSTAAFL remains in effect. The price you may have to pay for a guarantee of anomaly-free relations might be higher than you want to pay.

What does normalization cost? Think about what you do when you normalize a relation. You split it into two or more relations that contain the same information. More tables require more space. You must duplicate one or more of the columns of the original table to provide links among the newly created tables. Having more tables involves additional overhead. However, the biggest cost is likely to be reduced performance.

When you created the original unnormalized relation, the attributes it contained were grouped together for a reason. They were related to each other and probably would be used together to generate reports and to respond to queries. If, by normalizing the relation, you separate attributes that should appear together in either reports or query responses, you lengthen the time required to generate those reports or run those queries. What was split apart will have to be joined together again, at least temporarily, to produce the desired reports and query results. For large relations and complex retrievals, the performance degradation can be significant.

For some projects, you face the real possibility that putting all the relations in a database into DKNF will drive system performance to an unacceptably low level. How can you maintain high data integrity and still have acceptable performance?

Trading Off Data Integrity Against Performance

In any database development project, two important objectives are in direct conflict with each other:

- You want your database to be free of modification anomalies.
- You want operation to be speedy and results to be produced quickly.

To be sure that modification anomalies do not corrupt your data, you should put all relations in the database into DKNF. However, separating related data items into different relations will slow operations on those data items, and the performance degradation could be significant.

In an ideal world, you would want your database to be structured in such a way that no modification anomalies would be possible. Also in that ideal world, responses to queries and requests for reports would be instantaneous. Of course, you don't live in an ideal world, so the question becomes, "How close can you come to the ideal situation? Can you get data integrity and performance that are both good enough to meet your needs?" In most cases, yes, you can. Using good judgment and common sense, you can arrive at a compromise that will deliver satisfactory integrity and performance at the same time.

Consider the following CUSTOMER relation:

CUSTOMER(CustID, Fname, Lname, Street, City, State, Zipcode)

Key: CustID

Functional Dependencies: CustID → all non-key attributes

Zipcode → State

The CUSTOMER relation is not in DKNF because State is dependent upon a non-key attribute. If you know the zip code of an address, you know what state that address is in. You could break the CUSTOMER relation into two relations: CUST(CustID, Fname, Lname, Street, City, Zipcode) and CODE-STATE(Zipcode, State). Both relations would be in DKNF, and the possibility of modification anomalies having to do with states and postal codes would have been eliminated. However, this is not a sensible thing to do.

Most reasons for accessing the CUSTOMER relations involve retrieving the full address of the customer, including State. It is silly to break the State information off from the rest of the address if you are going to have to recombine the two relations almost every time you want to look at or use a customer record.

If you don't normalize the CUSTOMER relation, what trouble can you get into? What anomalies are possible? What if you want to delete a customer who happens to be the only customer in the relation that has the zip code 92683? If you delete that row from the table, you lose not only the information on that customer, but also the fact that the zip code 92683 is in the state of California. This is a deletion anomaly. Yes it is a deletion anomaly, but who cares? I don't. For the purposes of my business, if I don't have any customers in zip code 92683, I don't care what state that zip code is in.

Insertion anomalies are also not a concern in this case. You cannot record the fact that the zip code 97209 is located in the state of Oregon until you have a customer in that zip code. Big deal! If you don't have a customer there, you don't care about that anyway.

In this example, choosing not to normalize the CUSTOMER relation has consequences, but they are consequences that I don't care about. The message here is to use common sense when normalizing relations. Try to achieve an appropriate balance between data integrity and performance, keeping in mind which classes of anomalies can hurt you and which cannot.

Chapter 8

Using an Entity-Relationship Model to Design a Database

My goal in this book is to show you how to design and build robust, reliable databases and database applications that will do the job you want done. A database will be only as good as the model you create to capture what the users have in their minds about the system. The E-R model is probably the most popular model used by database designers as a basis for a relational database design.

After you translate the E-R model into a relational model, you probably need to normalize the relational model to ensure that your database will not experience modification anomalies. In this chapter, I describe how to convert an E-R model into a relational model, and how to normalize that model to produce a final database design. I describe different types of relationships, and then I present a detailed example, to show step-by-step how to design a highly functional, efficient, and reliable database.

Capturing the User's Model with an E-R Model

The first step in any database development effort is to recognize that the process has discrete steps. As I describe in Chapter 2, a robust design requires that you go through the stages of system development. Before you can even think about capturing the users' data model, you must get a very

clear picture of exactly what is required. You do this by spending the necessary time and effort in the definition phase, the requirements phase, and the
evaluation phase. (See Chapter 2 for details about these phases.) It is critically important that you give these phases their just due.

After you receive client signoff on the evaluation phase, you may enter the
design phase. The first part of the design phase is to convert the users' data
model that you gathered through research and interviews into an E-R model.
Make the E-R model match the users' data model as closely as possible. After
you have started building the E-R model, you will probably have to go back to
the client more than once with additional questions, in order to clear up any
ambiguities or fill in any missing facts.

Converting an E-R Model into a Relational Design

After you have an E-R model of the system you are building, most of the hard
work is done. Now all you have to do is convert the E-R model into an equivalent relational model. Although this is not exactly a no-brainer conversion, it
is close. Many of the features of the E-R model transfer directly to a relational
model.

Relations, attributes, keys, and relationships

In Chapter 4, I explain that an E-R model has four main elements: entities,
attributes, identifiers, and relationships. These four elements correspond to
the relations, attributes, keys, and relationships of the relational model.

In many cases, an entity from the E-R model translates directly into a relation
in the relational model. The attributes of that entity translate into the attributes of the corresponding relation. Identifiers in the E-R model translate into
keys in the relational model. Relationships between entities translate into
relationships between relations. Figure 8-1 represents this correspondence.

After you convert your E-R model into a relational model, inspect it for susceptibility to modification anomalies. See if any of your relations deal with
more than one theme. If they do, you can eliminate potential problems by
normalizing the relations to DKNF.

Figure 8-1:
Correspond-
ence
between the
E-R model
and the
relational
model.

E-R Model		Relational Model
Entities	→	Relations
Attributes	→	Attributes
Identifiers	→	Keys
Relationships	→	Relationships

Normalizing

Consider the AFFILIATE relation, in which the Zetetic Institute keeps contact information about other research institutions around the world. Figure 8-2 shows the AFFILIATE entity in the E-R model and the corresponding AFFILIATE relation in the relational model.

AFFILIATE entity contains

AffilNum
InstitutionName
Street
City
State
PostalCode
Country
ContactName
ContactPhone

Figure 8-2:
AFFILIATE
entity and
corre-
sponding
AFFILIATE
relation.

AFFILIATE (<u>AffilNum</u>, InstitutionName, Street, City, State, PostalCode, Country, ContactName, ContactPhone)

A close look at the relation's attributes should tell you whether it deals with more than one idea:

AFFILIATE(<u>AffilNum</u>, InstitutionName, Street, City, State, PostalCode, Country, ContactName, ContactPhone)

In this case, it does deal with more than one idea, and is thus not in DKNF. It could be subject to modification anomalies. The affiliate institution is one idea; the relationship between postal codes and addresses is a second idea; the institution's contact information is a third idea.

You can normalize the AFFILIATE relation by breaking it into three relations that carry the same information, each dealing with only one theme or idea. The three new relations are

> AFFILIATE(<u>AffilNum</u>, InstitutionName, Street, PostalCode, Country, ContactName)
>
> POSTAL(<u>PostalCode</u>, <u>Country</u>, City, State)
>
> CONTACT(<u>ContactName</u>, ContactPhone)

Each of these new relations deals with only one idea. AffilNum is the primary key of the AFFILIATE relation; PostalCode, Country, and ContactName are foreign keys. PostalCode and Country form a composite primary key for the POSTAL relation, while ContactName is the primary key of the CONTACT relation.

Now that you have normalized the AFFILIATE relation to DKNF, you can ask whether this is what you really want. If your most frequent use of the AFFILI-ATE relation is to extract the name and address of the contact person at an affiliate institution, you may choose not to normalize. You make this decision based on how badly performance degrades during such a use, when you switch from the unnormalized single-relation form to the normalized three-relation form. Perhaps the best approach is to build the database in the nor-malized form, and then monitor performance.

If performance becomes unacceptable, you may purposely denormalize the design. If you denormalize consciously, you recognize the potential risks of modification anomalies, and you can include code in your database applica-tions that will prevent them from happening. Alternatively, you can decide that anomalies that might be introduced will not cause problems. For exam-ple, if a deletion anomaly causes you to lose the fact that a particular postal code is located in a specific state, you may not care.

One-to-one relationships

The simplest form of binary relationship is the one-to-one (1:1) relationship, in which an entity of one type is related to one and only one entity of another type. An example of this type of relationship would be that between a Zetetic Institute researcher and his or her assigned computer. Every researcher at the Zetetic Institute is issued a laptop computer for use at the Institute and while traveling to seminars and symposia. Each computer is assigned to only one researcher. Figure 8-3 illustrates the relationship as an E-R diagram.

Figure 8-3:
One-to-one
relationship
example.

The ovals denoting minimum cardinality next to both the RESEARCHER entity and the COMPUTER entity show that a researcher need not accept a computer if he or she doesn't want one, and not every computer in the Institute's inventory need be assigned to a researcher at any given time.

You can translate this E-R model into a relational model. The relationship between the two relations is established by taking the primary key of one relation and placing it into the second relation as a foreign key. Figure 8-4 shows one way of doing this.

Figure 8-4:
Relational
model
represen-
tation of
one-to-one
relationship.

RESEARCHER(ResearcherID, Department, Location, Phone, CompID)

COMPUTER(CompID, Brand, Model, RAM, HD)

In Figure 8-4, the primary key of COMPUTER has been added to the RESEARCHER relation as a foreign key. Another way of forming the relationship would be to place the primary key of RESEARCHER into the COMPUTER relation as a foreign key. Figure 8-5 illustrates this structure.

Figure 8-5:
Relational
model
represen-
tation of
one-to-one
relationship.

RESEARCHER(ResearcherID, Department, Location, Phone)

COMPUTER(CompID, Brand, Model, RAM, HD, ResearcherID)

The two structures shown in Figure 8-4 and Figure 8-5 both represent the relationship accurately. However, one may be preferred over the other based on performance considerations. Look at the following queries:

- ✔ How much RAM does Schroedinger's computer have?
- ✔ List all researchers who have Sony computers.

The first query starts from the RESEARCHER relation, links to the appropriate row in the COMPUTER relation, and then returns the value of the RAM attribute. The second query starts from the COMPUTER relation, links to the appropriate rows in the RESEARCHER relation, and then returns the names of all the researchers who have been assigned Sony computers.

If queries of the first type are run more often than those of the second type, you may get better performance with the structure shown in Figure 8-4, because your link to the COMPUTER relation is via its primary key. The structure in Figure 8-5 would also work, but might be slower because access to the COMPUTER relation is via a foreign key.

The same logic applies, but in the reverse direction, if queries of the second type are more common. In this case, the query starts with the COMPUTER relation, and then links to appropriate rows in the RESEARCHER relation. By reasoning similar to that given previously, you may get better performance with the structure shown in Figure 8-5, because the link to the RESEARCHER relation is via its primary key. I say *may* because, depending on the specific implementation you are working with, and the sizes of your tables, the difference in performance due to how you link tables may or may not be significant.

One-to-many relationships

One-to-many relationships (1:N) are more complex than 1:1 relationships because one instance of the first entity type is related to multiple instances of the second entity type. This type of relationship occurs frequently in many different contexts. For example, in the Zetetic Institute, a DEPARTMENT may have many instances of RESEARCHER, but each RESEARCHER is affiliated with one and only one DEPARTMENT. Regarding the Institute's non-academic staff, each STAFFMEMBER reports to one and only one MANAGER, but a MANAGER may supervise multiple instances of STAFFMEMBER. Figures 8-6 and 8-7 show the E-R diagrams for these two relationships.

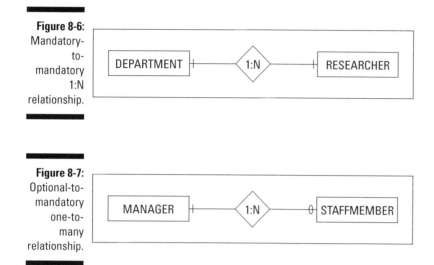

Figure 8-6:
Mandatory-
to-
mandatory
1:N
relationship.

Figure 8-7:
Optional-to-
mandatory
one-to-
many
relationship.

In Figure 8-6, a DEPARTMENT must have at least one RESEARCHER and a RESEARCHER must be affiliated with a DEPARTMENT, so the minimum cardinality is one on both ends of the relationship. In Figure 8-7, a STAFFMEMBER must report to a MANAGER, but a MANAGER need not have a STAFFMEMBER reporting to her in order to hold the rank of MANAGER. Thus, the minimum cardinality of the relationship is zero on the STAFFMEMBER side and one on the MANAGER side.

Sometimes, one-to-many relationships are called *parent-child* relationships. In this context, a parent can have many children, but a child can have one and only one parent. The analogy to biology breaks down a little here, but people use this terminology anyway, so don't be surprised if you see it.

To show the one-to-many nature of a parent-child relationship, you need a richer form of representation than the simple structure shown in Figures 8-4 and 8-5. *Data structure diagrams* provide this added richness, enabling you to distinguish between the one side and the many side of a relationship. Figure 8-8 is a data structure diagram that corresponds to the E-R diagram shown in Figure 8-6.

Each relation is shown enclosed in a rectangular box, and the line connecting the two relations has a splayed crow's foot at the many end, but no crow's foot at the one end. The primary key of the DEPARTMENT relation (DeptID) has been placed into the RESEARCHER relation as a foreign key. The DeptID attribute provides the link between the two relations.

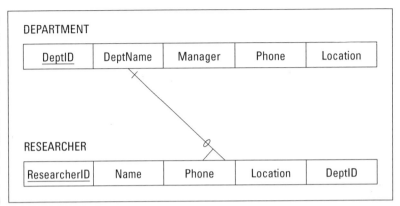

Many-to-many relationships

Many-to-many relationships (M:N) are the third and most complex type of binary relationship. One tuple in the first relation corresponds to multiple tuples in the second relation, and one tuple in the second relation corresponds to multiple tuples in the first relation. Figure 8-9 shows an example of this type of relationship. A RESEARCHER can work on more than one PROJECT at the same time, and each PROJECT can be staffed by more than one RESEARCHER.

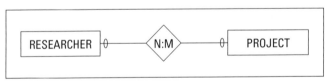

Minimum cardinality is zero at both ends of the relationship because you have found, by interviewing users, that a PROJECT can be started before a RESEARCHER has been assigned to it, and that a RESEARCHER may be on staff, but not currently assigned to any PROJECT.

Now you have a problem. You cannot easily draw a data structure diagram for a many-to-many relationship. You cannot place the primary key of PRO-JECT into the RESEARCHER relation as a foreign key, because a researcher may be involved in more than one PROJECT, each with its own primary key. Similarly, you cannot place the primary key of RESEARCHER into the PROJECT relation as a foreign key, because a PROJECT may employ more than one RESEARCHER.

More than one way exists to deal with M:N relationships, but the simplest and safest is to decompose a single M:N relationship into two 1:N relationships. You know very well how to translate 1:N relationships into the relational model.

The procedure for decomposing a M:N relationship into two 1:N relationships is straightforward. Create a third relation, called an *intersection relation*, whose attributes are the primary key of the M side and the primary key of the N side. Place this new relation between the original two, with 1:N links running from the original relations to the new one, as shown in Figure 8-10.

Now, you have more tables, which in one sense adds to the complexity of the database. However, the relationships between tables are much simplified. Overall, this makes the database much less subject to modification anomalies. It also makes the database much easier to understand.

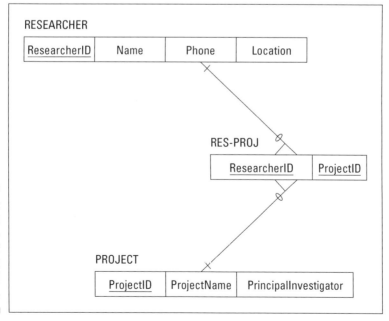

Figure 8-10: Relational representation of decomposed M:N relationship.

Subtype relationships

The relationships I describe in previous sections of this chapter all relate an entity of one type with a distinct entity of another type. Another kind of relationship is the supertype/subtype relationship. The supertype may be made up of several subtypes. An example of such a supertype might be EMPLOYEE at the Zetetics Institute. Subtypes might be EXEMPT salaried employees, NON-EXEMPT hourly employees, and RESEARCHER academic employees. The three subtypes share some attributes but not others:

> EXEMPT: EmployeeID, Fname, Lname, Phone, Title, Salary
>
> NON-EXEMPT: EmployeeID, Fname, Lname, Phone, Title, Wage
>
> RESEARCHER: EmployeeID, Fname, Lname, Phone, AcademicRank, Salary

Figure 8-11 shows the E-R diagram of this system.

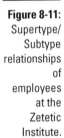

Figure 8-11: Supertype/ Subtype relationships of employees at the Zetetic Institute.

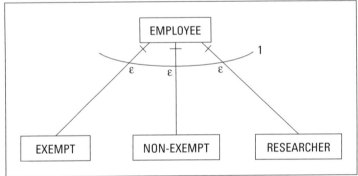

This E-R model translates directly into the following relational model:

> EMPLOYEE (<u>EmployeeID</u>, Fname, Lname, Phone)
>
> EXEMPT (<u>EmployeeID</u>, Title, Salary)
>
> NON-EXEMPT (<u>EmployeeID</u>, Title, Wage)
>
> RESEARCHER (<u>EmployeeID</u>, AcademicRank, Salary)

The relationship between the supertype (EMPLOYEE) and any one of its subtypes (EXEMPT, NON-EXEMPT, or RESEARCHER) is one-to-one.

An example

The best way to understand how to translate an E-R model into an equivalent relational model is to work your way through illustrative examples that show typical situations that are similar to those you might encounter as a developer. In this section, I take one of the examples of E-R diagrams given in Chapter 4 and step through its translation into a relational model.

Figure 8-12 shows the E-R diagram of the Mistress Treasure business model. You need to translate this model into a relational model that can be directly realized as a database.

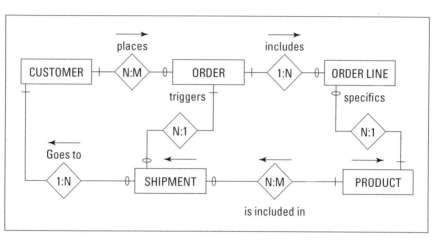

Figure 8-12:
E-R model
of order
processing
for the
Mistress
Treasure
online
business.

The E-R diagram in Figure 8-12 shows the entities and primary keys listed in Table 8-1.

Table 8-1	Entities and Keys in the Mistress Treasure Database
Entity	**Primary Key**
PRODUCT	ProductID
ORDER	OrderNo
ORDER LINE	OrderNo, LineNo
CUSTOMER	CustomerID
SHIPMENT	ShipmentNo

Looking at the maximum cardinality diamonds, you can conclude

- ✔ One CUSTOMER can place more than one ORDER (1:N).
- ✔ One ORDER can include more than one ORDER LINE (1:N).
- ✔ One ORDER LINE specifies one PRODUCT, but a product may appear on more than one ORDER LINE (1:N).
- ✔ More than one PRODUCT can be included in one SHIPMENT, and one PRODUCT can be included in more than one SHIPMENT (N:M).
- ✔ More than one SHIPMENT can go to one CUSTOMER (N:1).

This model has one N:M relationship, and the rest are 1:N relationships.

To convert the E-R model to an anomaly-free relational model, you need to make sure that all the relations are in DKNF and that the N:M relationship has been decomposed into two 1:N relationships with an intersection relation in the middle. Because you know how to normalize relations to DKNF, assume that the relations in Figure 8-12 all deal with a single theme and are already in DKNF. After the relations are in DKNF, the next step is to make sure that the relationships between relations form proper relational links.

You can establish the 1:N relationship "ORDER LINE specifies PRODUCT" by placing the primary key of PRODUCT (ProductID) into the ORDER LINE relation as a foreign key. You can handle the other 1:N relationships in a similar fashion:

- ✔ The primary key of ORDER (OrderNo) is already in ORDER LINE, so you don't need to add anything.
- ✔ Place the primary key of CUSTOMER (CustomerID) into ORDER as a foreign key.
- ✔ Place the primary key of CUSTOMER (CustomerID) into SHIPMENT as a foreign key.

Create the intersection relation PRODUCT-SHIPMENT (ProductID, ShipmentNo) between the PRODUCT and SHIPMENT relations. The primary key of PRODUCT (ProductID) is in PRODUCT-SHIPMENT as a foreign key. The primary key of SHIP-MENT (ShipmentNo) is also in PRODUCT-SHIPMENT as a foreign key. One tuple in the PRODUCT relation may correspond to multiple tuples in the PRODUCT-SHIPMENT relation, but each tuple in the PRODUCT-SHIPMENT relation corresponds to one and only one tuple in the PRODUCT relation. Similarly, one tuple in the SHIPMENT relation may correspond to multiple tuples in the PRODUCT-SHIPMENT relation, but each tuple in the PRODUCT-SHIPMENT relation corresponds to one and only one tuple in the SHIPMENT relation.

At this point, you have a fully normalized relational design that matches the users' data model, and can be implemented with a relational database management system.

Chapter 9

Using a Semantic Object Model to Design a Database

In This Chapter

▶ Transforming your SOM into a relational design

▶ Handling different object types

*I*f you have chosen to convert your client's users' model into a semantic object model (SOM), you are well on your way to having a database design. As I show you in this chapter, the conversion from a semantic object model to a corresponding relational model, in most cases, is quite straightforward.

In Chapter 5, I describe seven different types of semantic objects. Each of those object types has a direct translation into one or more relations. Furthermore, because each semantic object, by definition, represents a single idea, any relational model derived from a SOM will most likely already be in DKNF. You do not need to expend any further normalization effort.

Converting an SOM into a Relational Design

Chapter 5 describes the seven different types of semantic objects:

- ✔ Simple objects
- ✔ Composite objects
- ✔ Compound objects
- ✔ Hybrid objects
- ✔ Association objects
- ✔ Supertype/subtype objects (parent/child objects)
- ✔ Archetype/version objects

Each type has its own translation into relations. In the following sections, I illustrate each of the seven translations with an example.

Simple objects

A simple object contains only single-value, nonobject attributes. As you might expect, it is the easiest type of object to convert into a relational equivalent. In fact, it is a direct translation. One simple object in the semantic object model translates to one relation in the relational model. Figure 9-1 shows a diagram of the VEHICLE simple object that I describe in Chapter 5, as well as the equivalent VEHICLE relation.

Figure 9-1:
VEHICLE
simple
object and
VEHICLE
relation.

VEHICLE
ID VehicleID 1.1
ID LicenseNo
ID LicenseState
Make
Model
Engine
Color

VEHICLE (VehicleID, LicenseNo, LicenseState, Make, Model, Engine, Color)

In general, the unique identifier of the simple object becomes the primary key of the relation. The attributes of the simple object become the attributes of the relation.

Composite objects

Composite objects are like simple objects, but in addition, they can contain one or more multivalue, nonobject attributes. The receipt generated by the cash register at Steve's Market can be modeled with a composite object. The RECEIPT semantic object has single value attributes, such as date and total, as well as a multivalue attribute for each item sold.

A composite object in the semantic object model translates into multiple relations in the relational model: one relation for the composite object, and one relation for each repeating group within the object. A multivalue attribute is another name for a repeating group.

From the definition of a relation, you know that a relation may not contain any repeating groups. Thus, you must create a new relation for each such repeating group. Figure 9-2 diagrams the RECEIPT semantic object and shows the two relations that it translates into: RECEIPT and ITEM.

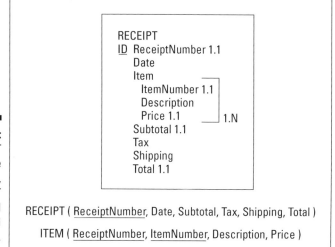

Figure 9-2: RECEIPT composite object, RECEIPT relation, and ITEM relation.

The unique identifier of the composite object (underlined in Figure 9-2) becomes the primary key of the RECEIPT relation. The unique identifier of the RECEIPT relation (ReceiptNumber), combined with the unique identifier of the repeating group (ItemNumber), form a composite primary key for the ITEM relation (underlined in Figure 9-2). The attributes of ITEM are the attributes of the semantic object's repeating group plus the primary key of the RECEIPT semantic object, and the attributes of the RECEIPT relation are the attributes of the RECEIPT semantic object, excluding the attributes in the repeating group.

Because minimum and maximum cardinality are specified for a composite object, you must also translate that information to the relational representation. The minimum cardinality of the repeating group may be 0 or 1. You indicate a minimum cardinality of 0 with an oval on the data structure diagram representing the corresponding relation. For a minimum cardinality of 1, you show a slash mark on the data structure diagram. Figure 9-3 shows a data structure diagram of the relational representation of the RECEIPT composite object.

The data structure diagram shows the link between the RECEIPT and the ITEM relations, and also shows the maximum and minimum cardinality. Primary keys are underlined. Maximum cardinality of 1 or N is shown by the absence or presence of a crow's foot on the line linking the two relations. Minimum cardinality of 0 or 1 is shown by an oval or a slash, respectively, on the connecting line.

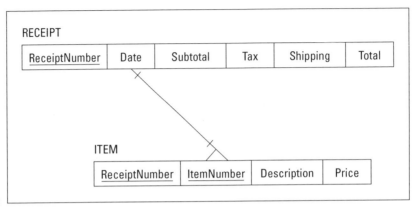

Figure 9-3:
Data
structure
diagram
corre-
sponding
to RECEIPT
composite
object.

Compound objects

A compound object contains at least one object attribute, but no multivalue attributes. The fact that it contains at least one object attribute implies that it is directly related to at least one other object. There are three different types of compound objects:

- ✔ **One-to-one:** One instance of the first object corresponds to one and only one instance of the second object, and one instance of the second object corresponds to one and only one instance of the first object.

- ✔ **One-to-many:** One instance of the first object corresponds to multiple instances of the second object, but one instance of the second object corresponds to one and only one instance of the first object.

- ✔ **Many-to-many:** One instance of the first object corresponds to multiple instances of the second object, and one instance of the second object corresponds to multiple instances of the first object.

One-to-one compound objects

I can illustrate the idea of a one-to-one compound object with another example from the Zetetic Institute. The Institute issues a computer to each researcher who joins the Institute. The researchers use the computers for making calculations, writing papers, sending and receiving e-mail, and various administrative tasks. Each researcher is assigned one and only one computer, and each computer is assigned to one and only one researcher. You can accurately model this situation with a pair of one-to-one compound objects, as shown in Figure 9-4.

Each object in the pair contains an object attribute referring to the other object in the pair. The maximum cardinality of both compound objects is 1, and the minimum cardinality is either 0 or 1 depending on whether the existence of that object is mandatory. In this example, a researcher might refuse to accept a computer, preferring to do all calculations, writing, and administration the old-fashioned way. In the interests of academic freedom, the Institute allows this choice, although it does not encourage it. So the minimum cardinality of the COMPUTER object attribute is 0. By the same token, a computer may be sitting in inventory, unassigned, so the minimum cardinality of the RESEARCHER object attribute is also 0.

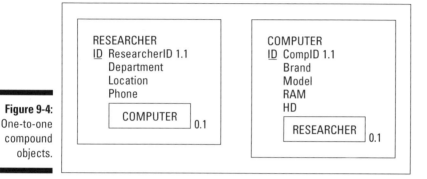

Figure 9-4:
One-to-one compound objects.

The compound object in Figure 9-4 translates into the two relations shown in Figure 9-5. The two relations are linked by the fact that the RESEARCHER relation contains the primary key of the COMPUTER relation (CompID) as a foreign key.

Figure 9-5:
Relational model representation of one-to-one compound objects.

RESEARCHER (ResearcherID, Department, Location, Phone, CompID)

COMPUTER (CompID, Brand, Model, RAM, HD)

Each relation deals with one and only one idea and is in DKNF. No additional normalization is needed, or even possible. Figure 9-6 shows the data structure diagram for the COMPUTER-RESEARCHER relationship. The primary key of COMPUTER has been placed into the RESEARCHER relation. Because this is a one-to-one relationship, it would have been equally valid to place the primary key of the RESEARCHER relation into the COMPUTER relation.

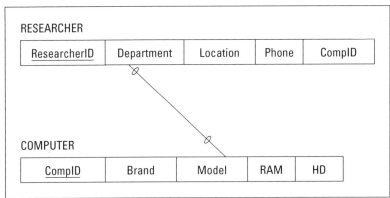

Figure 9-6:
Data
structure
diagram of
one-to-one
relationship
between
RESEARCHER
and
COMPUTER.

One-to-many compound objects

To illustrate the case of one-to-many compound objects, refer back to the fact that in the Zetetic Institute, a department may have many researchers, but each researcher is affiliated with one and only one department. Figure 9-7 shows the DEPARTMENT and RESEARCHER semantic objects.

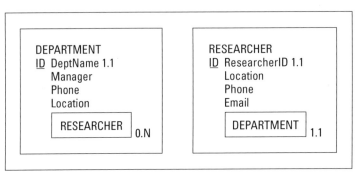

Figure 9-7:
DEPART-
MENT and
RESEARCHER
constitute a
one-to-
many
compound
object pair.

The DEPARTMENT object contains a RESEARCHER object attribute with a cardinality of 0.N. The 0 indicates that a department can exist even if it has no researchers. The N means that a department can employ multiple researchers.

The RESEARCHER object contains a DEPARTMENT object attribute with a cardinality of 1.1. The first 1 means that a researcher must be affiliated with a department. The second 1 means that a researcher can be affiliated with at most one department.

The semantic object model in Figure 9-7 translates into the relational model shown in Figure 9-8 as a data structure diagram.

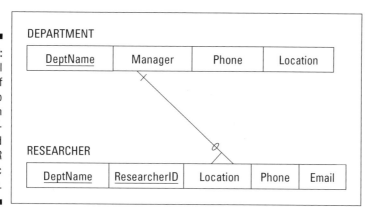

The diagram in Figure 9-8 shows the one-to-many nature of the relationship with the crow's foot on the RESEARCHER end of the line linking the two relations. Minimum cardinality is shown by the oval at the RESEARCHER end and the slash at the DEPARTMENT end.

Many-to-many compound objects

Generally, the real world is more complex and harder to model than we would prefer. Many-to-many relationships are common to a wide variety of contexts. You model these relationships with many-to-many compound objects, which you must then translate into their equivalents in the relational model. As you would expect, because many-to-many compound objects are more complex than one-to-one or one-to-many compound objects, they translate into more complex structures in the relational model.

Consider the organizational structure of the Zetetic Institute. A researcher may be assigned to several projects at the same time. Similarly, a project may be staffed by several researchers at any given point in time. This is an example of a many-to-many relationship. You can model this many-to-many relationship as shown in Figure 9-9.

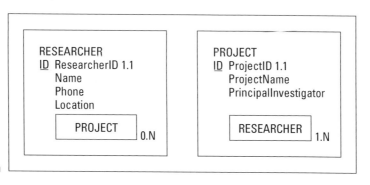

PROJECT is an object attribute in the RESEARCHER relation with a cardinality of 0.N, and RESEARCHER is an object attribute in the PROJECT relation with a cardinality of 1.N. The many-to-many nature of the relationship is shown by the cardinalities of the object relationships. Both object attributes have a maximum cardinality of N. The minimum cardinality of 0 for the PROJECT object attribute in the RESEARCHER relation shows that a researcher may not be assigned to any project. The minimum cardinality of 1 for the RESEARCHER object attribute of the PROJECT relation shows that a project cannot exist unless it has at least one researcher assigned to it.

Because you cannot represent a many-to-many relationship between two semantic objects by two normalized relations, you decompose the many-to-many relationship into an equivalent structure that has two one-to-many relationships feeding into an intersection relation that lies between the two relations that correspond to the two original semantic objects. Figure 9-10 illustrates this structure.

Between the PROJECT and RESEARCHER relations, you have the new intersection relation RES-PROJ. RES-PROJ is on the many side of a one-to-many relationship with PROJECT and is also on the many side of a one-to-many relationship with RESEARCHER. You have traded the conceptual complexity and susceptibility to anomalies of a many-to-many relationship for the relative simplicity and reliability of two one-to-many relationships. All the trade costs you is the addition of one relation to your schema. That is a small price to pay for a reliable design.

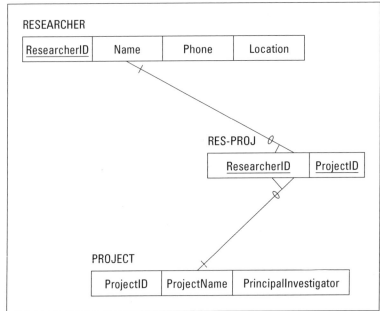

Figure 9-10:
Relational represen-
tation of
decomposed
M:N
relationship.

Hybrid objects

Hybrid objects combine the characteristics of composite objects and compound objects. A hybrid object contains at least one multivalue attribute and at least one object attribute.

The classic example of a hybrid object in a business context is the invoice. An invoice contains a multivalue attribute very similar to the ItemNumber attribute of the RECEIPT object that I use to describe composite objects earlier in this chapter. However, an invoice typically contains a lot more information than does a simple sales receipt. It usually has the name and shipping address of the customer, and may contain other pertinent information about the customer. It generally also names the salesperson that made the sale, so that a commission can be appropriately allocated. Customers and salespeople are significant enough to be represented by semantic objects of their own. Figure 9-11 shows a semantic object diagram of the semantic objects related to an invoice: INVOICE, ITEM, CUSTOMER, and SALESPERSON.

To translate the semantic object model into a relational model, create a relation for the original hybrid object, an additional relation for each multivalue attribute in the hybrid object, and an additional relation for each object attribute in the hybrid object. Figure 9-12 shows the resulting relational model.

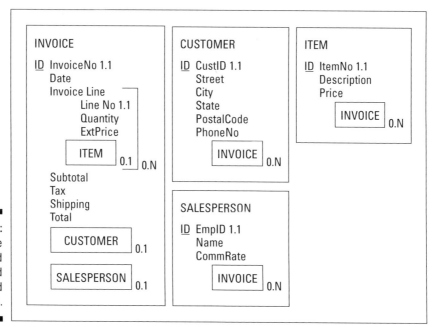

Figure 9-11: Example hybrid object and related objects.

Figure 9-12:
Relational
model of
hybrid
object
INVOICE.

INVOICE (<u>InvoiceNo</u>, Date, Subtotal, Tax, Shipping, Total, CustID, EmpID)

INVLINE (<u>InvoiceNo</u>, <u>LineNo</u>, ItemNo, Quantity, ExtPrice)

ITEM (<u>ItemNo</u>, Description, Price)

CUSTOMER (<u>CustID</u>, Street, City, State, PostalCode, PhoneNo)

SALESPERSON (<u>EmpID</u>, Name, CommRate)

All the relations are linked by columns that serve as the primary key in one relation and as a foreign key in the second relation. ItemNo links the ITEM relation to the INVLINE relation. InvoiceNo links the INVLINE relation to the INVOICE relation. CustID links the CUSTOMER relation to the INVOICE relation, and EmpID links the SALESPERSON relation to the INVOICE relation.

Association objects

Association objects are a special case of compound objects that often shows up in scheduling situations. Chapter 5 describes the example of tracking freight service on the Great Eastern & Nutley Railroad. A train pulled by an engine, driven by an engineer, makes a run from a starting point to a destination, on a given day. Figure 9-13 shows the semantic object diagram that captures this slice of life in the real world.

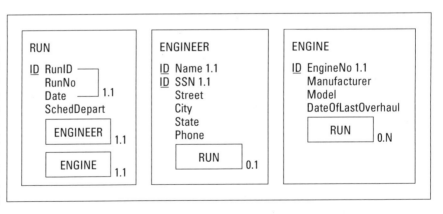

Figure 9-13:
RUN is an
association
object that
links the
ENGINE
object to the
ENGINEER
object.

The relations formed from association objects differ from the intersection relations formed from other compound objects that have a many-to-many relationship with each other Association relations carry additional information beyond merely containing the primary keys of the relations they are associating.

In the example, the RUN relation contains numerous attributes in addition to the primary keys of the ENGINE and ENGINEER relations. Figure 9-14 is a data structure diagram of the relations corresponding to the objects in Figure 9-13.

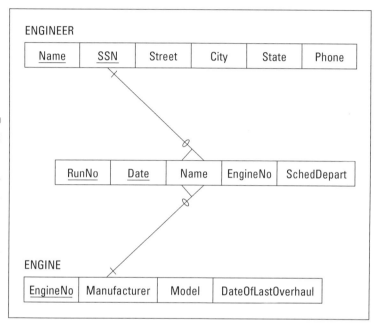

Figure 9-14: Association relation shows how resources ENGINE and ENGINEER combine to carry freight from one city to another.

Supertype/subtype objects

In Chapter 8, I use the example of employees of the Zetetic Institute to illustrate the idea of supertype and subtype objects. That example includes three types of employees: exempt, non-exempt, and academic. Exempt employees, generally professionals and managers, are salaried and cannot earn overtime pay. Non-exempt employees are paid by the hour and are paid time-and-a-half for any hours beyond 40 that they work in a week. Academic employees are paid according to a contract that runs for an academic year rather than a calendar year. Figure 9-15 is a semantic object diagram of the Zetetic Institute's three types of employees.

If you do a simple translation of this semantic object diagram into a relational model, you get the relations shown in Figure 9-16.

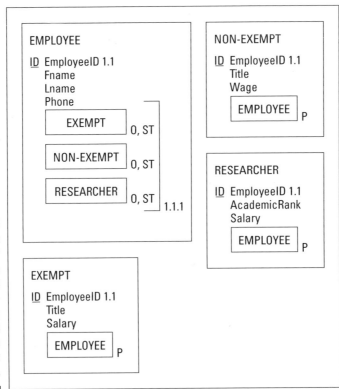

Figure 9-15:
Supertype/
subtype
objects
repre-
senting
employees
at the
Zetetic
Institute.

Figure 9-16:
Naive
relational
model of
Zetetic
Institute's
employee
types.

EMPLOYEE (EmployeeID, Fname, Lname, Phone)

EXEMPT (EmployeeID, Title, Salary)

NON-EXEMPT (EmployeeID, Title, Wage)

RESEARCHER (EmployeeID, AcademicRank, Salary)

The relationship between the supertype (EMPLOYEE) and any one of its sub-types (EXEMPT, NON-EXEMPT, or RESEARCHER) is one-to-one. This model is valid, but it has a problem nonetheless.

Say you know the name of a Zetetic Institute employee, and you want to know her compensation, but you don't know whether she is exempt, non-exempt, or a researcher. To find the information you want, you have to scan the EXEMPT, NON-EXEMPT, and RESEARCHER relations sequentially until you find her record in one of them. If the subtype relations have many records, this could be a slow process.

One solution to this problem would be to add an EmployeeType field to the EMPLOYEE relation, in which an EmployeeType of 'E' would denote an exempt employee, a type of 'N' would denote a non-exempt employee, and a type of 'R' would denote a researcher. The resulting model, shown in Figure 9-17, would permit quick retrieval of data located in the subtype relations. No time would be wasted searching tables that do not contain the target record.

Figure 9-17:
Improved
relational
model of
Zetetic
Institute's
employee
types.

EMPLOYEE (<u>EmployeeID</u>, Fname, Lname, Phone, EmployeeType)

EXEMPT (<u>EmployeeID</u>, Title, Salary)

NON-EXEMPT (<u>EmployeeID</u>, Title, Wage)

RESEARCHER (<u>EmployeeID</u>, AcademicRank, Salary)

The relationship between a supertype and any of its subtypes is always one-to-one, so maximum cardinality of a supertype/subtype relationship is 1. Minimum cardinality must be 1 on the supertype side, and may be either 0 or 1 on the subtype side, depending on whether existence of the subtype is mandatory.

Archetype/version objects

In Chapter 5, I illustrate the idea of archetype/version objects with software. Operating systems or application programs are released, then as improvements are made newer versions are released. For example, Windows NT is the archetype of an operating system. Windows NT 3.51, Windows NT 4.0 and Windows 2000 are examples of versions of the Windows NT operating system. Figure 9-18 shows the semantic object diagram for a versioned software product.

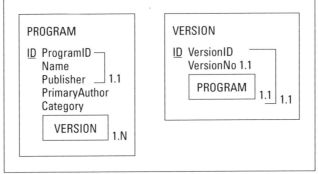

Figure 9-18:
Archetype/
version
objects
repre-
senting a
software
product.

As you can see from Figure 9-18, archetype/version objects constitute a specific type of compound object. The PROGRAM object contains an object attribute for the VERSION object and vice versa. Figure 9-19 shows the data structure diagram corresponding to the objects in Figure 9-18. Name and Publisher together form a composite key for the PROGRAM relation. To link the PROGRAM relation to the VERSION relation, Name and Publisher must be added to the VERSION relation, where together they constitute a foreign key.

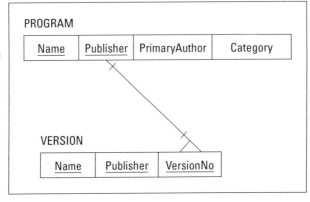

Figure 9-19:
Data
structure
diagram for
PROGRAM
and
VERSION
objects.

There is only one software product, but there could be multiple versions, so the maximum cardinality from the PROGRAM relation to the VERSION relation is one-to-many. For the relationship to exist at all, the software must exist, and furthermore, at least one version of the software must exist, so minimum cardinality is one on both ends of the relationship.

An Example

In this section, you look at the same Mistress Treasure business that I analyze in Chapter 8, but this time in the context of the semantic object model rather than the entity-relationship model. There are similarities and differences in the way you translate the two models into equivalent relational models, but you should end up with a relational model that is equally valid, regardless of which approach you take.

Figure 9-20 shows the semantic object diagram of the Mistress Treasure business model. You need to translate this model into a relational model that can be directly realized as a database.

The semantic object diagram in Figure 9-20 shows the semantic objects and primary keys that I list in Table 9-1.

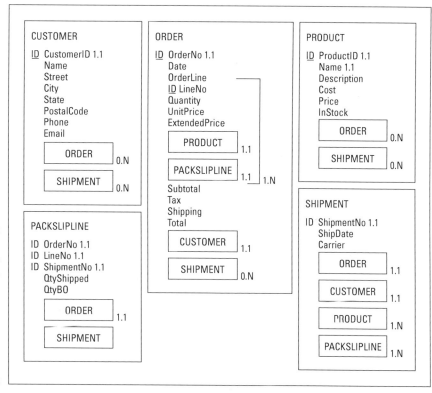

Figure 9-20: SOM of order processing for the Mistress Treasure online business.

Table 9-1	Semantic Objects and Keys in the Mistress Treasure Database
Semantic Object	*Primary Key*
PRODUCT	ProductID
ORDER	OrderNo
PACKSLIPLINE	OrderNo, LineNo, ShipmentNo
CUSTOMER	CustomerID
SHIPMENT	ShipmentNo

Looking at the maximum and minimum cardinality subscripts, you can come to the same conclusions that I describe in Chapter 8:

✔ One customer can place multiple orders (1:N).

✔ One order can include multiple order lines (1:N).

✔ One order line specifies one product (1:1).

✔ Multiple products can be included in one shipment, and one product can be included in multiple shipments (N:M).

✔ Multiple shipments can go to one customer (N:1).

This model has one N:M relationship, and the rest are 1:N relationships.

All the semantic objects in the Mistress Treasure model are compound objects. To convert the semantic object model to an anomaly-free relational model, you need to make the translations described earlier in this chapter for compound objects.

The repeating group in the ORDER semantic object requires you to create a new ORDERLINE relation. You can establish the 1:N relationship between PRODUCT and ORDERLINE by placing the primary key of PRODUCT (ProductID) into the ORDERLINE relation as a foreign key. You can handle the rest of the relationships in a similar fashion:

✔ The primary key of ORDER (OrderNo) is already in ORDERLINE, so you don't need to add anything.

✔ Place the primary key of CUSTOMER (CustomerID) into ORDER as a foreign key.

✔ Place the primary key of CUSTOMER (CustomerID) into SHIPMENT as a foreign key.

✔ Place the primary key of ORDER (OrderNo) into SHIPMENT as a foreign key.

Create the intersection relation PACKSLIPLINE between the ORDERLINE and SHIPMENT relations. The primary key of ORDERLINE (OrderNo, LineNo) is in PACKSLIPLINE as a foreign key. The primary key of SHIPMENT (ShipmentNo) is also in PACKSLIPLINE as a foreign key. One tuple in the ORDERLINE relation may correspond to multiple tuples in the PACKSLIPLINE relation, but each tuple in the PACKSLIPLINE relation corresponds to one and only one tuple in the ORDERLINE relation. Similarly, one tuple in the SHIPMENT relation may correspond to multiple tuples in the PACKSLIPLINE relation, but each tuple in the PACKSLIPLINE relation corresponds to one and only one tuple in the SHIPMENT relation. Figure 9-21 is a data structure diagram of the resulting relational model.

This model is now ready for implementation using a database management system or SQL.

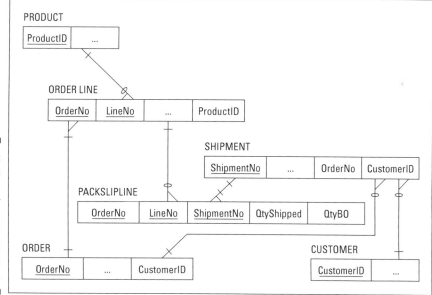

Figure 9-21: Mistress Treasure order processing relational model derived from the SOM.

Part IV
Implementing a Database

The 5th Wave   By Rich Tennant

"THIS SECURITY PROGRAM WILL RESPOND TO THREE THINGS:
AN INCORRECT ACCESS CODE, AN INAPPROPRIATE FILE REQUEST,
OR SOMETIMES A CRAZY HUNCH THAT MAYBE YOU'RE JUST
ANOTHER SLIME-BALL WITH MISAPPROPRIATION OF SECURED
DATA ON HIS MIND."

In this part . . .

*P*art IV takes the general principles of relational database design that I explain in Part III and applies them to three specific development environments. In the first case, I show you how to use a database design to create a Microsoft Access database. Access is probably the most popular DBMS running on personal computers. It is appropriate for small- to moderate-sized database systems. Next, I show you how to take a database design and convert it into a Microsoft SQL Server database. SQL Server is the most popular DBMS for building large database systems based on the Windows operating system. Finally, I describe how to build a database using pure command-driven SQL.

Chapter 10

Using DBMS Tools to Implement a Database

*A*ny database development project has two parts: developing the data-base itself, and developing the application that uses the database to accomplish some purpose. You can create a database in two ways: directly, by using SQL statements invoked from within a host program; or, by using development tools supplied by your DBMS vendor. In this chapter, I describe the process of developing a database using the tools included with one of the more popular database management systems. (I explain how to build a data-base with SQL in Chapter 12.)

Microsoft Access is an entry-level database management system, designed for relatively inexperienced developers who need to build small- to medium-sized database applications for use by individuals or small organizations. For larger jobs, Microsoft has a more powerful DBMS product named SQL Server. Knowledgeable developers and administrators use SQL Server to build and maintain large, complex applications. I discuss SQL Server in Chapter 11.

Before you can implement a database and expect it to meet your needs con-sistently and reliably, you must pass through the earlier development phases that I describe in Chapter 2: definition, requirements, evaluation, and design. You should thoroughly and meticulously complete all these phases before you decide which DBMS would be the best to use in implementing your system. As you gain experience, you will probably be able to make a good guess at which will be best, but even then, you should reserve judgment until you complete all the phases up to and including the design phase. In the process of gathering the information that enables you to create a design that meets all the requirements, you may find that your initial choice of DBMS is not the best. You may even find that it will not meet your needs at all.

Don't choose your tools until you know what the task will require. It is discouraging and a waste of time to try to excavate for a skyscraper's foundation using a hand trowel. On the other hand, it is frustrating and a waste of money to use a backhoe to plant a half-dozen tulips.

Translating a Relational Model into a Database

Figure 10-1 shows the Mistress Treasure relational database model. (For details on developing this model, see Chapter 9.)

This simplified model has six relations. I can use this model to illustrate what you must do to create a practical database, but it probably does not capture enough detail to serve as a model for a real system.

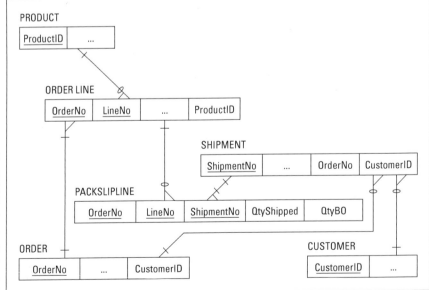

Figure 10-1:
Relational
model of
order
processing
for Mistress
Treasure
database.

Database models in the real world are always more complex than those you find in books. Models in books are designed to illustrate principles without obscuring those principles with unnecessary detail. On real projects, however, that detail is important, because it makes the model match the users' model. More detail means more relations and more relationships.

All the relationships in the model in Figure 10-1 are one-to-many, and in every case, you link the two relations in each relationship by putting the primary key of the relation on the 'one' side into the relation on the 'many' side as a foreign key.

The final relational design, based on the relationships shown in Figure 10-1 and the attributes shown in Figure 9-20, is as follows:

> PRODUCT (ProductID, Name, Description, Cost, Price, InStock)
>
> ORDER LINE (OrderNo, LineNo, Quantity, UnitPrice, ExtendedPrice, ProductID)
>
> SHIPMENT (ShipmentNo, ShipDate, Carrier, CustomerID)
>
> PACKSLIPLINE (OrderNo, LineNo, ShipmentNo, QtyShipped, QtyBO)
>
> ORDER (OrderNo, Date, Subtotal, Tax, Shipping, Total, CustomerID)
>
> CUSTOMER (CustomerID, FirstName, LastName, Title, Street, City, State, PostalCode, Phone, Email)

This system, with only six relations, straightforward relationships, and simple business rules, is a good match for the capabilities of Microsoft Access 2000. In the following sections, I describe how you can implement it using Access' development tools.

Access 2000

Microsoft Access today serves as the main introduction to database for many people. It is part of the Professional Edition of the Microsoft Office suite of basic applications, and is designed to integrate seamlessly with such other Office applications as Word, Excel, Outlook, and Front Page. Ease of use has been a primary consideration in the development of all the Office applications, but particularly so in the case of Access, because database management systems are inherently complex. Access is an appropriate tool for developing small- to medium-sized databases and database applications.

Do not consider this chapter to be a quick and easy way for you to find out everything there is to know about building databases with Access 2000. The purpose of this book is to explain the general principles of database development. I only use Access 2000 to illustrate those principles. As a result, I only scratch the surface here. For a treatment that focuses on Access 2000, read *Access 2000 Programming For Dummies*.

Building tables

Relations in the relational model translate directly into tables in a relational database. Each database management system has its own tools for building tables. To show how to use the table-building tools in Microsoft Access 2000, this section steps through the construction of the tables in the Mistress Treasure database. After you have a normalized database design for whatever project you are building, you can go through the same steps. The sequence of steps will be the same. Only the details that are specific to the system you are modeling will be different.

After you have an agreed upon and approved design for a table structure, which you do for the Mistress Treasure database (see the preceding section), you can proceed with database implementation:

1. **Launch the Microsoft Access application.**

   Access loads and then displays a screen similar to that shown in Figure 10-2.

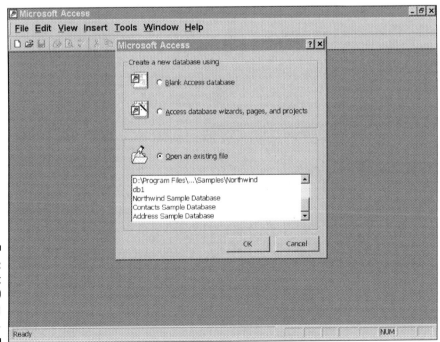

Figure 10-2: Microsoft Access 2000 opening screen.

2. **Specify whether you want to start with a blank Access database or use the Access database wizards, pages, and projects. Click OK.**

By using a wizard, you get step-by-step guidance throughout the entire process of creating a new database. However, using a wizard also inevitably means that you give up some flexibility and capability.

For the example I use throughout this chapter, selecting the wizard option does not offer any advantages. It just inserts some extra steps into the process. So the best choice is to select the Blank Access Database option and then click OK.

Access then displays the File New Database dialog box shown in Figure 10-3.

3. **Enter a name for your database and then click Create.**

This produces a screen similar to the one displayed in Figure 10-4.

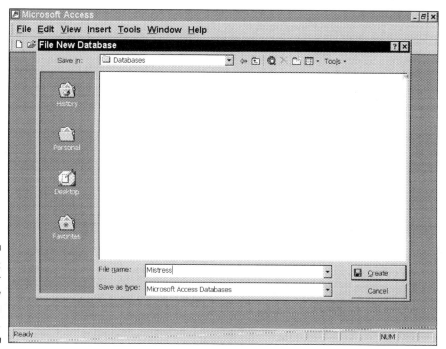

Figure 10-3:
Giving your
new
database
a name.

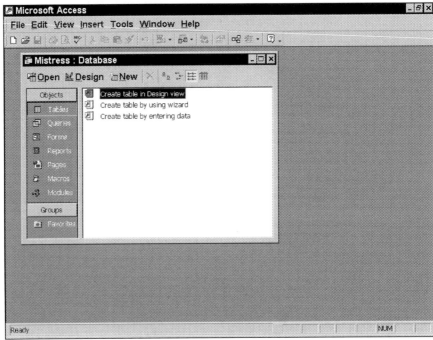

Figure 10-4:
Selecting
a table
creation
method.

4. **In the pane on the right side of the dialog box, select Create Table In Design View by double-clicking that option.**

   Access displays the Table1 dialog box shown in Figure 10-5. Table1 is the default name given to the first table you create. You can change this name to something more meaningful later.

   The data entry form has three columns: Field Name, Data Type, and Description. On the left edge of the form, an arrowhead indicates that the top row is selected.

5. **Enter the name of your first attribute in the Field Name column, and its type in the Data Type column.**

   In this example, I put ProductID in the FieldName column and Number in the Data Type column. The Description field is optional. If you have something descriptive and helpful to enter here, it is a good idea to do so. If the purpose of a field is obvious from its name, you may not want to bother putting anything into the Description field.

   You need to let Access know which attribute is the table's primary key. In this example ProductID is the primary key.

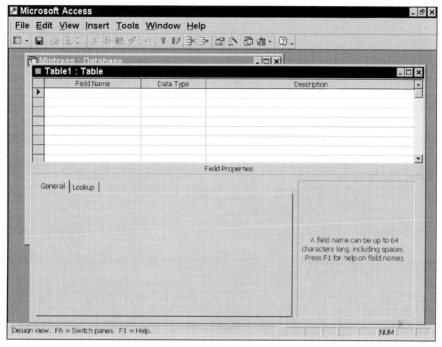

Figure 10-5:
Table
creation
dialog box.

6. **With the pointer still in the ProductID row, click the key icon in the icon bar.**

    This puts a key symbol in the slender column at the left edge, showing that Access now considers ProductID to be the primary key of the table you are building.

    Some default values will appear in the General tab at the lower left of the dialog box. Generally, you have to change at least some of these values, regardless of what database you are building.

7. **Make changes in this area to reflect what is shown in Figure 10-6.**

    The default Field Size of Long Integer is all right, as is the Decimal Places of Auto. Zero is an acceptable Default Value for this field. Because ProductID is the primary key of this table, the value of Required should be Yes and the value of Indexed should be Yes (No Duplicates). A table's primary key must have a non-null unique value.

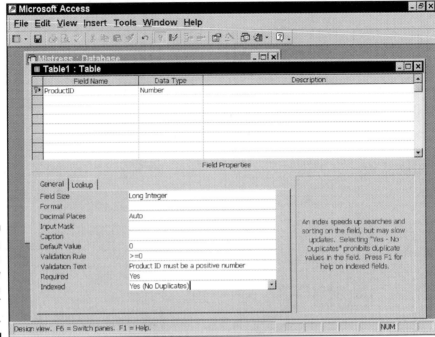

Figure 10-6:
Entering the
primary
key of the
PRODUCT
table.

Table 10-1 shows the values that should appear for the characteristics listed on the General tab. In this example, I do not specify some of the characteristics. In databases you build, you may or may not want to use them. I display all characteristics in Table 10-1 but in subsequent tables leave out characteristics for which no value is specified.

Table 10-1	Characteristics of ProductID Field in PRODUCT
Characteristic	*Value*
Field Size	Long Integer
Format	
Decimal Places	Auto
Input Mask	
Caption	
Default Value	0
Validation Rule	>= 0

Characteristic	Value
Validation Text	Product ID must be a positive number
Required	Yes
Indexed	Yes (No Duplicates)

Access checks the validation rule for a field whenever a user enters something into that field. If the entry violates the validation rule, Access rejects the entry and displays the Validation Text. This gives the user the opportunity to recognize the mistake and make a valid entry.

8. **After finishing the ProductID row, proceed to enter the rest of the attributes of the PRODUCT relation to successive rows in the Table1 table.**

When you are building your own database tables, you have to determine the appropriate values for the characteristics of each field. Tables 2 through 6 show the values I have chosen for the characteristics of the remaining fields in the PRODUCT table.

Table 10-2	Characteristics of Name Field in PRODUCT
Characteristic	**Value**
Field Size	30
Required	Yes
Allow Zero Length	No
Indexed	Yes
Unicode Compression	Yes

Because Name is a Text field, I specify the maximum Field Size as 30. Names longer than 30 characters will be truncated. I have decided that the Name field must contain a value, so Required has a value of Yes. I index the Name field because I will frequently want to retrieve records by a product's name. I specify Unicode Compression as Yes to save storage space. With compression, every character in the Text field takes up one byte of storage. Without compression, every character takes up two bytes. If you are storing lots of text, this could make a big difference in the size of your database. Because storage isn't free yet, smaller is better.

Although I use *Name* as an attribute name in the Mistress Treasure database design, it is not a good idea to do so. DBMSs often reserve words such as "Name," "Date," and "Order," and those words may have restricted meanings. It would be better to use something less common, such as ProdName.

Table 10-3	Characteristics of Description Field in PRODUCT
Characteristic	*Value*
Field Size	50
Required	No
Allow Zero Length	No
Indexed	No
Unicode Compression	Yes

For the Description field shown in Table 10-3, I set Field Size at 50, because a description of the product might conceivably be that long. A description is not Required, however.

Table 10-4	Characteristics of Cost Field in PRODUCT
Characteristic	*Value*
Format	Currency
Decimal Places	Auto
Default Value	0
Validation Rule	>= 0
Validation Text	Cost must be positive number
Required	Yes
Indexed	No

The Cost field has the Currency data type. Required is Yes because I want the user to enter a cost for every product Mistress Treasure carries, even if the cost is zero.

Table 10-5	Characteristics of Price Field in PRODUCT
Characteristic	*Value*
Format	Currency
Decimal Places	Auto
Default Value	99999
Validation Rule	>= 0

Characteristic	Value
Validation Text	Product ID must be positive number
Required	Yes
Indexed	No

The Price field also has the Currency data type. Default Value is not zero, because I do not want to inadvertently give away a product for free. Required is Yes because I want the user to enter a suggested price for every product Mistress Treasure carries.

Table 10-6	Characteristics of InStock Field in PRODUCT
Characteristic	**Value**
Field Size	Integer
Format	Standard
Decimal Places	0
Default Value	0
Validation Rule	>= 0
Validation Text	Product ID must be positive number
Required	Yes
Indexed	No

The Integer data type takes up less space than the Long Integer data type, so it is good practice to use Integer if you know that the largest value that will be stored in a field is less than the maximum for the Integer type. Unless you think you might stock more than 32,767 of an item, you can save space by using the Integer type. If you might stock more than that, the Long Integer type is good for over two billion copies of an item. Standard Format means commas are used to separate groups of three decimal places and periods are used to separate the integer part from the fractional part of a number (for example, 99,999.99).

9. **After you enter the proper data into all the fields of Table1, save the table specification you have just entered by choosing File⇨Save.**

   Access displays the dialog box shown in Figure 10-7, asking you for the name you want to give this table.

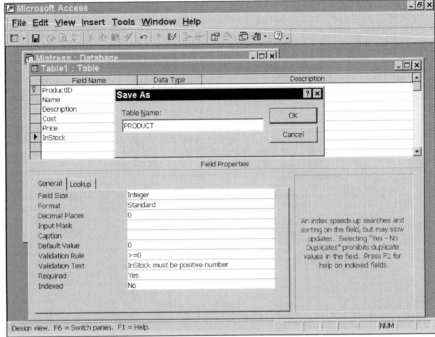

Figure 10-7:
Saving the
completed
specification
for the
PRODUCT
table.

10. **Enter a name (in my example, it's PRODUCT) and then click OK.**

You can turn the other relations into database tables in the same manner, with perhaps a few small differences. For the ORDER LINE table, one important difference is that the table has a composite key, made up of OrderNo and LineNo.

Specifying a composite key is a little tricky:

1. **Enter the information for OrderNo and LineNo on the first two lines of the entry form for the ORDER LINE table.**

2. **Select both lines by putting the cursor in the narrow column at the left edge of the form.**

   The cursor changes shape to a little right-pointing arrow.

3. **With the Ctrl key depressed, click one row and then the second.**

   Access highlights the selected rows, as shown in Figure 10-8.

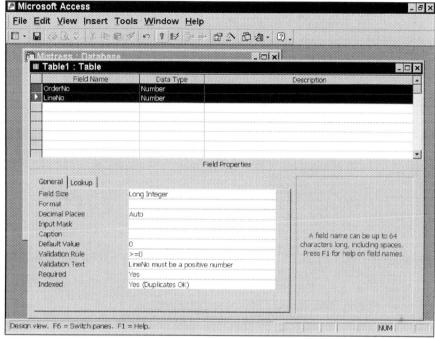

Figure 10-8:
First two rows of the ORDER LINE table are selected.

4. **Click the key icon in the icon bar.**

   Access puts key icons into the narrow left-hand column of both selected rows, indicating that they are both parts of a composite key.

You may now fill in the rest of the rows of the ORDER LINE specification, giving each field the appropriate characteristics. Tables 10-7 through 10-12 show the values of the characteristics of the fields in the ORDER LINE table.

Table 10-7	Characteristics of OrderNo Field in ORDER LINE
Characteristic	**Value**
Field Size	Long Integer
Decimal Places	Auto
Default Value	0
Validation Rule	>= 0
Validation Text	OrderNo must be a positive number
Required	Yes
Indexed	Yes (Duplicates OK)

Because OrderNo is part of a composite key, it is Required and Indexed. Duplicates are OK because OrderNo by itself is not the primary key.

Table 10-8	Characteristics of LineNo Field in ORDER LINE
Characteristic	*Value*
Field Size	Long Integer
Decimal Places	Auto
Default Value	0
Validation Rule	>= 0
Validation Text	LineNo must be a positive number
Required	Yes
Indexed	Yes (Duplicates OK)

Like OrderNo, LineNo is part of a composite key. It is Required and Indexed, and Duplicates are OK.

Table 10-9	Characteristics of Quantity Field in ORDER LINE
Characteristic	*Value*
Field Size	Integer
Decimal Places	0
Default Value	0
Validation Rule	>= 0
Validation Text	Quantity must be a positive number
Required	Yes
Indexed	No

Because Mistress Treasure does not anticipate that anyone will order as many as 32,767 of anything, I set Field Size to Integer rather than the default Long Integer. Quantity should always be a whole number so I set Decimal Places to zero. On any order line, the quantity being ordered is Required. There is no point in indexing on the Quantity field, because there are likely to be many duplicates. Also, it is unlikely that anyone would want to make a retrieval based on the quantity of items ordered. It is much more likely that people would retrieve information based on OrderNo.

Table 10-10	Characteristics of UnitPrice Field in ORDER LINE
Characteristic	*Value*
Format	Currency
Decimal Places	Auto
Default Value	99999
Validation Rule	>= 0
Validation Text	UnitPrice must be a positive number
Required	Yes
Indexed	No

UnitPrice is in the currency format, and a value is required, even if it is zero. I set Default Value to a high number, to prevent accidentally giving a product away for free.

Table 10-11	Characteristics of ExtendedPrice Field in ORDER LINE
Characteristic	*Value*
Format	Currency
Decimal Places	Auto
Default Value	99999
Validation Rule	>= 0
Validation Text	ExtendedPrice must be a positive number
Required	Yes
Indexed	No

ExtendedPrice is the product of UnitPrice and Quantity. Because both UnitPrice and Quantity are required to have values, ExtendedPrice also must have a value.

Table 10-12 Characteristics of ProductID Field in ORDER LINE

Characteristic	Value
Field Size	Long Integer
Decimal Places	Auto
Default Value	0
Validation Rule	>= 0
Validation Text	Product ID must be a positive number
Required	Yes
Indexed	Yes (Duplicates OK)

Every line in an order must be for a product, so ProductID is required. ProductID is a foreign key referring back to the PRODUCT table, so it has the same characteristics as it has in the PRODUCT table, except for the fact that it need not be unique in the ORDER LINE table. Figure 10-9 shows the completed specification for the ORDER LINE table.

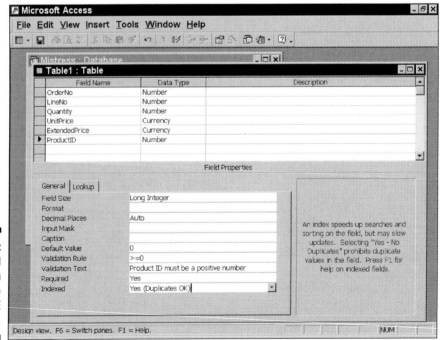

Figure 10-9: Completed specification for the ORDER LINE table.

If you want to follow along with the example that I use throughout this chapter, create the remaining tables in much the same way as you created the PRODUCT and ORDER LINE tables, specifying reasonable values for the characteristics of each field. Figure 10-10 shows the specification for the SHIPMENT table.

Figure 10-11 shows the specification for the PACKSLIPLINE table. The composite key of this table consists of three attributes.

Specifying the ORDER table is pretty straightforward. CustomerID is a foreign key that refers to the primary key of the CUSTOMER table. Figure 10-12 shows the completed specification.

The CUSTOMER table has a primary key of CustomerID, which is both Required and Indexed (No Duplicates).The management of Mistress Treasure also wants LastName and Email to be required fields so the company can maintain contact will all its customers.

After you define all six tables in the database, Access lists them in the Database dialog box, which has been on the screen all the time, although hidden behind the table specification forms. It shows all the objects currently defined in the system, as shown in Figure 10-13.

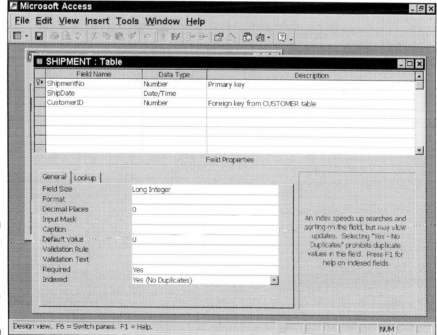

Figure 10-10:
Completed
specification
for the
SHIPMENT
table.

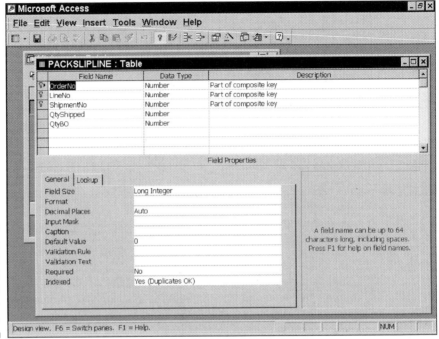

Figure 10-11: Completed specification for the PACKSLIP-LINE table.

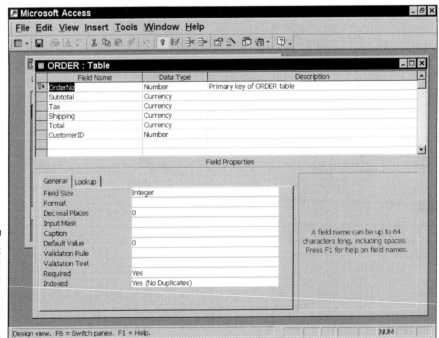

Figure 10-12: Completed specification for the ORDER table.

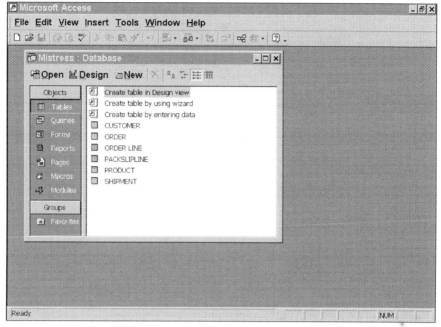

Figure 10-13:
All tables
have been
created.

Showing the relationships between tables

After you define the tables in a database, you need to look at the relationships that interconnect them:

1. **Choose Tools⇨Relationships.**

   Access displays the empty Relationships window.

2. **Choose Relationships⇨Show All.**

   As shown in Figure 10-14, Access displays the relationships among the tables in your database.

In this example, Access shows links between tables, based on the fact that you have used the same names for foreign keys and their corresponding primary keys. If you had used different names for foreign keys, you would now have to explicitly specify the links. As it is, Access has made a default assumption of what those links should be.

In the graphical model displayed, the arrangement of tables isn't the best, because some of the relationship links run behind tables to reach tables farther away. To make things clearer, drag the tables around so that relationships are clearer. Figure 10-15 shows the relationships unambiguously.

A bold font highlights primary keys, and lines represent links between corresponding fields in tables.

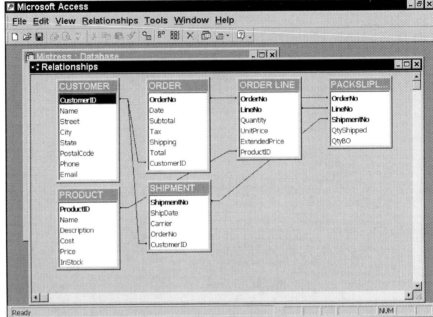

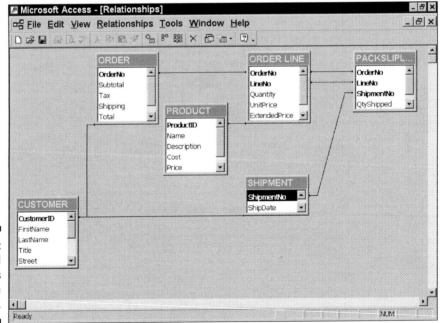

Adding data to tables

After you create a database's tables, you can fill them with data. Usually, you do this with the help of a custom data entry form embedded in an application. However, you can also enter data without a form. Access gives you the ability to add data directly to tables.

For example, to enter the Mistress Treasure products into the PRODUCT table, double-click PRODUCT in the dialog box shown in Figure 10-13. This brings up a generic data entry form similar to that shown in Figure 10-16.

This form has a column for each field in the PRODUCT table. Each column gets a default length, and the form already shows the default values that you entered for some of the fields. You will always have to change the default ProductID value to the actual ID for the product you are entering. You have to change the default cost of zero to the product's actual cost, and you need to change the default price of $99,999.00 to the suggested selling price. You also have to change the zero in the InStock field to reflect the actual number of this item that you have in stock.

As you finish entering each line, the cursor jumps down to the next line so you can make a series of entries without stopping. Figure 10-17 shows the Product data entry form after a few entries have been made.

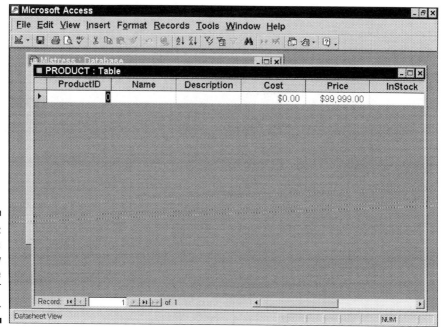

Figure 10-16: Generic data entry form for the PRODUCT table.

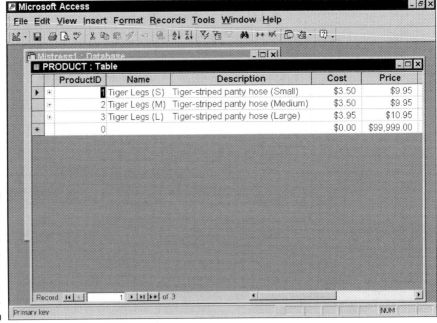

Figure 10-17:
PRODUCT
data entry
form after
several
entries have
been made.

As you enter each row, the row below it pops into existence, with the default values already present. When you finish entering data into this table, click the lower of the two X buttons in the upper-right corner of the Access window. A dialog box appears asking, Do you want to save changes to the layout of table 'PRODUCT? If you have made any layout changes, click Yes to save them. The data that you have entered is already saved in a temporary file. To store you entries permanently, close the database by choosing File➪Close from the Access menu bar.

You can enter data in the rest of the tables in the same way if you want. Enter customers in the CUSTOMER table. As they make orders, make appropriate entries in the ORDER and ORDER LINE tables. Then, as products ship, fill in the appropriate data in the PACKSLIPLINE and SHIPMENT tables.

Entering data this way works, but it is no way to run a business. It is much more complicated, slow, and error-prone than it needs to be. You can make the data entry process much more intuitive, which in itself would reduce errors. In addition, error-checking logic that prevents invalid entries would make things even better. With forms and applications, you can gain these important advantages.

Creating forms

Access gives you two ways to create a form:

- ✔ In Design view, as I demonstrate with the tables in the preceding section of this chapter
- ✔ With the Form wizard

Using the Form wizard is quicker and easier, but less flexible. You have less control over what the final form looks like. However, a wizard-generated form works just fine, and if the data-entry operators get accustomed to it, they can enter data into it just as fast as they could with a more ergonomically designed form.

Using the Form wizard

To understand the steps involved in using the Form wizard, and to see what the resulting form might look like, you can create the CUSTOMER form with the Form wizard. (For details on building the database that I use for the examples throughout this chapter, see the previous sections.) In the Mistress:Database dialog box (see Figure 10-13, earlier in this chapter), click Forms in the list on the left edge. The contents of the pane on the right change to what is shown in Figure 10-18.

Double-click the Create Form By Using Wizard option. Access opens the Form wizard shown in Figure 10-19.

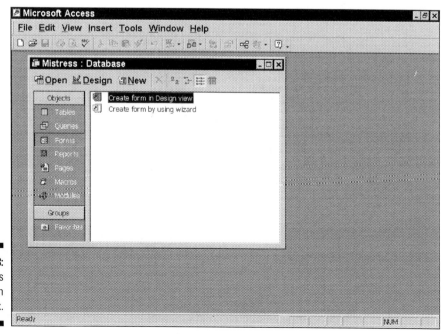

Figure 10-18:
Forms
creation
dialog box.

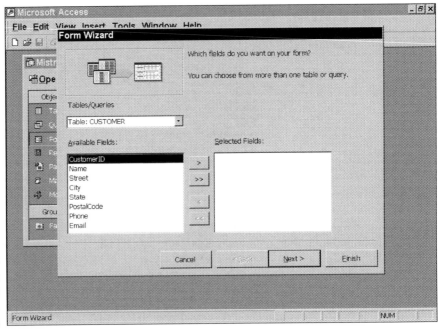

Figure 10-19:
The Form
wizard.

Because the CUSTOMER table is already selected in the Tables/Queries drop-down list, you don't need to select it. To create the entry form for the CUS-TOMER table, you want to select all the available fields because you will want to enter data into all of them. To select all the available fields in a single oper-ation, click the >> button in the middle of the Form wizard dialog box and then click Next. This action transfers all the fields from the Available Fields pane into the Selected Fields pane in a single operation.

Now the Form wizard asks you what kind of layout you want, giving you the options of Columnar, Tabular, Datasheet, and Justified. None of these choices are ideal, but Columnar is probably the best of the group, so select Columnar and then click Next.

Next, the Form wizard gives you a choice of several styles. A style defines a background pattern. The default style, Standard, is a solid gray background. It is not very aesthetic, but may well be the easiest on the eyes. Select Standard, or some other style that you fancy, and click Next. This brings up the Form wizard's final screen.

The last Form wizard screen asks what you want to name the form, assuming a default answer of CUSTOMER. This is a pretty safe guess for a form that takes fields from only one table. For forms that take data from multiple tables, you will probably have to think up an appropriate name. Finally, you are asked whether you want to open the form or modify its design. Assuming you are satisfied with what you have designed, select Open The Form and then click Finish.

The form you have just created pops onto the screen, with the default value of zero already in the CustomerID field. Figure 10-20 shows the new CUS-TOMER form, ready to accept data. It's not very pretty, but it will do the job.

Creating a form in Design view

Compared to using the Form wizard, creating a form in Design view takes more work and a higher level of skill. However, you may want to acquire that higher level of skill and take the extra time in development to build a better looking and more usable form. Assuming the Mistress database is open, from the screen shown back in Figure 10-18, double-click the Create Form In Design View option. Access displays the screen shown in Figure 10-21.

A blank form appears, waiting for you to fill it with content. On the left edge, a Toolbox also appears, giving you some of the tools you need to put content into the form. To build a form for entering data into the CUSTOMER table, choose View➪Properties. Access opens the form's property sheet, as shown in Figure 10-22.

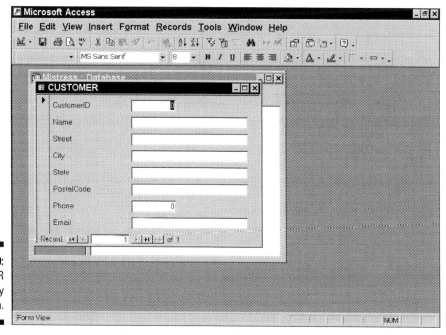

Figure 10-20:
CUSTOMER
data entry
form.

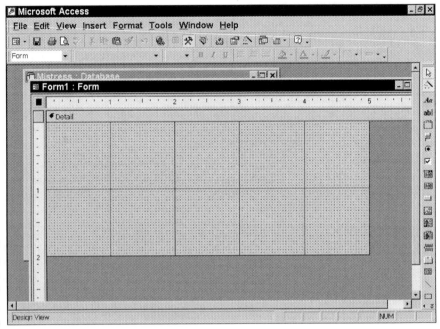

Figure 10-21:
Design view
of a new
form.

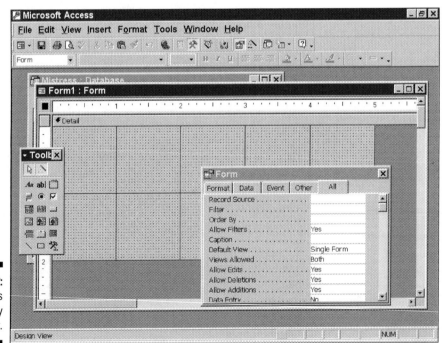

Figure 10-22:
The form's
property
sheet.

With the property sheet, you can specify in detail the properties of the form you are building. The first option, Record Source, specifies which table you want to link to the form. From the pull-down list, select CUSTOMER.

You want to add all the CUSTOMER table's fields to the form, so click the Field List icon in the toolbar. This pops up the field list window for the CUS-TOMER table, as shown in Figure 10-23.

You can select all the fields in the field list and drag them to the blank form. Hold the Ctrl key down while selecting each field in the list with a mouse click. When all fields are selected, drag them to the form and drop them where you want them. Don't try to place them exactly; you can move them to their final positions later. After the drag and drop, your screen should look something like Figure 10-24.

Now that the property sheet and the CUSTOMER field list have done their jobs, you can unclutter the screen by removing them. Click the X control in the upper-right corner of each. Expand the size of the form in its window by dragging the form's lower-right corner down and to the right. This will give you a little more room for making an easy to read placement of the form's fields. For an even larger form, you can expand the size of the form's window in the same way and then expand the form within it.

After you expand the form size, you can move around the fields and labels, resizing them as appropriate to give you the layout you want. You should also give the form a title. Select the Label tool from the Toolbox and then place a label at the top of the form. Size it appropriately and then type the title **Customers**. Give the title the Bold attribute and make it larger than the other text on the form. Figure 10-25 shows what the result might look like after you switch from Design view to Form view.

After you finish the form, exit it by clicking the X control in the upper-right corner of the form window. A dialog box appears, asking if you want to save changes to the design of the form 'Form1'. Click Yes. Access asks you to give the new form a name. Type **CUSTOMER** in the Save As dialog box and then click OK. The CUSTOMER form is ready to start accepting data. As you enter each record into the form, it is stored in the CUSTOMER table.

You can create forms for entering data into the other tables in the database. You can also create additional forms for other purposes. You may also use forms to view or modify the data in a database table, one record at a time.

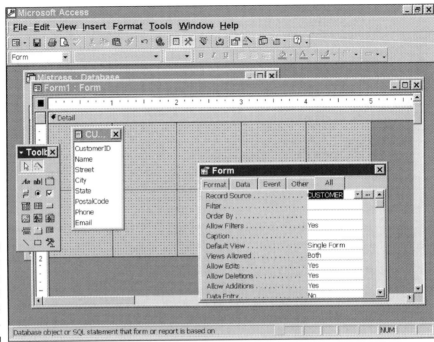

Figure 10-23:
The
CUSTOMER
field list is
displayed.

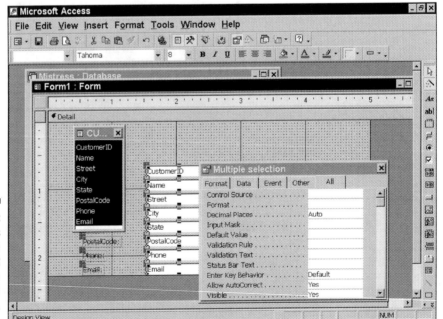

Figure 10-24:
Fields
from the
CUSTOMER
table have
been placed
on the form.

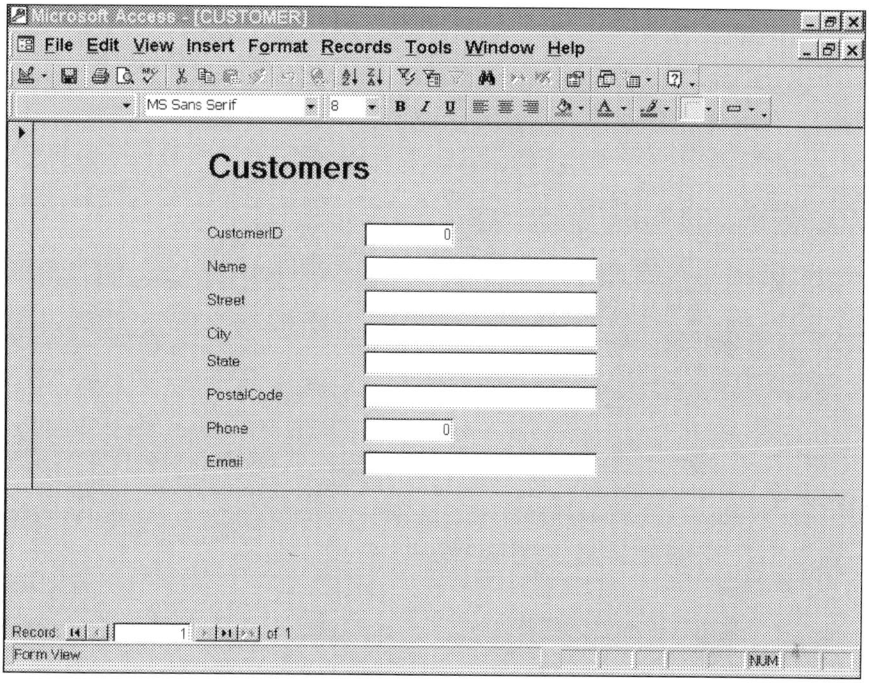

Figure 10-25:
CUSTOMER
form has
been laid
out and
given a title.

Creating queries

After you build your database and fill its tables with data, you can start using it to answer questions you have about the data it contains. These questions are called *queries*. Access provides a query by example (QBE) facility as the means for you to ask questions of the database. QBE is a graphical approach that does not require the user to understand any computer language.

You can pose a query that extracts information from one or more tables and puts the result in a new, temporary table. This result table can be read directly, or you can use it to provide the base information for a report. Reports put information retrieved by queries in a more readable and easily understandable form.

To illustrate how to use the QBE facility, this section shows you how to create a query to answer the question, "What is the total value of all orders written by customers in the state of Oregon?" This question requires information from the CUSTOMER table and the ORDER table. The CUSTOMER table contains the information about the state of residence of all customers. The ORDER table holds the values of all the individual orders. You can use Access's Query Design view to build the query to answer this question.

In the Mistress:Database dialog box (see Figure 10-13, earlier in this chapter), click Queries. You can choose to proceed either by creating a query in Design view or by using a wizard. Double-click the Create Query In Design View option. Access displays the Query Design grid and the Show Table dialog box, as shown in Figure 10-26.

In the Show Table dialog box, select CUSTOMER and then click Add. This adds the CUSTOMER table to the table/query pane of the Query Design Grid. Do the same thing to add the ORDER table to the query. Close the Show Table dialog box. Resize the Query Design grid and the tables in the table/query pane so that all the fields in both tables are displayed. The screen should look like the example in Figure 10-27.

In the Query Design grid, select CUSTOMER.CustomerID from the drop-down list in the first field position, CUSTOMER.State from the drop-down list in the second field position, and ORDER.Subtotal from the list in the third. Because you want to retrieve only those records for customers in Oregon, type ='**OR**' into the cell at the intersection of the Criteria: row and the State column. This produces the screen shown in Figure 10-28.

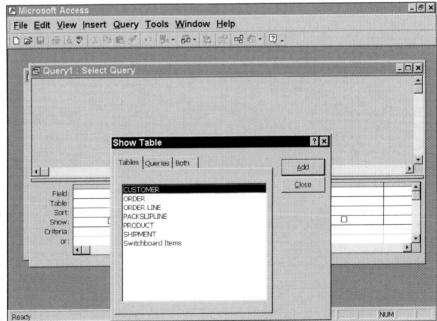

Figure 10-26:
The Query
Design grid
and the
Show Table
dialog box.

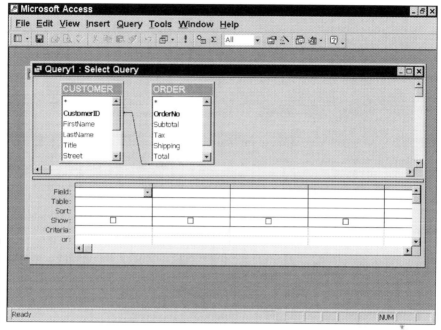

Figure 10-27:
Query
starting
point.

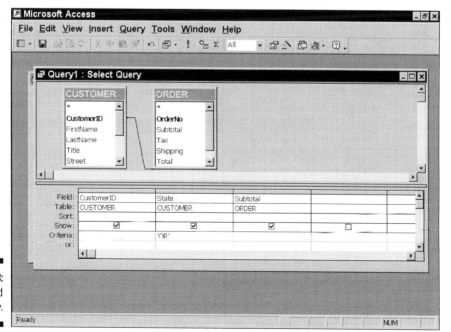

Figure 10-28:
Completed
query.

This query will return a table with three columns. The only rows in the table will be those in which the customer has an Oregon address. The first column will show the Customer IDs of all the Oregon customers. The second column will have 'OR' in every row. The third column will contain the total value of each order in the ORDER table.

This table is not a relation in the formal sense. If a customer has made multiple orders, the Customer ID field will be duplicated. The State field is definitely duplicated, because it contains 'OR' in every row. The Subtotal field could also contain duplicates. It is quite possible that the same customer might make two or more orders that have the same subtotal. This causes duplicate rows, so the table is not in first normal form. Nevertheless, it is still valuable in getting you where you want to go.

The query you have just created does not answer the question, "What is the total value of all orders written by customers in the state of Oregon?" but it does take you partway in that direction. To get what you want, you have to add up all the numbers in the third column of the result table. In addition to that, you don't really need to display the Customer IDs or the state information. You know the state will always be 'OR'.

SQL view

SQL is a database language that has been standardized by an international standards organization and adopted by relational database vendors around the world. All queries that you construct with QBE are translated into SQL before being submitted to the Access database engine for processing. Take a look at the SQL generated by the query shown in Figure 10-28. Choose View⇨SQL View. This command shows the SQL produced by the query:

```
SELECT CUSTOMER.CustomerID, CUSTOMER.State, ORDER.Subtotal
FROM CUSTOMER INNER JOIN [ORDER] ON CUSTOMER.CustomerID =
        ORDER.CustomerID
WHERE (((CUSTOMER.State)='OR'));
```

It is not the intent of this book to teach you SQL. For that read, *SQL For Dummies*. However, by analyzing an SQL statement such as this example, you can get some sense of how SQL works.

The SELECT clause specifies which fields to take from the source tables for inclusion in the result table. In this example, you are taking the CustomerID and State fields from the CUSTOMER table and the Subtotal field from the ORDER table. The FROM clause identifies where these columns come from: the CUSTOMER table joined to the ORDER table. (The nature of joins is beyond the scope of this book, but is fully explained in *SQL For Dummies*.) In this case, the only rows included in the result table are those in which CustomerID from the CUSTOMER table matches CustomerID from the ORDER table. The WHERE clause restricts the number of rows retrieved. Only those rows corresponding to customers in the state of Oregon go into the result table.

The preceding example is a valid SQL statement, but it does not produce the result you want. You don't need to *display* the CustomerID and State information, although the query has to know about them. Furthermore, you want to sum the Subtotal column. Returning to Design View, you can get rid of the unneeded columns by unchecking CustomerID and State in the Show: row of the Query Design grid. This change is immediately and automatically reflected in the SQL view, which becomes

```
SELECT ORDER.Subtotal
FROM CUSTOMER INNER JOIN [ORDER] ON CUSTOMER.CustomerID =
        ORDER.CustomerID
WHERE (((CUSTOMER.State)='OR'));
```

Now, only the column of subtotals will be displayed. At this point, all you have to do is add up that column. SQL provides just the tool you need to do that: the SUM function. By applying the SUM function to the Subtotal field, you arrive at a query that answers the original question:

```
SELECT SUM(ORDER.Subtotal)
FROM CUSTOMER INNER JOIN [ORDER] ON CUSTOMER.CustomerID =
        ORDER.CustomerID
WHERE (((CUSTOMER.State)='OR'));
```

In SQL view, modify the SQL generated by Access to include the SUM function as shown in this example. This statement will give the desired result. The change you have made is reflected immediately and automatically in Design view. If you switch back to Design view now, you will see how the QBE version of the query has changed.

Design view

Just by adding the SUM function to the SQL, you have substantially modified the way the Query Design grid looks. Figure 10-29 shows how it has changed.

The first column now has an expression in the Field: row (Expr1:Sum(ORDER. Subtotal)), and is the only column that has a check mark in the Show: field. The State column from the CUSTOMER table does not have a check mark in the Show: field, and has 'OR' in the Criteria field. Here's what all that means: Display the sum of all the subtotals of orders in the ORDER table where the customers who made those orders live in the state of Oregon.

The best of both worlds

In some cases, it is easier to express a query using QBE; in other cases, it is easier to use SQL. You do not have to choose one or the other. You can use them both, as the preceding example shows. For the parts that are easier to formulate with QBE, use QBE. Then switch to SQL view for the parts that are easier to express in SQL. You can go back and forth as many times as you like in the process of perfecting your query.

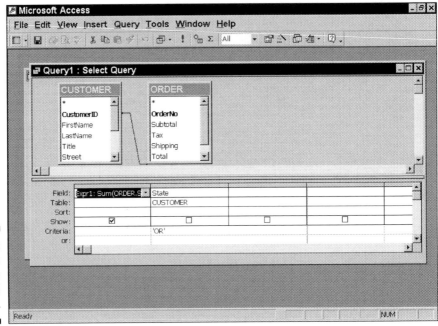

Figure 10-29:
QBE version
of the
modified
query.

Creating reports

Whereas forms provide a mechanism for entering raw data into a database, reports are designed to extract and display meaningful information from a database. You can either view a report on the computer screen or print it out on paper. Reports can be simple or elaborate, displaying information drawn from one table or many. Information can be grouped in a variety of ways, and can include computations such as subtotals and totals.

One of the better ways to find out how to create reports is to use Design view to examine an existing report that is similar to what you want to produce. Microsoft Access helps you with this strategy by providing several sample databases, each with a full complement of tables, queries, forms, and reports. One of these sample databases is the Northwind database, which concerns the business of a fictitious international trading company.

Figure 10-30 shows the Northwind:Database dialog box, with Tables selected. Eight tables have been defined, including one named Products.

A number of reports have been created to extract desired information from the Northwind database. By clicking the Reports option from the list on the left side of the dialog box, you can see the names of these reports, as shown in Figure 10-31.

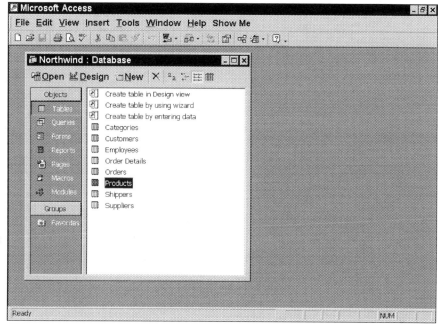

Figure 10-30:
Northwind database tables.

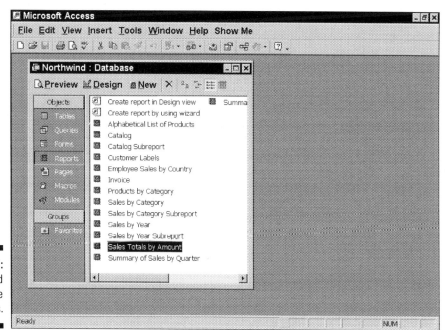

Figure 10-31:
Northwind database reports.

The Northwind example has quite a few reports, some simple and some quite complex. One of the simpler reports is the Alphabetical List of Products report. Figure 10-32 shows what this report looks like when displayed on the screen.

The report has four columns, all taken from the Products table. The products are sorted alphabetically, with a horizontal line separating the products whose names start with the letter 'a' from those starting with the letter 'b' and so on. A report header identifies the report, and a page footer gives the page number. To see how this report was built, switch to Design view. Figure 10-33 shows the Design view specification that created the report shown in Figure 10-32.

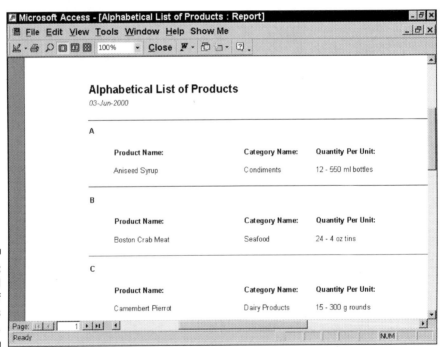

Figure 10-32:
Alphabetical List of Products report.

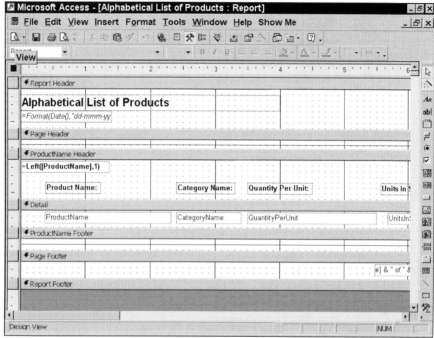

Figure 10-33:
Design view
of the
Alphabetical
List of
Products
report.

The Access Report generator is a band-oriented report writer. The Alphabetical List of Products report shows seven bands:

- The Report Header band contains information that appears at the top of the report. In this case, it includes the title of the report and the date it was printed.

- The Page Header band contains items that appear at the top of every page. For this report, the Page Header band is empty.

- The ProductName Header contains the identifier of each group of products (A for those starting with the letter A, B for those starting with the letter B, and so on) and the column heading of each column.

- The Detail band contains the actual list of products.

- The Product Name Footer contains a horizontal line to separate the products starting with one letter from the products starting with the next letter.

- The Page Footer holds whatever will be at the bottom of every page. In this case, it holds the page number.

- The Report Footer is empty in this example. Normally, it holds items designed to appear at the end of the report.

By studying this report, you can get a good idea of how to build a report that is based on a single table, with no calculations or other complications involved. Some of the other Northwind reports are examples of reports that draw upon multiple tables and have other complications, too. Use these reports as models that you can copy when you are building your own reports.

Creating applications

Previous sections in this chapter examine database tables, relationships, forms, queries, and reports. These are the major components of a database system. A database application is the 'glue' that binds these components together in a form that is easily and efficiently used by people who are not database experts. Ideally, database application users need to know nothing about database theory at all. They only need to know how to use the application. The application designer can make that task as easy as necessary. A tradeoff exists between ease of application programming and ease of use. The more effort you put into developing the application, the less the user needs to know. Because you develop an application only once, but it gets used many times, it pays to put in the effort needed to make the application as intuitive and fail-safe as possible. Chapter 13 looks at application development in more detail.

Chapter 11

Addressing Bigger Problems with SQL Server 2000

As I explain in Chapter 10, you can build a database in either of two ways: using development tools supplied by your DBMS vendor; or directly, by using SQL statements invoked from within a host program. In Chapter 10, I demonstrate how to develop a database using the tools included with Microsoft Access, one of the more popular database management systems. In this chapter, I describe the process for building a database with the development tools in Microsoft SQL Server 2000. Chapter 12 examines the process of implementing a database via SQL statements.

Getting to Know SQL Server 2000

Microsoft SQL Server 2000 is not just a larger, more robust product than Access; it is aimed at a different audience, and thus has different features. It is important to have a clear idea of what SQL Server is and what it is good for. Whereas Access is designed to support a relatively small number of users, running primarily noncritical applications, SQL Server is designed to support anywhere from dozens to thousands of users, running applications that may be vital to an organization's continued existence.

The developers of Access assumed that the people creating and maintaining Access databases would not be database professionals, and would have little or no knowledge of database theory or reliable design. The developers of SQL Server, on the other hand, assumed that those who would be called upon to develop and maintain SQL Server databases would be highly trained professionals, whose primary job would be working with SQL Server. This difference in audience dictated a major difference in features offered and user interface.

SQL Server has a much less intuitive user interface than Access does. Furthermore, where Access is an integrated package that you can use to build databases, forms, reports, and applications, SQL Server provides basic database functions, but assumes that you will use other tools to generate forms, reports, and applications.

Because Access and SQL Server are both Microsoft products, they have several things in common. For example, you can create a database design in Access, but specify that the data file be in SQL Server format. Consequently, you can design and build the database using the user-friendly Access tools and then run it in the more robust SQL Server environment.

If you do use Access to design a database that will later be operated upon by SQL Server, it may not be as full-featured as a database built from the ground up with SQL Server. You may have to make some fairly extensive modifications using the SQL Server tools, before you can use it in an enterprise-class application.

Translating Your Relational Model into a SQL Server Database

To provide a direct comparison of database implementation in SQL Server with database implementation in Access, this chapter uses the Mistress Treasure model again. Figure 11-1, the same as Figure 10-1, shows the model that I use for the examples in the following sections of this chapter.

This model has six relations and fairly simple one-to-many relationships. The challenge now is to implement the model using SQL Server. I assume that SQL Server has already been successfully installed on your Windows 98, Windows NT, or Windows 2000 machine.

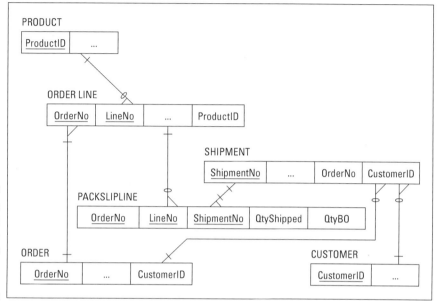

Starting SQL Server

Even the simple act of starting SQL Server running is not as easy as it is for Access:

1. **Click Start⇨Microsoft SQL Server.**

   A submenu pops up with a number of options. The option you want is Enterprise Manager.

2. **Click Enterprise Manager to display the Enterprise Manager screen shown in Figure 11-2.**

The screen you see may look a little different from Figure 11-2, depending on what SQL Server Groups have already been created, but the general appearance should be similar to that shown here.

As with Access, the first step in transforming a relational design into an implementation is to create tables. Creating tables with SQL Server is similar in general to creating them with Access, but with differences in detail.

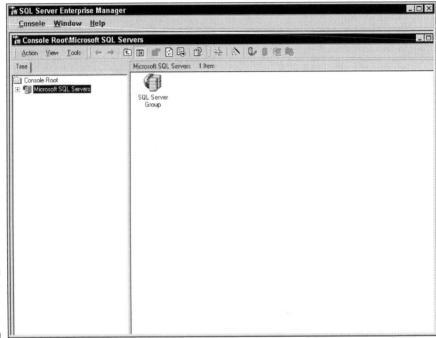

Figure 11-2:
Enterprise
Manager.

Building tables

To create database tables with SQL Server, go through the following steps:

1. **In the left-hand pane of the Enterprise Manager, click the + sign to the left of the Microsoft SQL Servers icon.**

   The SQL Server Group icon drops down.

2. **Click the + sign to the left of the SQL Server Group icon.**

   The icon for your server drops down. (My server is named Byzantine.)

3. **Click the + sign to the left of your server icon.**

   A whole list of things drops down, as shown in Figure 11-3.

4. **Double-click the Databases icon.**

   Several database icons drop down. These include databases that Microsoft delivers along with SQL Server, plus any that people in your organization may have created. You don't want to deal with any of the databases that already exist; you want to create a new one.

5. **Click the New icon, shaped like a starburst, in the toolbar.**

   SQL Server displays the Database Properties dialog box shown in Figure 11-4.

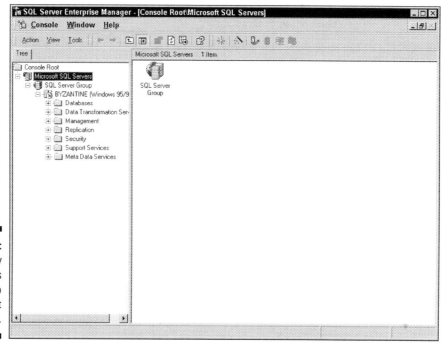

Figure 11-3:
The directory
tree has
started to
sprout
branches.

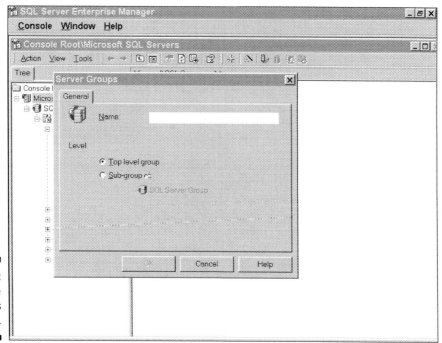

Figure 11-4:
Database
Properties
dialog box.

6. **Enter the name you want to give to your new database. (I named mine Mistress.)**

   SQL Server adds an icon representing your new database to the display of databases in the right pane of the Enterprise Manager window. The database has been created, but as yet it contains no tables.

7. **Right-click the icon for your database, and choose New.**

   SQL Server displays a submenu, as shown in Figure 11-5.

   This submenu offers a whole list of new things that you can create.

8. **Choose Table from the submenu.**

   SQL Server displays the window shown in Figure 11-6, which is waiting for you to enter the specifications for the first table in your new database.

   If you try to follow along with the Mistress Treasure database example that I use throughout this chapter, you will find that you cannot define the PRODUCT table in exactly the same way as you define it in the Access database (see Chapter 10). For one thing, SQL Server has some-what different data types from those in Access. For another, the proper-ties you can assign to a column differ.

9. **Fill in the values for the PRODUCT table so the table definition form looks like Figure 11-7.**

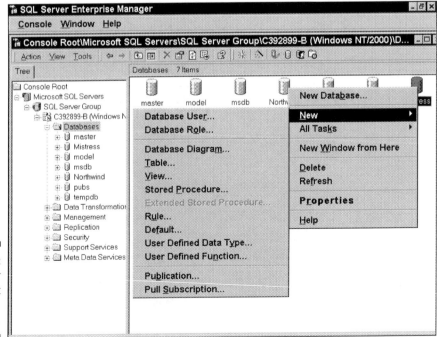

Figure 11-5:
Menus for actions that affect a database.

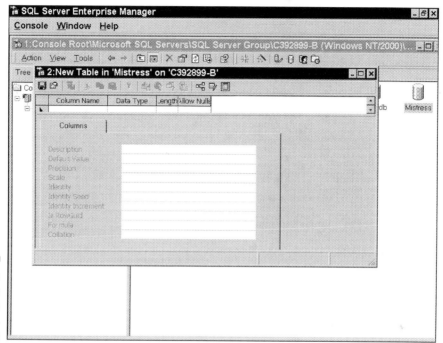

Figure 11-6:
Table
definition
form.

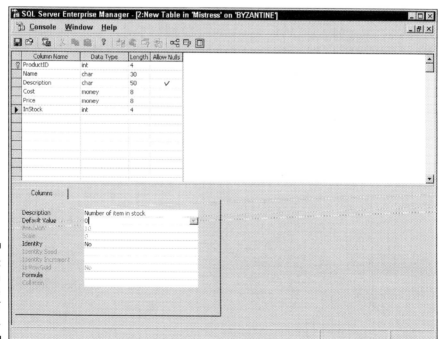

Figure 11-7:
Definition
of the
PRODUCT
table.

As you can see in Figure 11-7, ProductID is the key and is of the integer type (not long integer as is the case with Access). Access and SQL Server define their data types differently, and the `int` type in SQL Server is the closest equivalent to the `long integer` type in Access.

I unchecked the Allow Nulls column for all fields except the Description field. All other fields must have some value, even if it is zero.

10. **To save the newly defined table, click the diskette icon in the upper-left corner of the screen.**

    A dialog box pops up asking for a name to give the new table.

11. **Enter the name PRODUCT and then click OK.**

    This creates the PRODUCT table in the Mistress database.

12. **Return to the Enterprise Manager by clicking the lower of the two X controls in the upper-right corner of the screen.**

You can define the rest of the tables in the same way. To define another table, either click the New icon as you did last time, or choose Action⇨New Table. SQL Server responds by displaying a blank table definition screen, which you can populate as you did the PRODUCT definition screen.

Figures 11-8 through 11-12 show the definition screens for the other tables in the Mistress Treasure database.

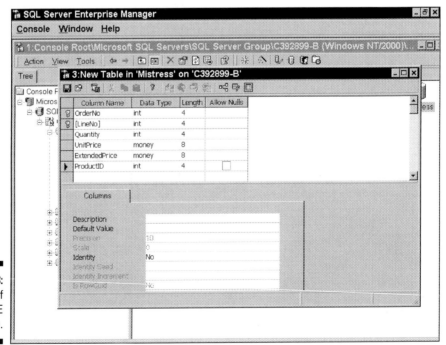

Figure 11-8:
Definition of
ORDER LINE
table.

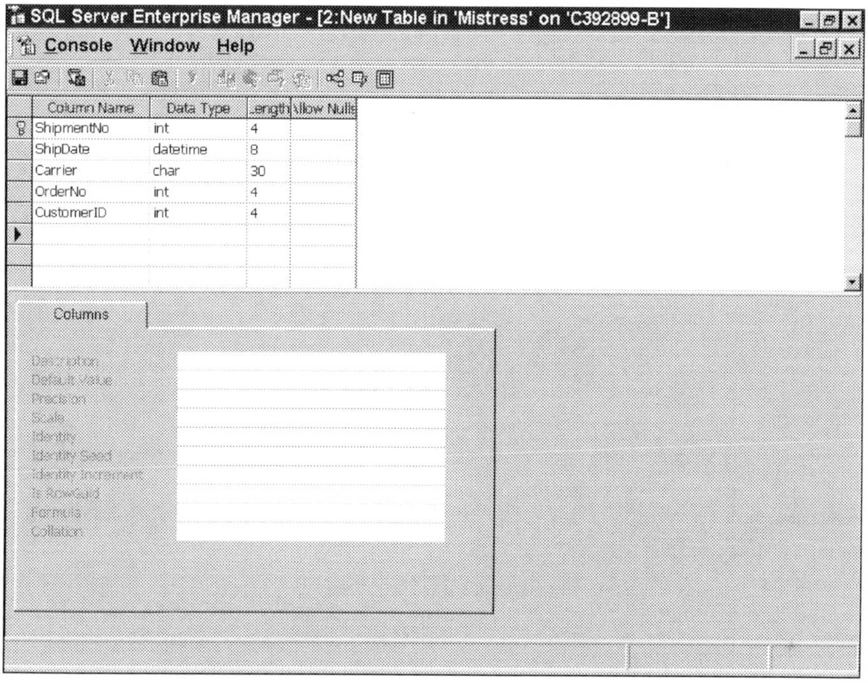

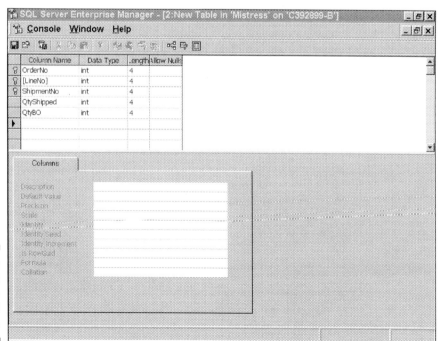

Figure 11-9:
Definition of
SHIPMENT
table.

Figure 11-10:
Definition
of PACK-
SLIPLINE
table.

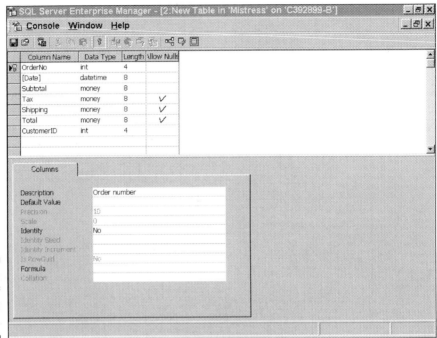

Figure 11-11:
Definition of
ORDER
table.

Figure 11-12:
Definition of
CUSTOMER
table.

Establishing the relationships among tables

After you define the tables, you must specify the relationships among them. In the Mistress Treasure example, just because the CUSTOMER table and the ORDER table both include an attribute named CustomerID, SQL Server does not assume that they refer to the same thing.

With ORDER selected in the right pane of the Enterprise Manager, choose Action➪Design Table. SQL Server opens the definition screen for the ORDER table. At this point, you could modify the table definition if you wanted to. However, you only want to establish its relationships to the tables to which it is linked by virtue of sharing a key field. In this case, it is linked to the CUSTOMER table by the CustomerID field. Click the Manage Relationships icon to display the Properties dialog box shown in Figure 11-13.

Click the New button. SQL Server assumes you want the relationship with the CUSTOMER table, and fills in the dialog box's fields, as shown in Figure 11-14.

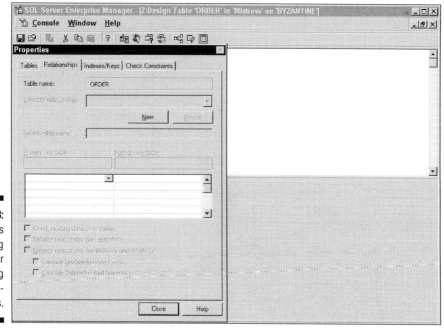

Figure 11-13: Properties dialog box for managing relation- ships.

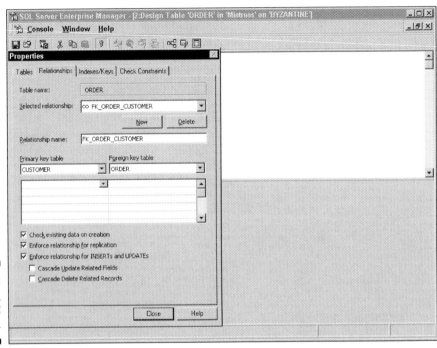

Figure 11-14:
ORDER_
CUSTOMER
relationship.

The selected relationship, FK_ORDER_CUSTOMER, indicates that ORDER is on the many (∞ side of the relationship. FK refers to the fact that ORDER is linked to this relationship by a foreign key. CUSTOMER is the primary key table, and ORDER is the foreign key table.

To establish the relationship, in the Primary Key Table column, under CUSTOMER, click in the first row and then pull down the field menu. Select CustomerID. Next, move to the Foreign Key Table column, pull down the field menu, and select CustomerID. In this way, you specify that CustomerID in the primary key table CUSTOMER is the same as CustomerID in the foreign key table ORDER. Figure 11-15 shows the dialog box after these selections have been made.

The three checked boxes, Check Existing Data On Creation, Enforce Relationship For Replication, and Enforce Relationship For INSERTs and UPDATEs, mean that you want this relationship to be enforced under all circumstances. The two unchecked boxes require a little more explanation.

Cascade Update Related Fields means in this case that if the CustomerID for a customer is changed in the CUSTOMER table, it will also be changed in all the entries for that customer in the ORDER table. Cascade Delete Related Records means that if the record for a particular customer is deleted from the CUSTOMER table, all records for that customer in the ORDER table also will be deleted.

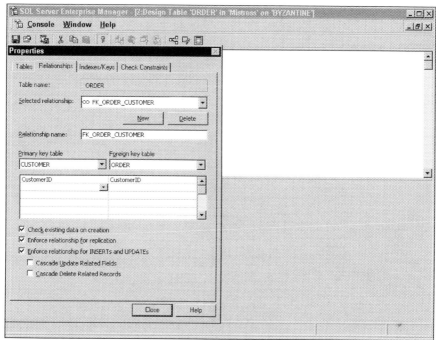

Click Close to establish the relationship.

In a one-to-many relationship, the table on the one side is called the *parent,* and the table on the many side is called the *child.* A parent can have multiple children, but (in this usage anyway) a child can have one and only one parent. When a parent is updated or deleted, the effects of that update or deletion may or may not cascade to its children, depending on whether the Cascade Update Related Fields checkbox or the Cascade Delete Related Records checkbox holds a checkmark.

Establish the other relationships between tables to match the relationships as specified in the relational model shown in Figure 11-1. After you enter all the relationships, you can show them graphically, using the Create Database Diagram wizard. Right-click the Diagrams icon in the tree in the left pane of the Enterprise Manager. When the wizard appears, follow its directions, and it will automatically create a diagram of your database, as shown in Figure 11-16.

The diagram shows the relationships among the tables, with a key symbol on the one side of each relationship and an infinity sign on the many side of each relationship.

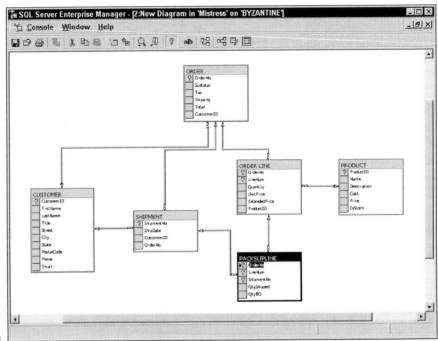

Figure 11-16:
Diagram of
the Mistress
database.

Is that all there is to it?

After you have defined tables and established the relationships among them, are you finished with building the database structure, and ready to start filling the tables with data? Probably not. SQL Server is much more robust than Access and can handle much larger, more complicated systems. That power comes at the price of added complexity however.

The Design Table screens, such as those shown in Figures 11-7 through 11-12, have several icons in the icon bar in addition to the Set Primary Key icon: Triggers, Show Permissions, Show Dependencies, and Generate SQL Script. (You used the Manage Relationships icon in the preceding section of this chapter.)

The icon bar also has a Manage Indexes/Keys icon and a Manage Constraints icon. By clicking the Manage Constraints icon, you can apply constraints to a table field in much the same way that validation rules work in Access. The permissions function enables you to specify what level of access a particular class of user may have to a table. You can prevent a given class of users from accessing a table or selectively allow them to view the contents of a table, add rows to a table, change existing rows in a table, or delete rows from a table.

The details of these options are beyond the scope of this book, which is not a tutorial on how to use SQL Server 2000. I use SQL Server and Access merely to illustrate two different tools that you might use in converting a relational design into a functional database. I also hope to give you some sense of the differences in complexity between two products that have the same general purpose.

Adding data to tables

After you create your tables and establish the relationships among them, you can add data. You perform this task in much the same way as you do in Access. In the Enterprise Manager, with Tables selected in the tree pane on the left, right-click the table you want to fill with data, and choose Open Table⇨Return All Rows, as shown in Figure 11-17.

SQL Server returns a tabular view of the table you specified. If the table does not yet contain any data, it will be waiting for you to enter some. Figure 11-18 shows the table after a couple rows have been entered.

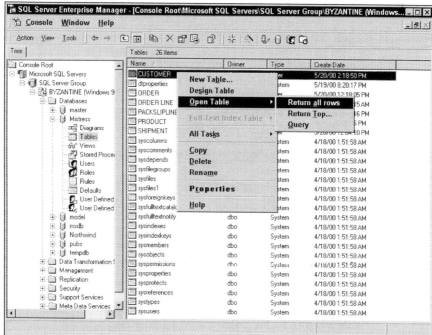

Figure 11-17: Choosing to add data to the CUSTOMER table.

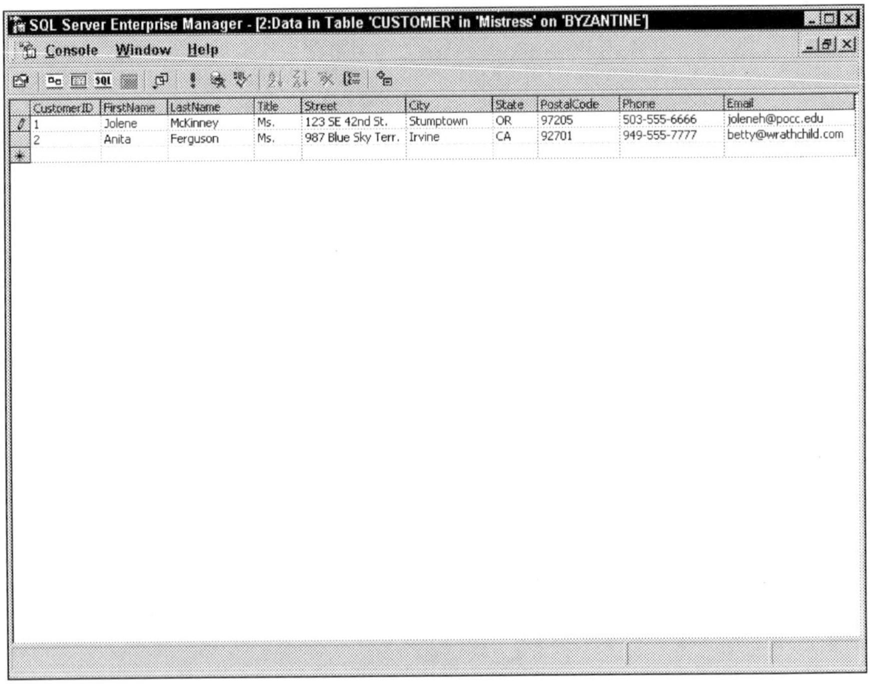

SQL Server Enterprise Manager - [2:Data in Table 'CUSTOMER' in 'Mistress' on 'BYZANTINE']

Figure 11-18:
Two rows
have been
added to the
CUSTOMER
table.

Creating queries

After you have your database populated with data, you can start getting some value out of it by asking some questions. These questions are called *queries*. Whereas Access enables you to pose queries either by using the graphical QBE approach or the command-driven SQL approach, SQL Server expects its users to be fluent in SQL, and so does not provide QBE.

To formulate a query, choose Tools➪SQL Server Query Analyzer from the Enterprise Manager menu bar. SQL Server displays the Query Analyzer screen, as shown in Figure 11-19.

The cursor is blinking in the blank window on the right, waiting for you to enter an SQL statement. You can type in a valid SQL statement or a series of such statements. Then from the menu bar, choose Query➪Execute. SQL Server executes the statements you have entered and displays the result. Figure 11-20 shows the result for a simple query that requests the display of all the records in the CUSTOMER table.

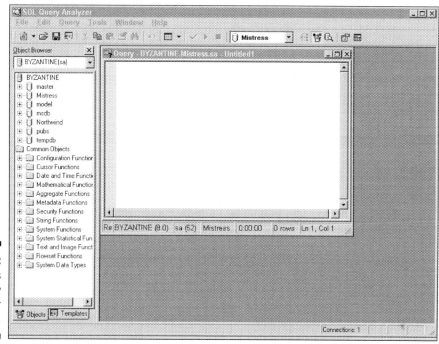

Figure 11-19:
SQL Server's Query Analyzer screen.

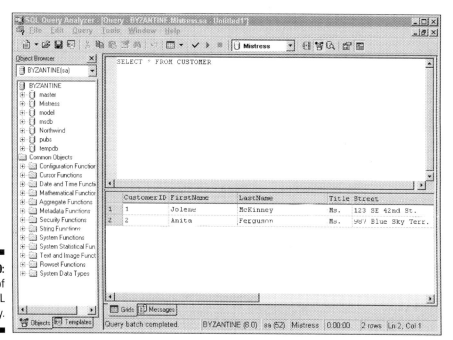

Figure 11-20:
Result of simple SQL query.

This example demonstrates how you get data out of a SQL Server database. You can enter and execute the query manually as in this example, or you can write a program in some host language such as C, C++, Java, or Visual Basic that contains SQL embedded in it. In most cases, you would not expect users to retrieve data manually. Rather, they would use an application that you or someone else would write. The application would give them data entry forms, choices of reports that they could print out, or the ability to display the results of queries that you know in advance will be needed on a frequent basis.

This book is not meant to show you how to formulate and use SQL queries. For that, refer to *SQL For Dummies* by Allen G. Taylor.

Creating forms, reports, and applications

SQL Server 2000 does not provide tools for creating forms, reports, or applications. The assumption is that these things are not database functions, but rather are application functions. Tools such as report writers are available to help you perform some of this application work, but much of it must be done by writing application program code and interfacing it to your SQL Server database. These activities are way beyond the scope of this book, so I will leave the matter there.

Chapter 12

Using SQL to Implement a Database

*I*n Chapters 10 and 11, I show you how to create a database and fill it with data, using two popular database management systems. After you become proficient in their use, these DBMS tools can save you lots of time. However, you don't absolutely need to have such tools to create databases. You can create a database from a design without any fancy tools, using nothing more than the SQL language. This raises a question. Just what is the SQL language anyway?

The Evolution of SQL

Shortly after E. F. Codd described relational database structure in his seminal paper on that subject, database researchers and professionals recognized that a language was needed to create and operate on relational databases. Various companies involved in the development of relational database management systems developed several such languages. Codd's own employer, IBM, developed a prototype relational database system named System R and a language to work with it named SEQUEL. SEQUEL was an acronym for Structured English QUEry Language. The label was appropriate because SEQUEL statements were much like English language sentences, but were more structured than most English sentences are. You could build queries with SEQUEL that looked like a kind of structured English.

IBM eventually released a relational database product on the market, based on System R. The language IBM delivered with that product was enough different from SEQUEL that IBM wanted to give it a name that was different, yet related to the older name. IBM opted to drop the vowels out of SEQUEL and call it SQL, pronounced 'ess-que-ell.' Many people today persist in pronouncing SQL as 'sequel' even though this pronunciation is not correct. Even book authors will state that SQL is an acronym for Structured Query Language, which it is not. SQL is not a structured language in the commonly accepted meaning of that term. The original association with structured English has nothing to do with true structured programming languages such as Pascal or C++.

ANSI Standard SQL

Over time, IBM's SQL became a *de facto* standard in the industry, gradually displacing other database query languages. The *de facto* standard became a standard *de jure* when the American National Standards Institute (ANSI) issued the SQL-86 specification in 1986. The idea was to specify a common core of SQL syntax that everyone would follow, to facilitate portability of code from one DBMS to another. The 1986 specification was revised and expanded in 1989 and again in 1992. SQL-92 is also an international ISO standard. Most recently, SQL:1999, the most comprehensive version to date, has been released. DBMS manufacturers are working to bring their products into compliance with it, but have a long way to go before they can claim complete compatibility.

The standards conflict

Producers of database management system software face a difficult dilemma: Should they make their DBMS completely compliant with the international standard or not? There are strong arguments for both conclusions.

Adhering to the standard makes a lot of sense. This way, database programmers all over the world will know how to build applications using your DBMS. If your SQL is nonstandard, they will have to go through a costly and time-consuming learning process to become familiar with your product's idiosyncrasies. They may decide not to bother, and use a different DBMS instead. So database management system vendors face significant pressure to adhere to the standard.

On the other hand, if your DBMS product has exactly the same capabilities as the products of all the other DBMS vendors, why should anyone choose yours? It would be nice if your product had distinctive capabilities that no other product had. Then, in order to make use of these capabilities, a database application developer would have to buy your DBMS over all the others. It is in a vendor's interest to offer capabilities that competitors do not offer. These extra capabilities differentiate your product from others in the marketplace.

Now take the point of view of database developers. Should they restrict themselves to using only standard SQL or should they make use of one or more of the nifty nonstandard features offered by one of the DBMS vendors? There are arguments both ways.

By writing your applications entirely in standard SQL, you insure yourself against the obsolescence of any single DBMS product or the demise of the vendor that produces it. Your application will run in a variety of environments with little or no alteration as you move it from one platform to another. This is good.

However, if you make a conscious decision not to use a powerful nonstandard tool that is offered by the DBMS system that you are using anyway, you will without a doubt spend more time and effort in building your application than you otherwise would. Because deadline pressure is common and time to market critical to profitability in many cases, it may be difficult to avoid using every tool at your disposal, in order to deliver on time. Having to make tough decisions such as this gives application developers and their managers premature gray hair. You must evaluate each case on its individual merits, and make a decision as to whether or not to use a nonstandard feature.

Interactive SQL

You can use SQL to create or manipulate data in a database in either of two ways: directly from a terminal, or embedded in a program written in some host language, such as C++ or Visual Basic. With interactive SQL, you enter a SQL statement from your keyboard, and it gets executed right away. Alternatively, you can enter a series of SQL statements and execute them as a batch. In either case, you hold a conversation with SQL, and it responds to your instructions immediately.

This mode of operation is appropriate if you are performing an operation that you will do only once, or at most a few times. You might use interactive SQL when you are creating a database. You might use it if you are doing system administration tasks such as modifying permissions for a particular user or class of users. You might also use it if you are making an unusual query that you probably will not need to repeat any time soon.

Because there is a human in the loop, operating with interactive SQL is not particularly fast. It is most appropriate for tasks that you will do only once.

Embedded SQL

As the name implies, embedded SQL consists of SQL statements that you embed in a program written in some general-purpose programming language such as C++ or Visual Basic. SQL by itself is not a full-featured language, concentrating as it does on database manipulations. SQL does not include a complete set of flow of control structures and mathematical operators. The host language supplies such features.

Embedded SQL is most appropriate when the task at hand is something that you must do on a regular basis — for example, querying a transaction database on a monthly basis to determine a company's current profitability. The query is the same every time; only the data is different.

Using embedded SQL is faster than interactive SQL and assures consistent results. After you verify that the code is correct, you can use it repeatedly without fear of errors creeping in due to a keyboarding mistake.

Programs containing embedded SQL pass through a preprocessor that translates the SQL into equivalent code in the host language. The resulting code is then fed to the host language compiler, which reduces it to machine code. The machine code is executed by the computer, returning the results specified by the original SQL statements.

SQL Variants

The SQL standard does not specify everything normally needed to create a robust, commercial-grade database application. Some things have been left unspecified. To cover these items, DBMS vendors have developed their own implementations, which are not necessarily compatible with the implementations of other vendors. In addition, vendors are motivated to add unique features to their products that they think will give them an advantage over their competitors. These factors cause the syntax of one DBMS product's SQL to differ to a greater or lesser extent from the syntax of another product's SQL. Because Access and SQL Server are both Microsoft products, it is reasonable to assume that although the SQL of each may not be identical to the other, they are probably more similar than either would be with, for example, the syntax of Oracle's SQL or that of IBM's DB/2.

I doubt that you are interested in the gory details of exactly which keywords or syntactical variants apply to which DBMS product. Whichever product you are looking at will have documentation about its capabilities and how to use them. If you are interested in whether a particular feature of a DBMS complies with the SQL standard, you can consult the SQL specification or *SQL For Dummies*.

Creating a Database with SQL

In Chapters 10 and 11, I show you how to create a very basic database using Access and SQL Server development tools. You can also create databases without any such tools using pure SQL.

SQL is logically divided into three components: the Data Definition Language (DDL), the Data Manipulation Language (DML), and the Data Control Language (DCL). Use the commands that make up the Data Definition Language to create a database structure. After you create the structure, use the Data Manipulation Language to add data to tables and manipulate it. The Data Control Language gives you the capability to protect the security of your database.

Creating the table structure

SQL's Data Definition Language comes close to the ultimate in simplicity. It contains only three commands: CREATE, ALTER, and DROP. These commands apply to tables, views, and a few other things that I do not cover here. Furthermore, you don't have to be a rocket scientist to figure out what these commands do:

- ✔ Use CREATE to create a new table.
- ✔ Use ALTER to change the structure of an existing table.
- ✔ And finally, use DROP to eliminate a table from a database.

To find out how to use SQL's DDL, you can create the CUSTOMER table for the Mistress database, using ANSI Standard SQL. (For details on designing this sample database, see Chapter 9.)

```
CREATE TABLE CUSTOMER (
    CustomerID      Integer            NOT NULL,
    FirstName       Character (15),
    LastName        Character (20)     NOT NULL,
    Title           Character (5),
    Street          Character (25),
    City            Character (20),
    State           Character (2),
    PostalCode      Character (10),
    Phone           Character (15),
    Email           Character (30) );
```

This DDL statement creates the same CUSTOMER table that I show you how to build using Access and SQL Server in Chapters 10 and 11, respectively. The only difference is the way you specify the attributes. Because CustomerID is the primary key, you specify that it not be null. You also specify that LastName not be null because you want at least to know the last name of anyone entered into the CUSTOMER table.

As a second example, create the Mistress PRODUCT table:

```
CREATE TABLE PRODUCT (
    ProductID      Integer           NOT NULL,
    Name           Character (25)    NOT NULL,
    Description    Character (30),
    Cost           Numeric (10,2),
    Price          Numeric (10,2),
    InStock        Integer           NOT NULL );
```

In this case, you want to guarantee not only that ProductID and Name are non-null, but also that InStock is required to have a value. The NOT NULL entry in the third column of these column specifications is called a *constraint*. A column constraint specifies some property that entries into that column must or must not have. Constraints can apply to a single column, a table, or an entire database.

Defining business rules and constraints

Generally, constraints in a database directly relate to business rules in the system the database is modeling. Some such constraints apply only to a single column; others can apply to an entire table. Some constraints, called *assertions,* apply to multiple tables.

Column constraints

Table 12-1 gives some typical business rules for the products of Mistress Treasure and the corresponding column constraints in the database.

Table 12-1	Business Rules and Associated Constraints
Business Rule	**Constraint**
Product item must have a name	NOT NULL
Cost must have positive value	Cost >= 0
Price must be greater than or equal to Cost	Price >= Cost

To incorporate these constraints into the definition of the PRODUCT table, you must add a couple of lines:

```
CREATE TABLE PRODUCT (
    ProductID          Integer              NOT NULL,
    Name               Character (25)       NOT NULL,
    Description        Character (30),
    Cost               Numeric (10,2)
        CHECK (Cost >= 0),
    Price              Numeric (10,2)
        CHECK (Price >= Cost),
    InStock            Integer              NOT NULL );
```

The CHECK clauses enforce constraints on the Cost and Price fields, respectively.

Table constraints

A table constraint applies to an entire table. In the preceding section, you could use a table constraint in the definition of the CUSTOMER table rather than the NOT NULL constraint you apply to the CustomerID field. Here is an example of this usage:

```
CREATE TABLE CUSTOMER (
    CustomerID       Integer              PRIMARY KEY,
    FirstName        Character (15),
    LastName         Character (20)     NOT NULL,
    Title            Character (5),
    Street           Character (25),
    City             Character (20),
    State            Character (2),
    PostalCode       Character (10),
    Phone            Character (15),
    Email            Character (30) );
```

The only difference between this definition and the previous one is that the PRIMARY KEY constraint has replaced the NOT NULL constraint on the CustomerID field. The PRIMARY KEY constraint is actually a stronger constraint, because it implies the NOT NULL constraint, but also establishes that this field is the primary key of the table.

Assertions

Assertions apply to multiple tables. Consider the following example:

```
CREATE TABLE ORDER (
    OrderNo         Integer            PRIMARY KEY,
    OrderDate       Date,
    Subtotal        Numeric (10,2),
    Tax             Numeric (10,2),
    Shipping        Numeric (10,2),
    Total           Numeric (10,2),
    CustomerID      Integer );

CREATE TABLE SHIPMENT (
    ShipmentNo      Integer            PRIMARY KEY,
    ShipDate        Date,
    CustomerID      Integer,
    OrderNo         Integer );

CREATE ASSERTION
    CHECK (NOT EXISTS SELECT * FROM ORDER, SHIPMENT
        WHERE ORDER.OrderNo = SHIPMENT.OrderNo
        AND SHIPMENT.ShipDate < ORDER.OrderDate);
```

This assertion guarantees that when an entry is made into the SHIPMENT table corresponding to a particular order, the date of the shipment of the goods cannot come before the date the order for the goods was placed. This kind of constraint prevents one class of data entry errors.

Adding data to tables

Whereas SQL's Data Definition Language deals with the structure of a database, its Data Manipulation Language (DML) deals with the data that resides in that structure. Where the DDL has only three commands (CREATE, ALTER, and DROP), SQL's DML is much more complex, with four commands (INSERT, UPDATE, DELETE, and SELECT):

- ✔ Use the INSERT command to put new data into a database table.

- ✔ Use the UPDATE command to change the contents of rows already in a database table.

- ✔ Use the DELETE command to remove selected rows from a database table.

- ✔ And finally, use the SELECT command to retrieve selected rows from a database table or a combination of database tables.

In this chapter, I only look at the INSERT command, to show how adding data to a table with SQL compares to adding the same data to a table using the Access or SQL Server tools that I cover in Chapters 10 and 11.

After you define your tables using SQL CREATE statements, you can start adding data to them. When you are using a DBMS such as Access or SQL Server, you can do this by entering data into the fields of a table on the screen. In an application, you can enter each new row of the table into a screen form. When you finish entering a row and accept it by clicking an OK button, the application clears the form to prepare it to accept the next row. Because SQL provides a command-driven interface rather than a graphical one, entering data in SQL is not as convenient. In fact it is so *inconvenient* that you would probably never do it, unless your DBMS's graphical user interface suddenly broke and you were left with only SQL capability. It does work however, so I will show you how to enter data into tables using SQL alone.

The INSERT command has the following general form:

```
INSERT INTO TABLENAME [(Column1, Column2, ... ColumnN)]
    VALUES (value1, value2, ... valueN);
```

The square brackets around the column names indicate that the listing of column names is optional. If you do not list the column names, SQL assumes that the values you are inserting are in the same order as the columns in the table are. If for some reason you want to enter the values in a different order from the order of the columns in the table, you must list columns in that same different order. This ensures that the values you enter go into the correct columns.

In some cases, you may not have all the data needed to completely fill in a table record. You can still do an INSERT as long as you have data for the primary key and any other fields that have the NOT NULL constraint. Here is an example of such a partial insertion:

```
INSERT INTO CUSTOMER (CustomerID, FirstName, LastName)
    VALUES (:vcustid, 'Dayna', 'Aronson');
```

You want to be sure that the CustomerID you assign to this new customer is different from all the values of CustomerID that are already in the CUSTOMER table. One way to do this is to maintain a counter, and increment it every time you add a new customer. Put the current value of the counter into the vcustid variable before issuing the INSERT statement. After you have Mr. Aronson in the table, you can fill in the rest of his information later with an UPDATE statement.

Building security and reliability into your databases

Most data that is important enough for people to put into databases is important enough to protect from loss or corruption. Threats to a database come in various forms:

- ✔ The hardware your system is running on might fail.
- ✔ The software you are using to access your database might be buggy.
- ✔ Two users accessing the same data at the same time might interfere with each other.
- ✔ A user might accidentally make a mistake that alters or destroys data.
- ✔ A user might maliciously alter or destroy data.

To protect your database against these threats, SQL provides a set of commands that collectively are referred to as the Data Control Language (DCL). Different defenses apply to different threats.

To protect against the malicious user, SQL incorporates a system of user access levels. The person in charge of maintaining the database, called the database administrator (DBA), can assign different privilege levels to different people. Highly trusted people, with the appropriate need, can be given the right to view, insert, update, and delete rows from tables that they are authorized to work on. People who do not require that level of access might be granted the right to view a table, but not insert new rows into it.

The DML has the SELECT, INSERT, UPDATE, and DELETE commands, which allow a person to view a table, add rows to a table, change the contents of rows in a table, or delete rows from a table. The DBA can selectively GRANT the privilege of using one or more of these commands to an individual or a group of individuals. Furthermore, the owner of a table (generally the person who created it) automatically has these privileges, and also has the power to GRANT them to others.

As an example of the granting of privileges, say the sales manager at Mistress Treasure is the owner of the CUSTOMER table. She can grant access to that table to the assistant sales manager as follows:

```
GRANT SELECT INSERT UPDATE DELETE
    ON CUSTOMER
    TO AssistantSalesManager;
```

Now the assistant sales manager can take care of business while the sales manager is in Hawaii on vacation. This is fine, but perhaps not enough. The sales clerks that report to the assistant sales manager have a legitimate need to see the customer list, but perhaps not to alter it in any way. The sales manager can meet this need by giving the assistant sales manager the right to delegate access privileges. This can be accomplished by modifying the GRANT statement as follows:

```
GRANT SELECT INSERT UPDATE DELETE
    ON CUSTOMER
    TO AssistantSalesManager
    WITH GRANT OPTION;
```

This revised statement gives the assistant sales manager the right to grant the SELECT, INSERT, UPDATE, and DELETE privileges on the CUSTOMER table to anyone she wants. Here is a typical use of this right:

```
GRANT SELECT
    ON CUSTOMER
    TO Valerie, Melody;
```

If you grant privileges to people, you must also have a way of revoking them. For example, an employee may resign and go to work for a competitor. It would be a good idea to revoke any access privileges that employee might have. Do this with the DCL REVOKE command, as follows:

```
REVOKE SELECT
    ON CUSTOMER
    FROM Valerie;
```

Establishing user access levels can provide significant protection against malicious attacks by users who have no business accessing the database. Such access levels, however, do not protect the database from mistakes made by authorized users. You must rely on validity checks and constraints to help with that class of problem.

Hardware failures and software bugs happen, and user access levels provide no protection against these types of problems. SQL uses a transaction structure as a defense against such threats. Whenever an SQL statement that could make a change to a database is executed, it is encapsulated in a transaction. Either the transaction will complete successfully or it will fail. If it completes successfully, no problem. If the transaction fails, everything that was done to the database up to the point of failure is rolled back. After a rollback, the database is returned to the condition it was in before the transaction started. At this point, the user or DBA can address the problem, and after fixing it, rerun the transaction.

Even though modern DBMS products encapsulate your SQL statements in transactions, it is a good practice to back up your databases frequently, just to be on the safe side. What is a reasonable backup interval depends on how many changes are made to it per unit time. If the database is receiving thousands of updates per hour, it should be backed up more often than a database that receives only a few dozen updates per week.

Part V
Implementing a Database Application

The 5th Wave   By Rich Tennant

"HE SAID THE ONLY HEAVY METAL HE WAS INTO WAS MAINFRAMES."

In this part . . .

A database is only half the solution to an organization's data management problems. The other half is the application (or applications) that makes the data in the database accessible to the users in a meaningful form. Using the tools in Microsoft Access, I show you how to build the forms and reports that the users see and interact with. Then I show how to bind those elements together with a menu system to create an easy-to-understand, easy-to-navigate application.

SQL is the language that the database understands, but by itself, SQL is not powerful or flexible enough to create a total application. It must either be combined with features of a development environment such as Access or with a programming language such as Visual Basic, C, or C++. Part V describes how two basically incompatible things (SQL and any procedural programming language) can be made to work together seamlessly.

Chapter 13

Using DBMS Tools to Implement a Database Application

In This Chapter

▷ Creating a forms-based application with Access

▷ Developing a more sophisticated application with Visual Basic for Applications (VBA)

*A*fter you have a database (see the Chapters in Part IV of this book), you need an application to retrieve and otherwise manipulate the data in it. This chapter describes tools that database management systems provide to establish a communication link between a database and its users. Most people need an easier way to enter data into a database than typing UPDATE statements. They also need an easier way of retrieving information from a database than typing SELECT statements.

Access 2000 provides easy to use tools that enable you to create applications without being a programmer. You can build an entire, but admittedly modest, application, just using the facilities provided by Access. If you can program a little, you can build more powerful applications using Access's programming language, called Visual Basic for Applications (VBA). VBA is also the language in Microsoft's Visual Basic development environment.

SQL Server, on the other hand, as well as other enterprise-class database management systems, does not provide as many user-friendly tools. The vendors of such major league DBMS products assume that their products' users are experienced programmers who will write programs to provide the needed user interface. SQL Server does not have forms generator or report generator facilities. It assumes you will either use external tools to build these things or code them from scratch yourself. I talk about that scenario in Chapter 14.

Building a Forms-based Application with Access

In Chapter 10, I give a step-by-step procedure for building a form using the tools Access provides. You can use such forms for entering data, displaying the results of queries, and changing the contents of database records. Those three uses of forms, along with the printing of reports, constitute the main things that a user sees and interacts with. If you make those forms and reports easily accessible by, for example, menu selections, you have a database application. For many jobs, that is all you need.

With Access, you can build a special kind of form that acts as a wrapper around other forms, providing a context in which they live. This special kind of form is called a *switchboard form*. You can use a switchboard form to bind together the various components you create for an application, converting a collection of components into a real application. In the following sections, I show you how to create this type of application, using the Mistress Treasure database as an example. For more information about the design and development of the Mistress Treasure database, see Parts III and IV in this book.

Doing justice to the stages of system development

In any development project, you must perform all the phases of the system development process, as I describe in Chapter 2. By the time you actually start using Access in the implementation phase, you have already spent significant time and effort in the definition, requirements, evaluation, and design phases. Every detail of the user interface should already be decided. You should make sketches of all the screen forms, and the users should buy off on them before you build them. The same goes for the switchboard form. Carefully document what it contains and how it will work before you start to build it.

Building the application's forms

In Chapter 10, I show you how to build the CUSTOMER form for entering data into the CUSTOMER table. In this section, you fill out the Mistress database by creating forms for PRODUCT and ORDER.

The ORDER form will contain a subform with which you can enter data into the ORDER LINE table. Using a subform is convenient when you want to display on the same form, the data from two tables that bear a one-to-many relationship with each other. Because a one-to-many correspondence exists between a SHIPMENT and the lines on the packing slip that goes with that shipment, the SHIPMENT form will contain a subform for PACKSLIPLINE. I do not go into building the SHIPMENT form here, because the procedure is the same as that for building the ORDER form.

You can build the PRODUCT form in exactly the same way that you build the CUSTOMER form (see Chapter 10). Figure 13-1 shows the completed PRODUCT form.

The ORDER form, interfacing as it does with two tables, deserves a closer look. To create the ORDER form, complete the following steps:

1. **In the dialog box shown in Figure 13-2, double-click Create Form In Design View.**

   Access displays the screen shown in Figure 13-3.

   A blank form appears. Somewhere on the screen, a Toolbox may also appear, giving you some of the tools you need to put content into the form.

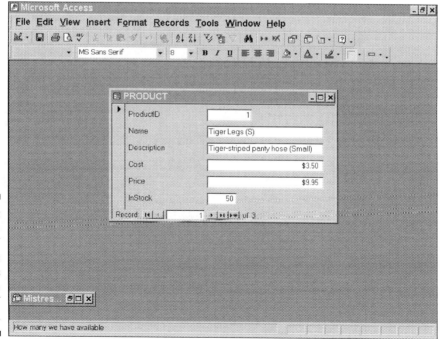

Figure 13-1:
The PRODUCT form accepts data into the PRODUCT table.

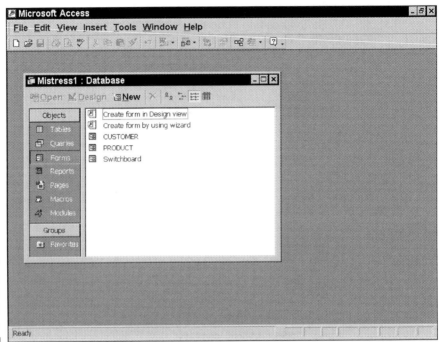

Figure 13-2:
Forms
creation
dialog box.

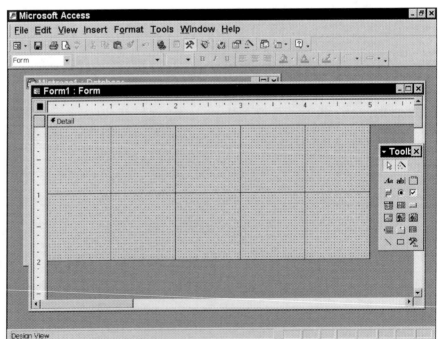

Figure 13-3:
Design
view of a
new form.

2. **If the Toolbox does not pop up, click the Toolbox icon in the toolbar to display it.**

3. **To build a form for entering data into the ORDER table, choose View⇨Properties.**

   Access opens the form's property sheet, as shown in Figure 13-4.

   With the property sheet, you can specify in detail the properties of the form you are building.

4. **Select the All tab if it is not already selected.**

   The first option, Record Source, specifies which table you want to link to the form.

5. **From the pull-down list, select ORDER.**

6. **You want to add all the ORDER table's fields to the form, so if it does not appear automatically, click the Field List icon in the toolbar (next to the Toolbox icon).**

   Access pops up the field list window for the ORDER table, as shown in Figure 13-5.

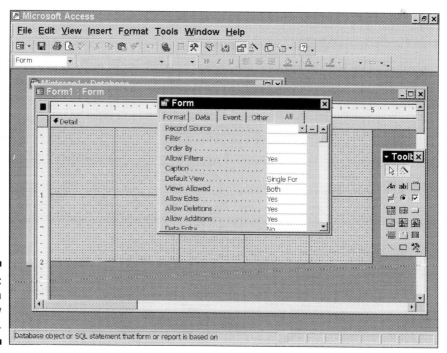

Figure 13-4:
Form property sheet.

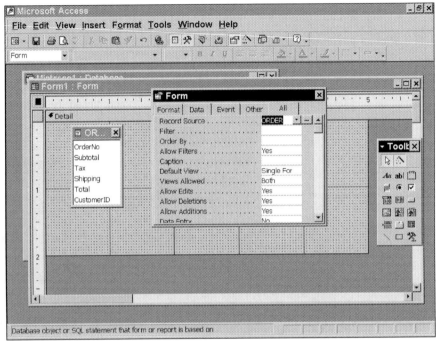

Figure 13-5:
ORDER field
list is
displayed.

7. **You can select all the fields in the field list and drag them to the blank form: While holding the Ctrl key down, select each field in the list with a mouse click.**

8. **When all fields are selected, drag them to the form and drop them where you want them.**

   Don't try to place them exactly; you can move them to their final positions later. After the drag and drop, your screen should look something like Figure 13-6.

9. **The property sheet and the ORDER field list have done their jobs, so you can unclutter the screen by closing them.**

10. **Expand the size of the form in its window.**

    Because you are going to add a subform for multiple lines of ORDER LINE data, you need to provide extra room. For an even larger form, you can expand the size of the form's window in the same way and then expand the form within it.

11. **After you expand the form size, move around the fields and labels from the ORDER table, resizing them as appropriate to give you the layout you want.**

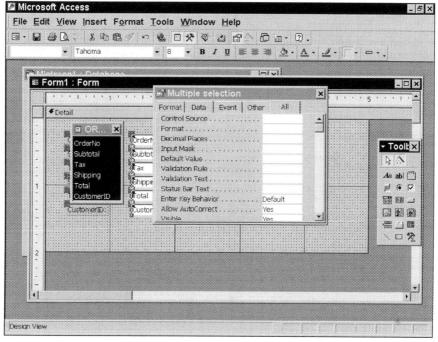

Figure 13-6:
Fields from
ORDER table
have been
placed on
the form.

12. **You should also give the form a title.**

    Do this by selecting the Label tool from the Toolbox and then placing a
    label at the top of the form. Size it appropriately and then type the title
    ORDER. Give the title the Bold attribute and make it larger than the
    other text on the form.

13. **Add the ORDER LINE subform: Make sure the Control Wizards button
    in the Toolbox is depressed, then drag the ORDER LINE table from the
    Database window and drop it on the ORDER form.**

    The SubForm wizard appears, as shown in Figure 13-7.

    Access already knows that ORDER LINE is on the many side of a one-to-
    many relationship with ORDER, linked by the OrderNo field. The wizard
    presents you with the opportunity to link the ORDER LINE subform into
    the ORDER main form, using OrderNo as the linking field, or to define
    some other link.

14. **In this case, the default that Access has chosen is the one you want, so
    click Next.**

    The SubForm wizard's next dialog box is displayed, asking you for the
    name of the subform.

15. **Enter a name, as shown in Figure 13-8, and then click Finish.**

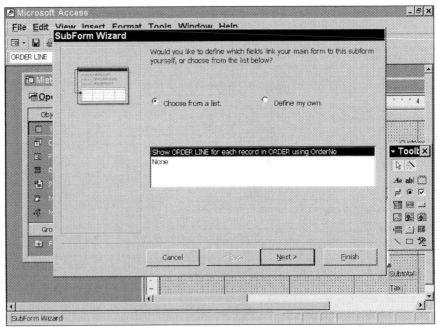

Figure 13-7:
The
SubForm
wizard.

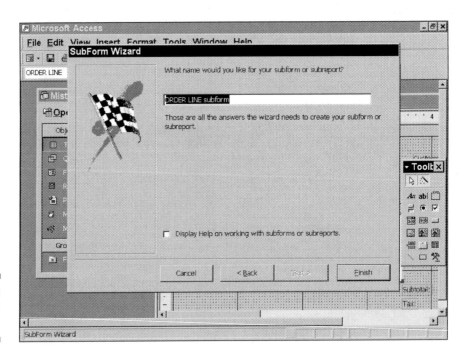

Figure 13-8:
Naming the
subform.

At this point, the subform appears in the form you are creating. After resizing, it appears, in Design view, something like the example shown in Figure 13-9.

16. **The default layout of the ORDER LINE subform is not the best, so resize and rearrange labels and fields into a more logical order, as well as remove the OrderNo field from view.**

OrderNo is displayed in the main form and it would be redundant to repeat it in the subform. Figure 13-10 shows the redesigned subform, again in Design view.

17. **Switch to Form view, so you can see how the form will look to a user, as shown in Figure 13-11.**

Access fills in fields with their default values, which hopefully would never appear on a real ORDER form.

You also see that the fields in the subform are not sized and aligned the way you want, but you can rearrange the order of the fields as shown in Figure 13-12.

If you want to force the user to make an entry in a particular field, do not give that field a default value.

18. **Rearrange other fields and resize them to produce the arrangement shown in Figure 13-13.**

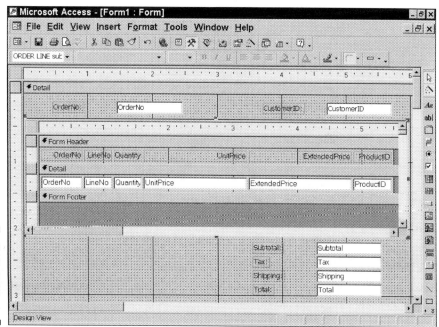

Figure 13-9:
ORDER form
containing
ORDER LINE
subform.

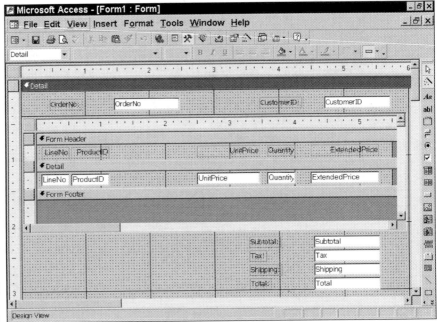

Figure 13-10:
ORDER
form with a
redesigned
ORDER LINE
subform.

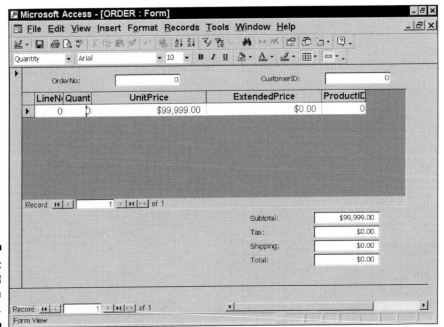

Figure 13-11:
ORDER
form in
Form view.

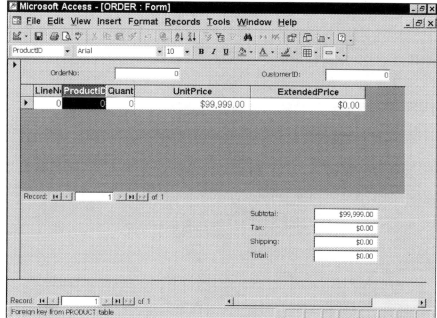

Figure 13-12: ProductID field has been moved to the left.

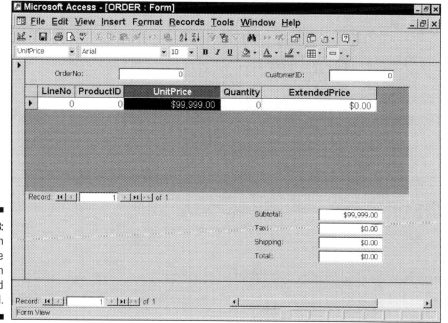

Figure 13-13: Subform fields have been rearranged and resized.

19. **Now that the form is finished, exit it by clicking the X control in the upper-right corner of the form window.**

    If you have not already saved the form, a dialog box appears, asking if you want to save changes to the design of the form Form1.

20. **Click Yes.**

    Access asks you to give the new form a name.

21. **Type** ORDER **in the Save As dialog box and then click OK.**

    The ORDER form is ready to start accepting data. As you enter each record into the form, Access stores appropriate parts of it in the ORDER table and in the ORDER LINE table.

22. **Build the SHIPMENT form, which also contains a subform, the same way that the ORDER form was built.**

    You can build all the application's forms the same way, either with or without subforms.

Aside from forms, the other main element of an application is reports. I take a brief look at how to build reports in Chapter 10.

After you create all the forms and reports you need, you can embed them in a wrapper that makes them easy to access. That wrapper is a switchboard form.

Tying things together with a switchboard form

Access can make a switchboard form for you, if you build your system using the Database wizard. Alternatively, you can build your own switchboard form in one of two ways:

- ✔ You can navigate between forms using hyperlinks.
- ✔ You can write a custom program using VBA.

The following example uses the hyperlink method, which does not involve any programming.

From the Database window shown in Figure 13-2, double-click Create Form In Design View. Access puts a blank form on the screen in Design view. Populate it with labels as shown in Figure 13-14.

Create the Customer Operations menu first. This menu provides hyperlinks to all the different operations you want to perform on the CUSTOMER list. You can insert the hyperlinks one at a time. To start, select the Add a new CUSTOMER label and then right-click it. Access displays the pop-up menu shown in Figure 13-15.

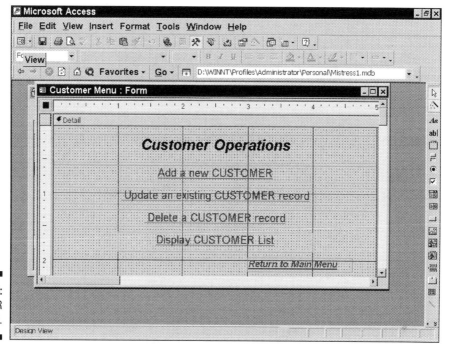

Figure 13-14:
CUSTOMER
switchboard.

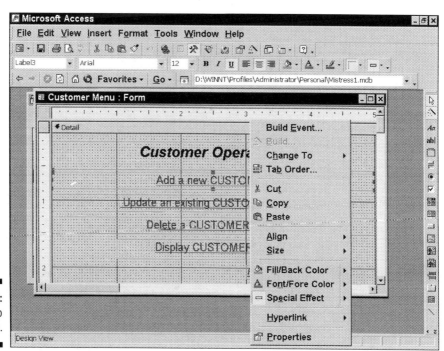

Figure 13-15:
Pop-up
menu.

Choose Properties from the menu, to display the Properties dialog box shown in Figure 13-16.

Click the small button to the right of the Hyperlink Address field in the Properties dialog box. Access displays the Edit Hyperlink dialog box, as shown in Figure 13-17.

You want to link to the CUSTOMER form, so select it as shown in Figure 13-17 and then click OK. In a similar fashion, make the appropriate hyperlinks for the rest of the options on the Customer Operations menu. Then, perform a similar process for the main menu shown in Figure 13-18.

Select the Operate on CUSTOMER records option, as shown in Figure 13-18, and then go through the process of editing its hyperlink, as shown in Figure 13-19.

Now that you have created the main menu, return to the Customer Operations menu and add the Return to Main Menu hyperlink (see Figure 13-20).

In Form view, the main menu just created looks like Figure 13-21.

The Customer Operations menu looks like Figure 13-22.

The first option on the Customer Operations menu links to the CUSTOMER form shown in Figure 13-23.

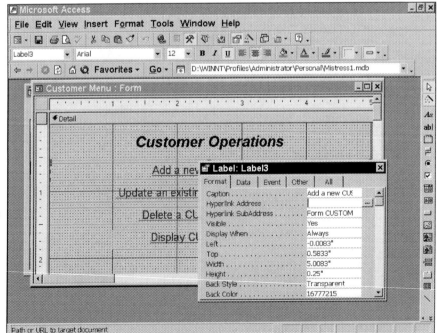

Figure 13-16:
Properties
dialog box
for the Add
a new
CUSTOMER
label.

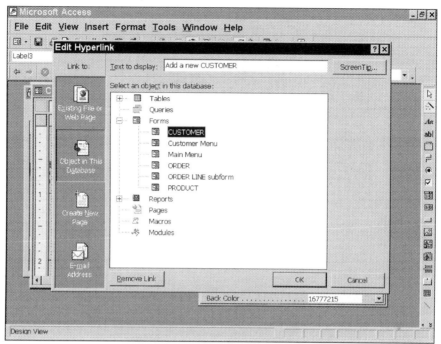

Figure 13-17:
The Edit
Hyperlink
dialog box.

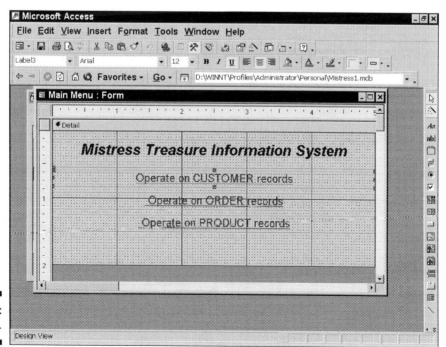

Figure 13-18:
Main menu.

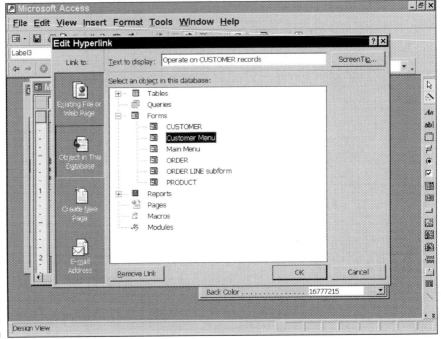

Figure 13-19:
Adding a
hyperlink
to the
Customer
Operations
menu.

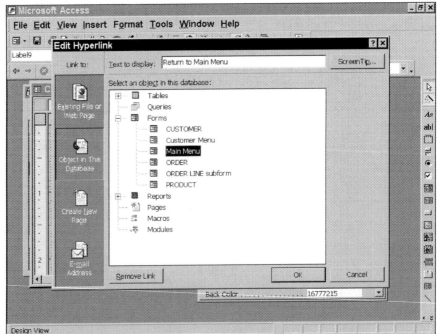

Figure 13-20:
The Edit
Hyperlink
dialog box
for Return to
Main Menu.

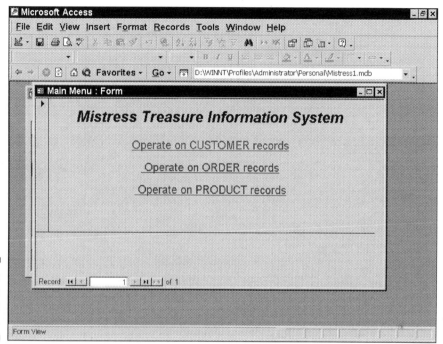

Figure 13-21:
Main
menu in
Form view.

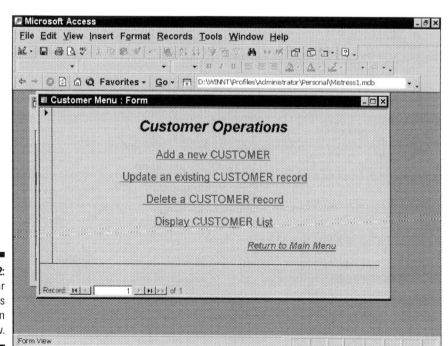

Figure 13-22:
Customer
Operations
menu in
Form view.

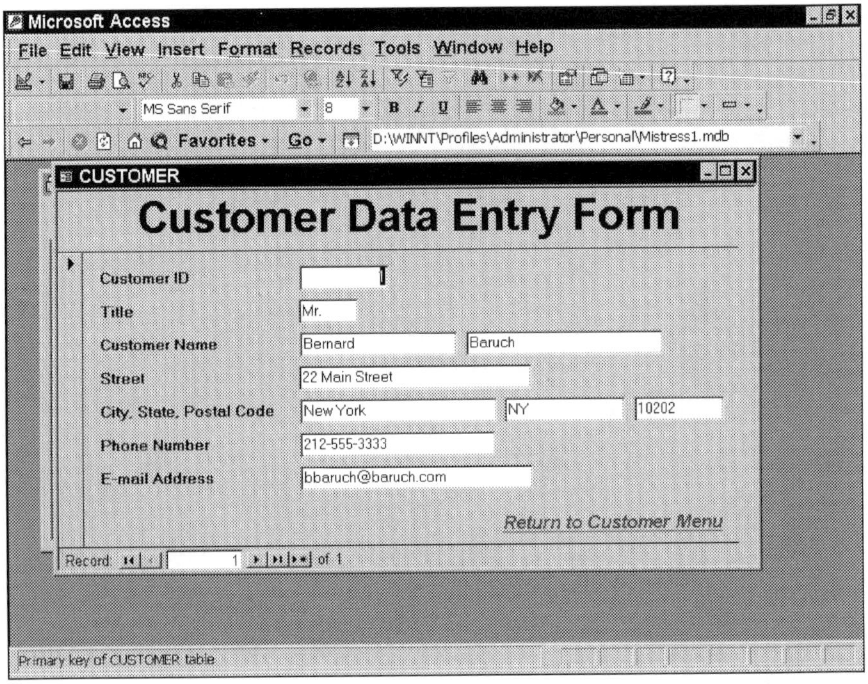

Figure 13-23:
CUSTOMER
form.

You now have a basic Access database application. You could still do much more to give it additional functionality or to make it more intuitive, but you have the essentials in place. Users unfamiliar with Access could use this application to maintain the data that is important to the Mistress Treasure company, after a short training session.

Using VBA to Create a More Sophisticated Application

As you might expect, you can also navigate among menus, forms, and reports by writing program code that performs these functions directly. With a programming language such as VBA or Visual Basic, you have finely detailed control over everything and thus can build an application that looks and acts exactly the way you want it to. This is great! However, remember TANSTAAFL. (There Ain't No Such Thing As A Free Lunch.) The price you pay for that extra power is that you must know how to program.

To become a truly adept VBA programmer takes months of training and years of experience. If you already have that training and experience, wonderful. I don't have to tell you what to do here, to build an application to wrap around your forms and reports. If you do *not* already have that training and experience, walking you through the code here would not do you any good. You might consider starting with a good book, such as *Visual Basic For Dummies.*

A good plan might be to start off building simple applications glued together with switchboard menus, gradually introducing snippets of VBA code as you come to understand how to use them. Eventually, you will become a full-fledged VBA programmer, and your Access applications will elicit gasps of awe from astounded users. Well, maybe not exactly gasps of awe. Most users will probably have no appreciation whatsoever of the creativity and cleverness that you have put into your applications. No matter. You and a small circle of cognoscenti will know and appreciate what you have accomplished.

Chapter 14

SQL and Database Applications

A s I demonstrate in Chapter 12, SQL is a great tool for building relational databases. You might even say that it is the only tool for building relational databases, because the logical structures you specify with user-friendly rapid application development environments, complete with graphical user interfaces and wizards, ultimately get translated into SQL, which is then fed into the DBMS to create the physical database structure on disk. However, database *applications* are something else.

Database applications are programs that automate the interactions between users and databases. Database applications are written to perform certain very specific operations on a database, to achieve predetermined results. You cannot write a database application program entirely in SQL, because SQL is not a complete programming language. In this chapter, I explain what a complete programming language is, as well as why SQL is not one. Then, I describe how you can use SQL in the building of a database application even though it is not a complete programming language.

Programs and Procedural Languages

A computer is a machine that follows instructions. Give it an instruction, and it performs an operation. Give it a second instruction, and it performs a second operation. Keep feeding it instructions, and it continues to perform operations. At the hardware level, the instructions that a computer understands are very simple — for example:

1. **Go to location 1000 in memory and retrieve what you find there, putting it in register A.**

2. **Go to location 1002 in memory and retrieve what you find there, putting it in register B.**

3. **Add the contents of register A to the contents of register B, putting the result back into register A.**

4. **Write the contents of register A to output port 220.**

Computers can execute instructions in a sequence, such as the sequence listed here. This sequence is a simple computer program, which performs a useful function. It adds two numbers together and then sends the result to a display device.

A sequence of instructions that performs some useful operation is called a *procedure*. A typical computer program contains numerous procedures, each one performing an operation that, when strung together, accomplishes a more complex purpose.

Computer languages that operate in this manner are called *procedural languages*. Visual Basic is a procedural language. C and C++ are procedural languages. In fact, most of the computer languages that you are probably familiar with are procedural languages.

Procedural languages contain instructions that perform operations. In a procedural language program, these instructions are written one after another, then executed sequentially. The flow of execution may be linear, with each instruction following the previous one from beginning to end. Or, it may branch down one of two or more paths, or the flow may loop back and execute a sequence of instructions multiple times.

In any of these cases, the intent of the program is accomplished by executing its instructions in an order that is partially determined by the programmer and partially determined by conditions at runtime. Not all computer languages are procedural, however, and SQL is an example of one that is not.

SQL and Set-at-a-Time Operations

Unlike Visual Basic or C, SQL, as defined by the international SQL-92 specification, is not a complete programming language. It does not have the flow of control structures that enable branching or looping back to repeat a sequence of instructions. It lacks some other features of a complete programming language, too, such as complex mathematical operations.

SQL was created for the purpose of interacting directly with a database. It was not originally intended to serve as a general-purpose programming language. Over the years, it has acquired additional features, but the SQL-92 version is still far from being a complete programming language. DBMS vendors, in anticipation of the rollout of the much-enhanced SQL:1999 specification, have incorporated many of the missing features into their implementations of SQL. Even so, in many cases, the power of a procedural language is still needed.

One difference between SQL and procedural languages is that you do not exe-cute a sequence of SQL statements to perform some single function. Each SQL statement performs a complete operation all by itself. For example, if you wanted a list of all the customers who had bought Tiger Legs panty hose, size small, between February 1 and February 14, you could produce such a list with a single SQL SELECT statement.

When you operate on a database with a procedural language, because of the nature of procedural languages, you must deal with the data one record at a time. To find all the people who bought a particular item during a particular span of time, you have to step through several tables, record by record. If the database is properly indexed, you don't have to touch all the records, but you still have to process all the records that you do touch, one record at a time. If you were a procedural language programmer, you would have to tell the computer not only what you wanted, but also exactly how to get what you wanted and how to return it to you.

SQL processes queries such as the previous example, a set of records at a time rather than a single record at a time. With SQL, you just tell the computer what you want and let the DBMS figure out the most efficient way to do it.

Because the DBMS knows, at any given point in time, how fast the system's storage devices are, and the relative speeds of all the other components of the system, it has a much better chance of choosing the best execution plan than does the application programmer, who may have never even seen the system on which the application runs. Even if the programmer has seen it, she proba-bly does not know much about its various performance parameters.

Knowing those parameters is the job of the database administrator (DBA). Based on that knowledge, the DBA tunes the DBMS to give the best perfor-mance on the SQL statements that occur most frequently. This generally involves a tradeoff. When you improve the performance of some operations, it is usually at the expense of other operations, which will perform worse. Such tuning is useful if the operations you improve occur frequently and the ones that get worse are used less often or not at all.

Combining the Procedural and the Nonprocedural

Here's the problem: Procedural languages such as Visual Basic or C++ are great tools for writing the skeleton of a database application. With them, you can create screens and controls, do complex math, make on-the-fly decisions, loop through a section of code multiple times, and do all the other things that are not directly related to communicating with the database. However, procedural languages are not very good for operating on the database. SQL is ideal for operating on the database, but cannot do those other things that procedural languages can do.

Wouldn't it be great if you could somehow combine SQL with a procedural language in a way that would take advantage of the strengths of both? The SQL could deal with the database, and the procedural language could deal with everything else. Happily, you can make such a combination. In fact, all relational database applications above a modest level of complexity are composed of just such a combination. You can combine SQL with a procedural language in two different ways: with embedded SQL and using module language.

Embedding SQL in a procedural program

What could be simpler? Write a procedural program in some powerful language such as C, and when you need to deal with your database, drop an SQL statement into the code, and then write some more C until you are done. It almost works that way, but there is one little problem with that idea. It comes from the fact that computers do not understand programs written in the C language (or Visual Basic, or Fortran, or COBOL, for that matter).

Computers understand only one language: machine language. In order for a C program to be executed, it must first be translated into machine language. That translation is performed by a program called a *C compiler.* C compilers are designed to recognize C commands in a source file and translate them into machine language commands in an object file. C compilers do not recognize SQL statements, and will produce an error if they encounter one.

To overcome this problem, programs containing embedded SQL must be passed through a preprocessor before they go to the compiler. The preprocessor finds all the SQL statements in the program and puts them in an external routine, replacing each embedded SQL statement with a CALL to the routine. The compiler recognizes the CALL command as legal and is happy. The SQL in the external routine performs the database operations as it should. By this simple device, you can enjoy the benefits of both procedural programming and SQL data manipulation in the same program.

Consider the following fragment of C code, which controls a user's logon to the Mistress database:

```
if (argc == 1) {
    EXEC SQL CONNECT TO mistress;
    CHECKERR ("CONNECT TO MISTRESS");
}
else if (argc == 3) {
    strcpy (userid, argv[1]);
    strcpy (passwd, argv[2]);
```

```
        EXEC SQL CONNECT TO mistress USER :userid USING
            :passwd;
        CHECKERR ("CONNECT TO MISTRESS");
    }
    else {
        printf ("\nUSAGE: login [userid passwd]\n\n");
        return 1;
    } /* endif */

    printf( "Connect to Mistress\n" );
    printf( "**********************************\n\n");
```

It is all C code except for two embedded SQL statements. The first of the two SQL statements is

```
EXEC SQL CONNECT TO mistress;
```

And here is the second SQL statement:

```
EXEC SQL CONNECT TO mistress USER :userid USING :passwd;
```

The EXEC SQL prefix to the SQL CONNECT statements is a flag to the pre-processor, telling it that the current line is an SQL statement rather than a C command. The preprocessor operates on only these lines, because the C compiler knows how to handle all the others.

Embedded SQL, such as that illustrated here, is the most common means of combining the strengths of procedural programming with those of SQL. Module language is a second method for accomplishing the same thing.

Using module language

Conceptually, using module language is very similar to using embedded SQL. The difference is that no SQL is embedded in the procedural code. Instead, you place all the SQL in a separate module. Each SQL statement is a proce-dure unto itself and is individually callable from the main procedural pro-gram. The procedural program contains only procedural code, with calls to specific SQL procedures in the SQL module, as needed.

Although module language is less popular than embedded SQL, it has some advantages:

> ✔ You don't need to have a super-programmer who operates at the guru level in both a procedural language and in SQL. Such dual expertise is rare. Your procedural language guru can concentrate on the main proce-dural program, and your SQL guru can concentrate on the SQL module.

✔ Standard code debuggers will work on the procedural language program, because it has no SQL present to confuse them. This can make a big difference in development time, not to mention program maintenance after release.

The downside is that you must jump back and forth between the procedural language program and the SQL module to follow the flow of execution of the program. TANSTAAFL.

Using SQL without a Host Language

It's fine that you can combine SQL with a procedural host language to write database applications, but wouldn't it be even better if you could extend SQL to do the things that the procedural language does as well as the traditional data handling functions of SQL? Yes, it would. Going through a preprocessor stage and then a compilation stage is complex and time-consuming. Having to keep two different kinds of expertise in-house to maintain a single application seems inefficient. Debugging or modifying a hybrid application will be more difficult than it would be if only a single language were used.

These issues give vendors of database management systems valid reasons to want to extend their versions of SQL to include some of the more commonly needed features of procedural languages, such as branching and looping instructions. However, they also have strong reasons to keep their implementations compatible with the international SQL standard, SQL-92. In light of this conflict, what are the vendors doing? Many have made extensions they felt were needed, not waiting for the SQL standard to specify them. Seven or eight years is a long time to wait.

Even though it may seem otherwise, the international SQL standard is not a static document. It has been under revision since 1992. The newest version of the standard, SQL:1999, is in the process of being rolled out in segments. The first two parts of it, called the *Framework* and the *Foundation,* were released in 1999, providing for added functionality. These two parts do not address the issues of branching and looping. Branching and looping are addressed in Part 4, named Persistent Stored Modules. Because the release of SQL:1999 is so recent, (some parts still have not been released), it will be a while before DBMS vendors make their syntax for flow control structures such as branching and looping compliant with the specification. They will have to continue to support their existing customers who bought their products using the proprietary versions of those flow control structures.

At any rate, as time goes on, the need to switch out of SQL and into a general-purpose procedural language will lessen. You will be able to do more and more without having to leave SQL.

Part VI
Using Internet Technology with Database

The 5th Wave — By Rich Tennant

"Your database is beyond repair, but before I tell you our backup recommendation, let me ask you a question. How many index cards do you think will fit on the walls of your computer room?"

In this part . . .

*T*he Internet has profoundly affected most computer-related fields, and database is no exception. Complex enough in its own right, a database presents even more challenges when it is accessible over the Internet.

Part VI describes the architecture of database on a local area network and then contrasts that with database over the Internet. A major difference between those two environments is in the area of security. The owner of an Internet database has limited control over who will access the database. This affects some design decisions. Aside from Internet security concerns, you must address basic reliability issues for any database installation. Some DBMS products have good solutions to these issues and others do not. It is good to have a full understanding of both the issues and the solutions when selecting a DBMS for your organization.

Chapter 15

Database on Networks

In This Chapter

▷ Accessing data over a client/server network

▷ Working with databases via the Internet

▷ Handling database processing on your company's intranet

*M*ost computers today are connected to other computers by some kind of network. As you might imagine, accessing data over a network involves complexities not present on a single-computer system. If you want to make your database accessible to computers other than the one that hosts it, you need to know something about how computers are connected to each other. Before the rise of the Internet, the most common way of connecting computers together was with so-called client/server architecture.

The Architecture and Functions of Client/Server Systems

In a client/server system, computers take on two different roles: client and server. The server is the computer that is physically connected to the database. It is typically optimized for hosting large databases. A server generally has

✔ Large, fast hard disks that hold the databases

✔ High-speed links between the hard disks and the processor

✔ A fast processing system, often consisting of multiple central processing units (CPUs)

✔ A very large, fast main memory

✔ High-speed cache memory

Servers are optimized for transferring large quantities of data into and out of disk storage, as fast as possible.

The client in a client/server system has a much different role from that of the server, and thus is configured quite differently. For one thing, you can connect multiple clients to a single server. The client computer serves as the user interface for the people who are running applications. Because providing a user interface places a relatively light demand on processing power, client computers generally include

- Relatively small, inexpensive hard disks
- Moderately powered, inexpensive processors
- Modest amounts of standard-speed, inexpensive memory

From a cost/benefit standpoint, minimizing the cost of clients makes sense because you have so many of them. On the other hand, putting extra money into the server to beef it up pays dividends, because you often have only one server. Even in a large system with multiple clustered servers, each server may support hundreds of clients.

By putting the database in one central place, the server, many people can have shared access to data that is important to them. Multiple shared access can lead to contention problems if two people try to access the same data at the same time. However, effective solutions to the problem exist and have been implemented by all DBMS vendors.

Another advantage of centralized data is that everyone is "working off the same page." If each client had its own personal copy of the organization's data, changes to one that were not reflected in all the rest would lead to inconsistencies that would ultimately render the database worthless. Which of the many disconnected versions was correct? Who knows? Probably none of them.

Aside from the high degree of data integrity that client/server architecture delivers, it also delivers a major cost savings over isolated, unconnected computers. Because the server does all the heavy lifting, the client machines are little more than data entry and display stations that do a little bit of local processing. That means they can be cheap. Considering the number of clients connected to each server, the cheaper you make the clients, the lower your overall costs will be.

Two-tier client/server architecture

The system that I describe in the preceding section is the original form of client/server architecture. A server is connected to some data source, usually one or more hard disks, by a high-speed bus. It also is connected to a local area network, and through the network to multiple client computers.

This configuration has come to be called the *two-tier client/server architecture.* The client is one tier and the server is the second tier. Figure 15-1 is a schematic representation of a two-tier client/server system.

The task of running a database application is divided between the client machine and the server machine. The client runs the user interface part of the application, does some local processing, and sends SQL statements to the server.

The server performs two distinct functions. On the one hand, it is a *network server,* which communicates with clients over the local area network. On the other hand, it is a *database server,* which translates the incoming SQL into low-level commands to the data source and receives back responses. The network server function then sends the responses on to the requesting client Two-tier client/server architecture worked well, but was replaced by three-tier client/server architecture, which has both cost and performance advantages.

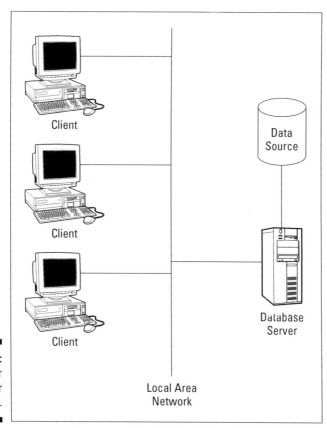

Figure 15-1:
Two-tier
client/server
system.

Three-tier client/server architecture

In a three-tier client/server system, network server and database server functions are separated. The network server concentrates on directing the traffic between the database server and the clients, and thus can take some of the processing load of both. Reducing the client's processing load allows the use of less powerful, less expensive client machines. Reducing the database server's processing load enables the database server to concentrate on processing requests and moving data into and out of the data source as fast as possible, improving overall performance. The network server, because its main function is to mediate the communication between the data source and the clients, is often called *middleware*. Figure 15-2 is a schematic representation of a three-tier client/server system.

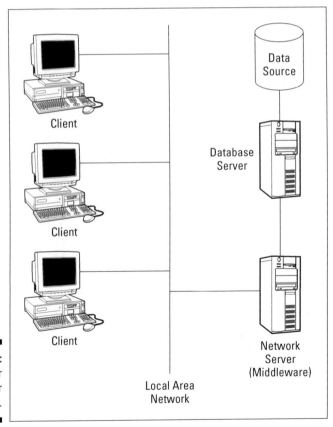

Figure 15-2:
Three-tier
client/server
system.

Comparing ODBC (Open Database Connectivity) and native drivers

It's amazing that client/server architecture works as well as it does. When you move beyond the fairly trivial case of a single server supporting multiple clients, all of whom are running code written specifically for that server, compatibility concerns assume mammoth proportions. What about the fairly common case in which clients are accessing multiple servers, each with a different application programming interface (API), sometimes even from the same application?

Theoretically, this should not be a problem. SQL is standardized, right? Well, yes and no. It is standardized, but DBMS vendors adhere to the standard to a greater or lesser degree. Furthermore, when you get down to the API level, the standard is not well defined.

API? What's that? Actually, the term *application programming interface* is pretty descriptive. A database management system, in order to communicate with mere mortals and thus be of use to them, must interface with an application program. Each DBMS has a standard way of providing such communication, its API. A problem arises because every DBMS vendor has its own idea of what the API should be like.

You can address this issue in two ways. One way is to accept the fact that different data sources are going to have different interfaces. This requires that the application have a different driver for each such source. These drivers, which are custom tailored to their data sources, are called *native drivers*. A native driver is optimized for the one data source it works with and thus provides the best performance available for that data source. The downside is that a native driver will not work at all with any other data source. If you have seven different data sources, you need seven different native drivers to talk to them.

The second way to address this issue is with ODBC (Open Database Connectivity). The ODBC code sits between the application and the data source. It presents the same interface to the application, regardless of which data source is being accessed.

On the data source side, the ODBC code presents a driver that is custom tailored for each data source it talks to. The advantage of ODBC is that the application program does not have to know the nature of the data source it is dealing with. The ODBC interface always looks the same, regardless of what data source is on the back end. This makes application programs that use ODBC much more portable than those that use native drivers. The same application can be used with multiple different data sources.

Front-end code

The client in a client/server system is often called the *front end,* and the
server is called the *back end.* This makes sense from the point of view of the
user. The user is sitting right in front of the client machine, and the server is
generally out of sight, perhaps in a back room or even in another building.

The code running on the client machine is the front-end code. The database
application, written in some procedural host language is the front-end code.
This code controls the flow of execution on the client machine, and provides
a context for the SQL statements that are either embedded in it or contained
in a separate module. The SQL doesn't execute on the client machine.
Instead, it is passed over the network to the server, where it is executed.

Back-end code

The back end code, running on the server, consists of the SQL that comes
over the network from the client. In addition, pieces of code called *stored procedures* also run on the server. Stored procedures are commonly used rou-
tines that might be called upon multiple times during the execution of an
application. Storing them on the server saves network bandwidth, because
they will not be repeatedly sent from the client every time they are invoked.
In addition to incoming SQL and stored procedures, the back end also runs
code that accepts data from the data source, formats it, and then sends it
over the network to the requesting client.

The Internet Changes Everything

Believe it or not, Al Gore did not invent the Internet. The Internet that is so
much a part of our lives today was originally developed by the United States
Department of Defense.

During most of the last half of the 20th Century, both the United States and
the Soviet Union lived in fear that the other would launch a pre-emptive
nuclear strike. The centralized command-and-control system that the United
States had during the 1950s and 1960s was susceptible to being knocked out
by a single well-placed thermonuclear bomb. Realizing this, military brass
put into place a decentralized command-and-control structure that could sur-
vive even if major segments of it were destroyed. Critical defense communications would be automatically rerouted over parts of the network that were
still functional. Originally, this network, called DARPANET (Defense Advanced

Research Projects Agency NETwork), connected military installations, defense contractors, and universities that were doing defense-related research.

As time went on, professors and students found the network so valuable for communicating with colleagues at other universities that they started to use it to talk about non-defense topics. Gradually, the civilian uses of the network overtook the military uses. The military migrated to other systems, using satellites and other communication channels. The DARPANET reflected the transformation to a substantially civilian communication system by changing its name to ARPANET. Finally with communication going to other countries on an ever-increasing basis, the name changed again to the Internet. In the latter half of the 1990s the graphically oriented World Wide Web took off, squeezing out the text-based services, such as gopher and veronica, which had preceded it on the Internet.

Two-tier Web architecture

It is interesting to draw parallels between the evolution of client/server architecture and Web architecture. Both started with a two-tier structure, and then migrated to a more capable three-tier structure. In the two-tier client/server case, a client computer running an application is connected by a local area network to a server computer hosting a database. In the two-tier Web case, a client computer running a browser is connected by the World Wide Web to a server computer hosting a Web site. Figure 15-3 diagrams how a two-tier Web system is connected.

The two-tier architecture is fine for informational or educational Web sites, but not useful for e-commerce or anything else that requires database access. Database access over the Web requires three-tier Web architecture.

Three-tier Web architecture

The three-tier client/server system separates the server into a network server (middleware) and a database server. To achieve a similar effect, the three-tier Web system adds a database server to the already existing Web server. The Web server also incorporates a server extension program that translates Web-speak (signals and protocols) to a language that the database server can understand. Figure 15-4 shows how a three-tier Web system is configured.

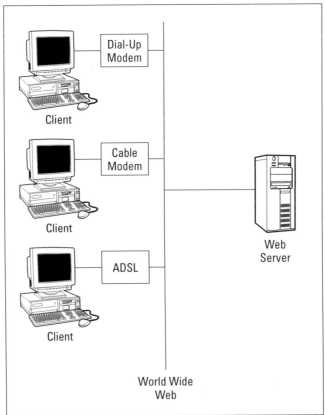

Figure 15-3:
Two-tier
Web
system.

The language of the Web

The language of the Web is HTML (HyperText Markup Language). Web servers communicate with Web clients using HTML. Database servers, however, do not understand HTML at all. Consequently, you need a server extension program to translate HTML to something the database server understands, and vice versa.

It should be no surprise that database servers do not understand HTML. HTML is not a programming language at all; it is a markup language. The purpose of HTML is to format text and graphics on a client's screen. HTML doesn't do anything at the server end of the connection. The server sends HTML to the client's Web browser for display. After it reaches the browser, the HTML determines the layout, colors, fonts, and so on of the display. That's all it does.

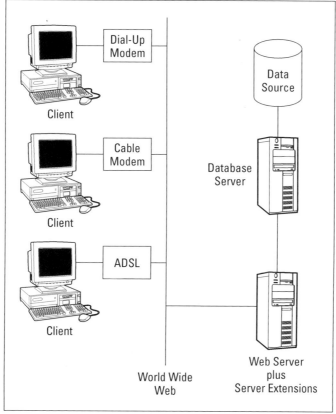

Scripting languages

For any kind of Web operation involving the transfer of data back and forth between the client and the server, you need more than a markup language such as HTML. Scripting languages allow a limited amount of conversation between the client and the server. For example, with HTML augmented by a scripting language such as JavaScript, you can display a data entry form on the client screen, accept entries into the form made by the user, and send them back to the server, where they can be processed. This is not anywhere near enough functionality to serve as a database front end, but it is a move in the right direction.

JavaScript

JavaScript was developed by Netscape as a means of giving some interactivity to the Netscape browser, beyond HTML's ability to follow hyperlinks that the user clicks. It does provide such interactivity, and Web pages that incorporate JavaScript can be much more engaging than those that only use static HTML (or even dynamic HTML, for that matter). JavaScript was never designed to facilitate heavy data transfer between a server and its clients.

Although the name JavaScript is suspiciously similar to the name of Sun's Java language, the two are not closely related. In fact, Netscape originally called its scripting language LiveScript. Later, for marketing reasons, Netscape made a deal with Sun and changed the name to JavaScript. Although Java and JavaScript exhibit some syntactical similarities, neither is derived from the other, and they are not compatible. JavaScript code is designed to be embedded in HTML documents to enhance client-side interactivity. Java is a full-fledged programming language that stands on its own.

VBScript

Although Microsoft supports JavaScript with its Internet Explorer browser, it does so begrudgingly. JavaScript suffers from the defect (from Microsoft's point of view) of not being a Microsoft invention. The fact that JavaScript was invented by Microsoft's rival Netscape makes matters even worse. To remedy this unseemly situation, Microsoft developed VBScript. VBScript, like JavaScript, is an interpreter that processes source code embedded in HTML documents. It has comparable functionality to JavaScript when run from within Internet Explorer.

One difference between VBScript and JavaScript has to do with compatibility. Whereas JavaScript is not a subset of Java, and has different syntax, commands, and rules, VBScript *is* a subset of VBA, which in turn is a subset of Visual Basic. If you are already a Visual Basic programmer, learning VBScript will be easy for you.

XML

XML (eXtended Markup Language), like HTML, is a scripting language derived from SGML. SGML (Standard Generalized Markup Language) is a standard for specifying markup languages rather than being a language itself. XML, like HTML, is characterized by content surrounded by tags. Unlike HTML, it is not involved with laying out content on a Web page, but rather with identifying by use of tags, the nature of the content being surrounded. XML provides a way to structure data as text. Because XML separates the data from the formatting of that data (which is done by HTML), it provides a way of exchanging data over networks that not only works well with the HTTP protocol, but also makes it easy for a receiving machine to extract the data, without having to strip off confusing formatting tags. HTTP (HyperText Transfer Protocol) is the protocol that defines the way information is formatted for transfer across the World Wide Web.

Data of interest can be stored in the form of XML files, but its best use is as a standard means of transporting data between machines, either over the Internet, an intranet, or a local area network. Because XML is not compatible with SQL-based relational databases, any content in XML format will have to be translated into a form a relational database can accept before true com-munication can take place using XML. Vertical market software packages exist and are under development that do just that. XML should become an important piece of the worldwide data/communications infrastructure in the years to come.

Java

Unlike scripting languages such as JavaScript and VBScript, Java is a *real* pro-gramming language. It was developed by Sun specifically for use on the Web. Java is based on C++, the high-powered, professional, workhorse language used by systems programmers, compiler writers, and other exalted beings who operate on a higher plane than most mortals. The developers of Java dropped some of the more arcane features of C++ to make Java development something that ordinary humans could do. They did succeed in broadening their audience. Java programming is not as easy as scripting, but not as hard as C++ programming.

Java is designed to be used in an unusual way. Initially, the Java code resides on the server, but typically is not executed there. When a client makes a con-nection to the server, the server downloads a Java *applet,* which is a small program designed to run on a client machine. The applet gives the client the ability to interact with a database on the server.

One of the prime advantages of using Java as opposed to say, Visual Basic, is that Java is platform-neutral. It will run under Microsoft operating systems, but will run equally well under UNIX. If you are developing an application and think it might run in a Sun Solaris environment, or under Linux, as well as under Windows 2000, it makes sense to use Java as your development language.

Serving Up Information Over the Organizational Intranet

Multinational corporations and other large organizations have been using computers for a long time. Initially, they employed large mainframe comput-ers that lived in raised-floor "glass houses," attended by acolytes, er . . . I mean computer operators. To have a program run, you had it keypunched into a card deck that you turned in at the vestibule of the glass house. An operator would then put your deck into the computer's card reader. Several hours later, your output would appear in your designated bin in the vestibule.

A big improvement in efficiency came about when tens or hundreds of dumb terminals (the ultimate thin client) were attached to the mainframe. This saved a lot of walking back and forth between your office and the glass house, although it was probably a blow to the cardiovascular fitness of the world's programmers. The mainframe/dumb terminal paradigm was eventually replaced by client/server architecture, another big improvement in performance, and at a lower overall cost.

The explosion of the World Wide Web in the mid-1990s exposed the world to the advantages of communicating with clients running browsers. The de facto standard browsers from Netscape and Microsoft would run on a wide variety of platforms, running a wide variety of operating systems. Unlike the front-ends of typical client/server applications, browsers were cheap. Today, they are even cheaper; you can download one for free. Not only that, converting from a client/server system to a browser-based intranet involves minimal hardware expense. The same computers and networking infrastructure can be used. These advantages were not lost on the people running organizational networks. If browser-based communication works well on the Internet, it ought to work even better on a network completely contained within a single organization. Better yet, all the experimenting and development had already been done. Thus, the intranet was born.

An intranet works just like the Internet, with servers serving up content, and clients accessing that content. It is a much safer environment than the Internet because the organization has physical control over all the machines on the net and can decide who has access to them. Security is much less of a concern, making the infrastructure for an intranet simpler than what is required for the Internet. As a result, databases storing sensitive corporate information can be safely placed on an intranet, without the fear that hackers will be able to access it.

Using an intranet for an organization's database operations offers the following advantages:

- This approach uses established technology pioneered on the Internet. No expensive development needed.

- Users are already familiar with the user interface, a standard browser.

- Browsers are the ultimate bargain, not just free, but also well supported.

- Because the intranet is isolated from the outside world, security worries are minimized.

Chapter 16

Database Security and Reliability

*I*f you have read this far, you know that databases are fairly complex things to create and maintain. You cannot go into a database development project lightly, and have any hope of succeeding. That being the case, people generally don't build a database unless the data they intend to put into it is important to them. If your data is important to you, you want to protect it from threats and preserve it from degradation. Thus, database security and reliability are major concerns of database developers.

So, what could threaten your database's safety? A number of things, including:

✓ Malicious people seeing your data, and based on that knowledge, hurting you or others

✓ Malicious people accessing your data and trashing it, thus depriving you of its use

✓ Malicious people accessing your data and changing it in subtle ways, causing you to make bad decisions

✓ Innocent people accessing your data and trashing it by mistake

✓ Two people corrupting your data by trying to access the same record at the same time

✓ Hardware failures while your database file is open

✓ Software failures while your database file is open

Lots of things could go wrong. If your data is important to you, you need to address all the concerns in the preceding list, and be alert to possible threats that you have not thought of yet. When it comes to maintaining databases, it helps to be a little paranoid.

Maintaining Database Security

For the purpose of maintaining database security, establish a set of categories of users, and assign different access privileges to different categories. That way, people will have access to the information and privileges they need to do their jobs, but will not have access to areas and functions that do not or should not concern them.

Users and privileges

As more and more databases are being made accessible over the Internet, the issue of security rises to primary importance. Malicious people, some of them very smart, are using the Internet. Even within an organization, malice might exist. A disaffected employee may have a private agenda that is not in agreement with the best interests of your organization. Earlier in this chapter, I list several bad things that malicious people can do to your database. You need protections against those bad things. You also need protections against the innocent mistakes of people who bear you no malice. What can you do?

Potentially, users can do five things to a relational database table. Each one is facilitated by a SQL keyword:

- They can see selected records in a table. The SQL SELECT statement does this.
- They can add a new record to a table. The SQL INSERT statement does this.
- They can change the contents of a record in a table. The SQL UPDATE statement does this.
- They can delete a record from a table. The SQL DELETE statement does this.
- They can link one table to another table. The SQL REFERENCES clause does this.

Your database will contain some information that you do not want unauthorized and potentially malicious people to see. Don't put that information on the Internet. It's possible that password protection and encryption will protect your information adequately, but I wouldn't count on it. Some awfully clever, persistent, and malicious people are out there. Because anyone anywhere in the world can access your Web site, and spend 24/7 trying to crack your security, I wouldn't bet against the forces of evil in cases like this.

On the other hand, your database may include some information that you don't mind even evil people seeing, such as your company's product catalog. As far as you are concerned, anybody can see your product catalog, but you don't want just anybody to be able to change it. With SQL, you can define different classes of users, and grant appropriate privileges to each class, withholding privileges that are not appropriate.

Classes of users and the privileges they have

In any database system, somebody must have broad, sweeping powers to do anything that can possibly be done to the database. If such an individual did not exist, situations would arise in which something needed to be done but no one would have the power to do it. Considering the power she wields, this person should probably be called "The Database Empress" or at the very least "The Database Queen." Computer scientists are not known for their imagination, however, so this exalted person goes by the mundane moniker of *Database Administrator,* abbreviated DBA. Who this person is depends on the size of the organization and the number of databases that must be maintained.

The database administrator

If you work in a small organization and are the only person that knows beans about computers, you are the DBA by default. You install the database management system, create database tables, write applications, and stack the empty soda cans. Because you installed the DBMS, you can grant yourself all the privileges that are available to be granted. You are the sovereign of an admittedly small empire, master of all you survey.

Having the immense powers of a DBA can be dangerous. Because a DBA can do anything, while in the course of working on an application or other project, you might inadvertently do something that irrevocably messes up your database. To protect yourself from that unhappy situation, create a second account for yourself that has limited powers. Use the limited account whenever you are doing database development. Log on as DBA only when you are doing administration tasks that require the power of the DBA. When you finish doing the administration, log off as DBA and log on again using your limited privilege logon.

Larger organizations will have multiple programmers creating databases and database applications. In this context, the DBA has expanded responsibilities. She must see that resources are shared equitably, that authorized people have the access they need, and that databases are protected. This can be a complex and demanding job, and people with the proper skills and experience are much in demand.

If you are responsible for an organizational database installation, make sure that you have at least one backup DBA. What would happen if your one and only DBA became unavailable for some reason, such as sudden illness or being hired away by a competitor? Without the DBA password, you would not be able to perform critical maintenance tasks and your database system would eventually become unusable. Play it safe. Make sure the DBA passwords, system maintenance information, and secret handshakes are shared with one or more highly trusted and well trained individuals.

Database object owners

One of the privileges the DBA can grant to someone else is the right to create database objects such as tables or views. Anyone who creates a table or view can specify who the owner of that object will be.

If you are creating a database for yourself, you will probably want to name yourself as owner of the objects it contains. If you are creating a database for a client, you may want to name the client as owner.

Database object owners have all rights with respect to the objects they own. They can fill tables with data, change the data, delete it, or merely look at it. They can even destroy the tables or views they own, if they want to. Furthermore, database object owners can grant access privileges to their objects to other people. The powers of a database object owner are second only to the powers of the DBA, when it comes to that owner's database objects.

Privilege grantees

Database object owners can pass on access rights to their objects, using the SQL GRANT statement. Consider the following SQL statement:

```
GRANT SELECT ON VENDOR TO PurchasingManager;
```

This statement allows the purchasing manager to view the VENDOR table, but not to change anything about it. To allow the purchasing manager to add new vendors to the list, the owner could issue the following statement:

```
GRANT INSERT ON VENDOR TO PurchasingManager;
```

Going one step further, the following statement not only allows the purchasing manager the privilege to view the vendor table, it also allows him to pass on that privilege to others:

```
GRANT SELECT ON VENDOR TO PurchasingManager
    WITH GRANT OPTION;
```

I do not go into further detail on using SQL to grant and revoke user privileges here. (Yes, any privilege that can be granted can also be revoked.) I cover this subject in *SQL For Dummies.* Suffice it to say that anyone who has a privilege and also has the grant option for that privilege, can pass the privilege on to someone else. Privilege owners can also revoke any privileges that they have granted.

The public

Any user who has not been specifically granted access privileges to a database object is considered a member of the public. In all likelihood, your database has tables or views that should be made available to anyone who wants to access them. Rather than naming everyone in the world with a very long GRANT statement, you can cover them all with a simple grant to the public, as in the following example:

```
GRANT SELECT ON PRODUCTLIST TO Public;
```

After this GRANT statement, anyone who has access to the database can view the contents of the product list table.

Controlling Concurrent Access

Early multi-user database systems ran into problems when two users tried to access the same data at the same time. Consider the following scenario:

Salespeople Roxie and Vera take telephone orders all day for the Mistress Treasure intimate apparel company. One Tuesday afternoon, Roxie receives a call from a customer who wants to buy three pair of Tiger Legs panty hose, size small. Roxie checks inventory on her computer terminal and sees that five pair are in stock. She informs the customer they are in stock and asks for the sale. The customer says, "I'll take them. Just a minute while I get out my credit card."

Meanwhile, Vera takes a call from a second customer. This customer asks if Vera has Tiger Legs panty hose, size small in stock. Vera queries the database and then replies that five pair are in stock. The customer has her credit card number ready and says she will take all five, so Vera executes the sale. Inventory for this item is decremented from five to zero.

Now Roxie's customer returns to the phone with her credit card number, but when Roxie tries to complete the transaction, she now finds that none are in stock. Roxie misses the sale, and Mistress Treasure has an unhappy customer, who will probably diss the company to her friends. Heaven forbid that the unhappy customer happens to be the lingerie critic for the local newspaper. There should be a way to prevent this kind of problem from happening. Such a way exists; it is called the transaction.

Transactions

A *transaction* is any one execution of a user program in a DBMS. Any transaction involves the use of one or more database objects, such as tables, columns within a table, or records within a table. After a transaction starts, the objects it uses are locked in such a way that any attempt by another transaction to access those objects will be blocked until the first transaction completes. How would the conflict between Roxie and Vera have been handled if transaction processing had been in effect?

1. Upon receiving the first call, Roxie locks access to the Tiger Legs, size small, record in the PRODUCT table.

2. Vera checks inventory and finds the table locked. She starts exchanging small talk with her customer while waiting for the lock to be lifted.

3. Roxie's customer gives Roxie her credit card number, triggering the sale of three pair of panty hose and the decrementing of the number in stock from five to two. The transaction completes.

4. Vera notices that the lock on the Tiger Legs record has been lifted and that two pair are in stock. She informs her customer, who purchases the two remaining pair.

In this scenario, Roxie's customer is happy, and Vera's customer is also reasonably happy, although she would have been willing to buy more if more had been available. Neither customer was given false hopes that were subsequently dashed. Transaction processing has brought about a happy result for everyone.

Serializability

The preceding example, in which transaction processing completely stops a second user while the first user has control of a database object, prevents concurrency problems, but can have a severe effect on overall system performance. Forcing transactions into a serial schedule in which one transaction cannot proceed until another completes is not absolutely required in order to guarantee database integrity. It is sufficient for transactions to be *serializable*, rather that strictly serial.

Serializable transactions are a set of transactions whose effect on the database state is identical to what the database state would be if the transactions had been executed in some serial order. In other words, transactions can be interleaved as long as the net effect on the database is the same as it would have been if they had been run serially.

Serializable transactions are just as safe as serial transactions and may in some instances provide better performance. Where performance is an overriding concern, it is also possible to set transaction processing such that serializability is not guaranteed. In these cases, anomalies in the data become possible. The DBA may choose to accept the possibility of anomalies in exchange for better performance. This requires an intimate knowledge of the data and how it will be used, as well as of what constitutes minimally acceptable performance. The DBA must exercise carefully considered judgment in order to provide the needed performance without invalidating results because of corrupted data.

Locking

In the discussion of transactions, I mention that a transaction would attempt to lock all the resources (database objects) that it needs to perform its designated function. Different kinds of locks exist — specifically, *shared locks* and *exclusive locks*.

If two users want to *look at* the same database record at the same time, no conflict exists. A shared lock allows both users access simultaneously. However, that same lock will prevent a third user from coming in and changing that record.

To change a record, a transaction needs to obtain an exclusive lock. If a record is already locked with a shared lock, an exclusive lock cannot be applied. Exclusive locks prevent the unfortunate conflict that Roxie and Vera experience in the example I describe in the previous section.

A potential problem exists with exclusive locks, however. Consider this example:

User 1 initiates a transaction that requires two resources: Table A and Table B. At the same time, User 2 initiates a transaction that requires the same two resources: Table B and Table A. User 1 gets to Table A first and puts an exclusive lock on it. User 2 gets to Table B first and puts an exclusive lock on it. User 1 now tries to lock Table B, but cannot. User 2 tries to lock Table A, but cannot. Both transactions keep trying to acquire the resource they lack, but can never succeed. This situation is called *deadlock*. Not realizing that they will never be able to acquire the missing resource, both transactions will keep trying forever, bringing the processor to its knees and slowing all other active transactions to a crawl.

Different DBMS systems have different solutions to the deadlock problem. As a database developer, you don't have to worry too much about this. It is the DBA's concern, and anyway, good workarounds exist. If you are working on an old legacy system, however, you might run into this problem. In such a case, the computer operator has to manually terminate one of the offending transactions, allowing the other to complete.

Database Crash and Recovery

Computer systems crash. On a Windows system, this event is often announced by the appearance of the infamous "Blue Screen of Death." At other times, the system just freezes, without any helpful announcement. If a system crash occurs while database transactions are active, the database will be corrupted. Any DBMS used for serious applications must be able to recover from any possible damage that might be done to a database, even if the crash occurs at the worst possible time. For a database in constant use, sooner or later, a crash will occur at the worst possible time.

How system crashes can hurt you

Computers have two kinds of storage, called volatile and nonvolatile. Volatile storage, also called main memory, comprises semiconductor memory chips. They are called *volatile* because when power is removed from the chips, the information they contain leaks away. Loss of power means loss of memory.

A computer's nonvolatile storage is principally in the form of hard disks. Hard disks store data in tiny magnetic domains that do not forget their contents when power is lost.

The volatility of main memory causes significant challenges to the recovery from system crashes. However, because memory chips are many orders of magnitude faster than nonvolatile hard disks, computer manufacturers continue to use volatile storage for their systems' main memory. Software remedies have been developed for recovery from crashes.

When a transaction has completed successfully, it is said to have *committed*. When a transaction has been abandoned short of completion, it is said to have *aborted*. Transactions that are still in progress are said to be *active*. These three conditions lead to three different problems when a crash occurs:

✔ A transaction that has committed, but has not yet been written to the stable storage of a hard disk when the crash occurs is a problem. No record of the database changes up to and including the transaction's successful completion exists.

✔ A transaction that has aborted, but for which record of the abort has not been written to stable storage when the crash occurs is a problem. No record of the database changes made since the transaction began exist, so the system does not know what to roll back.

✔ A transaction that is active may have made some changes to database tables but not others at the time of the crash. No record of how far the transaction got before the crash happened exists.

These are serious concerns. Small databases running on personal computers may not have to worry too much about crashes. Going to your last backup and redoing a few transactions may not be a very big problem for you. However, if you are running a large enterprise database system around the clock, 365 days a year, recovery from system crashes is a critical concern.

Recovering from a crash

The key to recovering from a crash is to have a relatively recent known good copy of your database and a record of all the transactions that had been applied to it up to the time of the crash. This requires an ironclad and rigidly adhered to backup policy. Ask yourself, "How often should I backup my data-base?" and then answer with another question, "How bad off would I be if my hard disk crashed one minute before my next scheduled backup?" If you are uncomfortable with the answer to that question, you need to consider back-ing up more frequently.

Even if you back up your system frequently, that still leaves the problem of how you will know all the changes that have been applied to the database since the last backup. The solution to that problem is logging.

Logging

When I talk about logging in the context of database systems, I am not refer-ring to the chopping down of large trees. Logging in database parlance is very eco-friendly. It refers to recording on stable storage (other than the hard disk that holds your database) every action that you perform on your database *before* you perform it. That way, if a system crash happens immediately after you have changed a database record, the fact that you made that change is recorded in the log, even though the change itself has been lost.

Logging enables you to go back to the last time when you knew the state of the database and reapply all the changes that took place between then and the time of the crash. You can then continue on, saving to stable storage the transactions that have committed, undoing the transactions that have aborted, and completing the transactions that were still active at the time of the crash.

Checkpointing

A *checkpoint* is a snapshot of the database state that is saved to stable storage. By taking checkpoints periodically, you decrease considerably the amount of work that must be done to recover from a system crash. Your log only has to go back to the last checkpoint before starting to redo the lost transactions, rather than back to the time just before the start of the oldest transaction at the time of the crash.

Mirroring

You mirror a database by maintaining two separate copies of it on two different stable storage devices. Every time you make a change to one, you change the other at the same time. Thus, if one of your hard disks crashes, you not only do not lose any data, you do not lose any time either, because processing can continue using the mirror disk.

Crash recovery facilities such as logging and checkpointing are effective but expensive. Mirroring is even more expensive. For mission-critical database environments such as those hosted by IBM's DB/2, Oracle's Oracle, or Microsoft's SQL Server, the reliability enhancement obtained with these techniques is often deemed worth the cost. You will not find such facilities on inexpensive personal computer database management systems such as Microsoft Access, however. This could be an important factor in your decision of what DBMS to choose for your organization.

Part VII
The Part of Tens

The 5th Wave — By Rich Tennant

"I TELL YA I'M STILL GETTING INTERFERENCE —
— COOKIE, RAGS? RAGS WANNA COOKIE? —
THERE IT GOES AGAIN."

In this part . . .

With the help of this book, you know how to design and build databases of distinction. I hereby exhort you to go forth and practice your craft. Design databases and then build them. However, before you do, read and take to heart the rules given in Part VII. They will remind you of the fundamentals and keep you from making major mistakes in the databases and applications you design. Even seasoned pros would do well to refresh their minds periodically with these basic principles.

Chapter 17

Ten Rules to Remember When Creating a Database

*I*n this book, I give hundreds of pages of detailed information on how to build efficient, reliable databases. It is a lot to remember. To make matters easier for you, I have distilled down the essence of this material to ten rules. If you follow these ten rules when building your databases, you can't go too far wrong.

Databases, Even Huge Ones Such as NASA's Bill of Materials for the Space Shuttle, Can Be Designed, Built, and Maintained

Large database projects may be intimidating due to their complexity and sheer size. However, by breaking the task up into phases and then dividing those phases into manageable tasks, you can get the job done.

Build Your Database Model to Accurately Reflect the Users' Data Model

It is impossible to build a database that accurately models a real, physical system, such as the Space Shuttle. That is all right, however, because you don't want to model real physical systems anyway. What you want to model is the way the users of a system think about it. This users' data model is an abstraction of the real system, that the user knows how to deal with.

Be Sure to Budget Enough Time to Do Justice to Every One of the Phases of Development

You will always face pressure from the client to deliver your product according to the schedule that was agreed to at the outset. Make sure that the schedule you agree to at that time allows for a full development including adequate time for all seven phases — definition, requirements, evaluation, design, implementation, testing and final documentation, and maintenance.

Build a Conceptual Model of Your Proposed Database

After you receive all the necessary input from users and other stakeholders, and come to a consensus that everyone agrees to, build a model of the system that agrees with that consensus. Use one of the popular, proven modeling systems such as the entity-relationship model or the semantic object model.

Make Your Model as Detailed as It Needs to Be, but Not More So

Make sure your model is rich enough to incorporate all the nuances that came out in the course of your discussions with the users. However, don't fall into the trap of trying to make your model more accurate than it needs to be. Design it so that it meets the users' requirements, then stop. The fact that you could build it to more closely reflect the physical system you are modeling is not important. You only want to go down to the level of detail that the user cares about.

Build Flexibility into Your Systems So They Will Adapt Easily When Requirements Change

If you build a database system to meet an organization's present day needs, it will probably not meet the users' needs five years from now. It might not be satisfactory even one year from now. Knowing that, build it so that it will be expandable. Make it easy to eliminate parts that are no longer needed, and to add new parts that meet requirements that were not anticipated during the initial development.

Accurately Assess the Project's Scope at the Beginning

It is absolutely critical to understand the scope of a project from the beginning. How big? How complex? How long will it take? The decision as to whether to move ahead with a project will depend on what it will cost in terms of time, materials, and money. If you estimate too conservatively, the client may decide not to proceed. If you estimate too aggressively, you will not be able to complete the project on time and on budget. That outcome could be even worse than the alternative. Spend all the time and effort necessary to come up with the best possible estimate of what the task will require.

Make Sure All the Relations in Your Model Deal With Only One Idea

Any relation that deals with more than one idea is probably subject to modification anomalies. Because modification anomalies can cause inconsistencies in your database, it makes good sense to avoid them by normalizing your relations to the point where they deal with only one idea.

Sometimes, for Performance Reasons, You Will Want to Denormalize Relations So They Deal With More than One Idea

You may not care about some modification anomalies. They do not affect you, based on how you are using your database. In such cases, you may be able to improve performance by combining fully normalized relations into a denormalized form. For example, in a CUSTOMER relation, the combination of the City and State attributes is redundant with the PostalCode attribute. You may want to keep them all in the same relation anyway, because they are usually used together in addressing an envelope.

Reduce Any Many-to-Many Relationships in a Model to Multiple One-to-Many Relationships

Many-to-many relationships in an entity-relationship model or semantic object model are difficult to convert into a relational model. By adding an intersection relation between the two relations that are connected by a many-to-many relationship, you transform one many-to-many relationship into two one-to-many relationships. The addition of one more relation to the model is a small price to pay for the reduction in relationship complexity.

Chapter 18

Ten Rules to Remember When Creating a Database Application

*A*fter your database is designed and implemented, you need a way for users to communicate with it. That is where the database application comes in. It is important that the database application be tailored to the people who will be using it. It is also important that the application function properly and efficiently. The following ten rules remind you of the important things to keep in mind when creating a database application.

Talk to Your System's Future Users a Lot

The database application displays the part of a system that users see and interact with. Make sure they can easily understand what they see. You must have a clear picture in your mind of who the users of your application are and how they think. Tailor the user interface of your system to these people and to the way they are accustomed to operating. The success or failure of your project depends not only on how good your system is, but also on how well this select group of people can use it.

Document Every Phase of the Development Process

Carefully document every phase of the development process, from your initial discussions with your client, all the way to final delivery and beyond. This will help to keep you focused on the primary objective and keep you from diverging off onto tangents. It will also help keep the client honest and reduce feature creep and scope creep.

Test Your Application Frequently

Start testing early in the implementation phase. No matter how good you are as a developer, your application programs are going to contain bugs. The bigger the project, the more likely it will have hidden problems. The more testing you do, the sooner you will find and eliminate those problems. The farther along in a development process you are before you find a bug, the more expensive it will be to fix.

Be a Consensus Builder

Any large database development project has multiple classes of users, each with its own perspective on what is required. You must act as a bridge between those divergent perspectives and bring them together. At the end of the project, you want *everybody* to be happy with the result, not just one class of user.

Pick the Right Tools for the Job

One size does not fit all, and you need to use a DBMS that is appropriate for the size of the system you are building. Some DBMS products, such as Microsoft Access, are designed for relatively small applications accessed by no more than a few dozen users. They assume that the people writing applications are not necessarily database professionals. The development tools are friendly, but the product is not designed to support large, complex systems. Other DBMS products, such as Oracle, DB/2, or SQL Server, do assume that developers are professionals. Development tools are not as friendly because the assumption is that they don't need to be. The products themselves are considerably more robust than are the Access-class products.

Database Applications Communicate with Databases Using SQL

You may write database applications in any programming language, such as C++ or Visual Basic, or you may write them using a rapid application development environment such as Borland Delphi or C++ Builder. Regardless of which tool you choose, any communication that takes place between the application and the database is done by means of SQL. The SQL may be embedded in the application code, or it may be in a separate module called by the application code.

Use Standard SQL Wherever Possible

DBMS vendors all try to offer SQL that complies with the international SQL standard. They also try to offer nonstandard features that will differentiate their product from the competition. If you stick to standard SQL, your applications will be more portable across different operating environments.

Optimize the Server for Fast Data Transfer

In a client/server system, the server's primary job is to retrieve requested data and send it to the requester as quickly as possible. Design every aspect of the server architecture and operating software to provide the fastest possible data transfer.

Configure the Client for Lowest Cost

The client in a client/server system doesn't have to do much beyond support the user interface. This does not require much processing power or memory. Because you probably have many more clients than servers on a system, you want to minimize client cost. Savings at the client end can be applied to making the server faster.

Pump Some Life into Web-based Applications

When building a Web-based database application, give the screen some dynamic elements. Web site visitors are generally not engaged by the static screens produced by plain vanilla HTML. This is just as true of a database site as it is of any other. Add some activity to your site by using a scripting language to provide some interactivity.

Glossary

ActiveX control: A reusable software component that can be added to an application, reducing development time in the process. ActiveX is a Microsoft technology, and ActiveX components can only be used by developers who work on Windows development systems.

aggregate function: A function that produces a single result based on the contents of an entire set of table rows. Also called a *set function.*

alias: A short substitute or "nickname" for a table name.

applet: A small application stored on a Web server that is downloaded to and executed on a Web client that connects to the server.

Application Programming Interface (API): A standard means of communicating between an application and a database or other system resource.

assertion: A constraint that is specified by a CREATE ASSERTION statement (rather than by a clause of a CREATE TABLE statement). Assertions commonly apply to more than one table.

attribute: A characteristic of an entity, semantic object, or relation.

back end: That part of a DBMS that interacts directly with the database.

business rule: A restriction on an organization's activities that must be reflected in any model of that organization.

catalog: A named collection of schemas.

checkpoint: A point of synchronization between a database and its associated transaction log.

client: That part of a DBMS that displays information on a screen and responds to user input (the front end).

client/server system: A multiuser system in which a central processor (the server) is connected to multiple intelligent user workstations (the clients).

cluster: A named collection of catalogs.

collating sequence: The ordering of characters in a character set. All collating sequences for character sets that have the Latin characters (a, b, c, ...) define the obvious ordering (a,b,c, ...). But they differ in the ordering of special characters (+, -, <, ?, and so on) and in the relative ordering of the digits and the letters.

column: A component of a table that holds a single attribute of the table.

commit: The successful completion of a database transaction.

composite key: A key made up of two or more table columns.

conceptual view: The schema of a database.

concurrent access: Two or more users operating on the same rows in a database table at the same time.

constraint: A restriction you specify on the data in a database.

constraint, deferred: A constraint that is not applied until you change its status to *immediate* or until you COMMIT the encapsulating transaction.

cursor: An SQL feature that specifies a set of rows, an ordering of those rows, and a current row within that ordering.

Data Control Language (DCL): That part of SQL that protects the database from harm.

Data Definition Language (DDL): That part of SQL used to define, modify, and eradicate database structures.

data integrity: Data that is logically consistent is said to have data integrity.

Data Manipulation Language (DML): That part of SQL that operates on database data.

data redundancy: Having the same data stored in more than one place in a database.

data source: A source of data used by a database application. It may be a DBMS or a data file.

data sublanguage: A subset of a complete computer language that deals specifically with data handling. SQL is a data sublanguage.

database: A self-describing collection of integrated records.

database, enterprise: Same as organizational database.

database, organizational: A database containing information used by an entire organization.

database, personal: A database designed for use by a single person on a single computer.

database, workgroup: A database designed to be used by a department or workgroup within an organization.

Database Administrator (DBA): The person ultimately responsible for the functionality, integrity, and safety of a database.

database application: Programs that work with a database to maintain and deliver desired information.

database engine: That part of a DBMS that directly interacts with the database (part of the back end).

database publishing: The act of making the contents of a database available on the Internet or an intranet.

database server: The server component of a client/server system.

DBMS: A database management system.

deadlock: Two transactions requiring the same resources each lock one resource while trying to lock the one already locked by the other transaction, freezing execution of both transactions.

deletion anomaly: An inconsistency in a database that occurs when a row is deleted from one of its tables.

denormalize: To purposely lower the normal form of a system of tables in order to improve performance. This is done with recognition of the fact that it could introduce anomalies into the data.

descriptor: An area in memory used to pass information between an application's procedural code and its dynamic SQL code.

diagnostics area: A data structure managed by the DBMS that contains detailed information about the last SQL statement executed and any errors that occurred during its execution.

distributed data processing: A system in which data is distributed across multiple servers.

domain: The set of all values that a database item can assume.

domain integrity: A property of a database table column where all data items in that column fall within the domain of the column.

driver: That part of a database management system that interfaces directly with a database.

driver manager: A component of an ODBC-compliant database interface. On Windows machines, it is a dynamic link library (DLL) that coordinates the linking of data sources with appropriate drivers.

entity: Something important to the user, that needs to be included in a database.

entity, ID-dependent: A weak entity whose identifier includes the identifier of the corresponding strong entity.

entity, strong: Any entity that is not a weak entity.

entity, weak: An entity that depends for its existence in a database on the existence of another (strong) entity.

entity class: A set of entities of the same type.

entity class, subtype: A set of entities that shares some attributes with one or more other sets of entities, but also has some attributes that it does not share.

entity class, supertype: A set of entities that includes two or more subtype entities.

entity integrity: A property of a database table that is entirely consistent with the real-world object that it models.

entity-relationship model: A formal, structured way of representing a users' model, developed by Peter Chen in 1976, that can be directly converted into a relational model.

feature creep: The tendency of the scope of a development project to gradually increase while development is in process. Often due to users "remembering" things that they absolutely need, but neglected to specify at the beginning of the project.

file server: The server component of a resource sharing system. It does not contain any database management software.

firewall: A piece of software or a combination of hardware and software that isolates an intranet from the Internet, allowing only trusted traffic to travel between them.

flat file: A collection of data records having minimal structure.

foreign key: A column or combination of columns in a database table that references the primary key of another table in the database.

front end: That part of a DBMS that interacts directly with the user.

functional dependency: A relationship between or among attributes of a relation.

hierarchical database model: A tree-structured model of data.

host variable: A variable that is passed between an application written in a procedural host language and embedded SQL.

HTML (HyperText Markup Language): A standard formatting language for Web documents.

HTTP (HyperText Transfer Protocol): The protocol that defines the way information is formatted for transfer across the World Wide Web.

identifier: One or more attributes that, when taken together, identify an entity instance.

identifier, object: One or more object attributes that, when taken together, identify a semantic object instance.

implementation: A particular relational DBMS running on a specific hardware platform.

index: A table of pointers used to locate rows in a data table rapidly.

information schema: The system tables, which hold the database's metadata.

insertion anomaly: An inconsistency introduced into a database when a new row is inserted into one of its tables.

Internet: The worldwide network of computers.

intranet: A network that uses World Wide Web hardware and software, but access is restricted to users within a single organization.

IPX/SPX: A local area network protocol.

Java: A platform-independent compiled language designed specifically for Web application development.

JavaScript: A scripting language used to add client-side functionality to HTML documents. Although JavaScript bears some syntactical similarity to Java, the two languages are not compatible with each other.

JDBC (Java DataBase Connectivity): A standard interface between a Java applet or application and a database. The JDBC standard is modeled after the ODBC standard.

join: A relational operator that combines data from multiple tables into a single result table.

key: A group of one or more attributes that identify a unique row in a relation.

lock, exclusive: The allocation of a system resource to a transaction in a concurrent processing system, such that no other transaction may either read or write to that resource.

lock, shared: The allocation of a system resource to a transaction in a concurrent processing system, such that other transactions may read the resource, but they may not write to it.

logging: Writing to a file a record of all changes made to a database system. The log should reside on nonvolatile media other than the media storing the database.

logical connectives: Used to connect or change the truth value of predicates to produce more complex predicates.

maximum cardinality: The maximum number of values that an attribute may have.

metadata: Data about the structure of the data in a database.

middleware: Software in a client/server system that translates traffic coming from the front-end client into a form understandable to the back-end data source, and vice versa.

minimum cardinality: The minimum number of values that an attribute may have.

modification anomaly: A problem introduced into a database when a modification (insertion, deletion, or update) is made to one of the tables in the database.

module language: A form of SQL in which SQL statements are placed in modules, which are called by an application program written in a host language.

nested query: A statement that contains one or more subqueries.

NetBEUI: A local area network protocol.

Netscape plug-in: A software component that is downloaded from a Web server to a Web client, where it is integrated with the client's browser, providing additional functions.

network database model: A way of organizing a database so that redundancy of data items is minimized by allowing any data item (node) to be directly connected to any other.

normal forms: A set of rules that specify how a relation may be structured.

normalization: A technique that reduces or eliminates the possibility that a database is subject to modification anomalies.

ODBC (Object DataBase Connectivity): A standard interface between a database and an application that is trying to access the data in that database. ODBC is defined by an international (ISO) and a national (ANSI) standard.

one-to-many relationship: A relationship between two relations where one row of the first table may correspond to multiple rows of the second table, but one row of the second table corresponds to one and only one row of the first table.

one-to-one relationship: A relationship between two relations where one row of the first table corresponds to one and only one row of the second table, and one row of the second table corresponds to one and only one row of the first table.

Oracle: A relational database management system marketed by Oracle Corporation.

parameter: A variable within an application written in SQL module language.

precision: The maximum number of digits allowed in a numeric data item.

predicate: A statement that may be either true or false.

primary key: A column or combination of columns in a database table that uniquely identifies each row in the table.

procedural language: A computer language that solves a problem by executing a procedure in the form of a sequence of steps.

query: A question you ask about the data in a database.

query by example (QBE): A type of query interface in which a user can express a query by providing examples of the values of some of the attributes of the desired records.

rapid application development (RAD) tool: A proprietary graphically oriented alternative to SQL. A number of such tools are on the market.

record: A representation of some physical or conceptual object.

referential integrity: A state in which all the tables in a database are consistent with each other.

relation: A two-dimensional array of rows and columns, containing single-valued entries and no duplicate rows.

relationship, many-to-many: A relationship between two relations where one row of the first table may correspond to many rows of the second table, and one row of the second table may correspond to many rows of the first table.

relationship, one-to-many: A relationship between two relations where one row of the first table may correspond to multiple rows of the second table, but one row of the second table corresponds to one and only one row of the first table.

relationship, one-to-one: A relationship between two relations where one row of the first table corresponds to one and only one row of the second table, and one row of the second table corresponds to one and only one row of the first table.

reserved words: Words that have a special significance in SQL and cannot be used as variable names or in any other way that differs from their intended use.

requirements document: A document generated at the beginning of a database development project that clearly states exactly what the proposed system will be required to do.

rollback: The process of undoing the effects of faulty or partially processed transactions.

row value expression: A list of value expressions enclosed in parentheses and separated by commas.

scale: The number of digits in the fractional part of a numeric data item.

schema: The structure of an entire database. The database's metadata.

schema owner: The person who was designated as the owner when the schema was created.

scoping: Determining the size of a project in terms of time and resources.

semantic object: A named collection of attributes that sufficiently describes a distinct entity.

semantic object model: A formal, structured way of representing a users' model, developed by David Kroenke and published in 1988, that can be directly converted into a relational model.

SEQUEL: A data sublanguage created by IBM that was a precursor of SQL.

serializable: A transaction execution schedule whose results are identical to the results of an execution schedule in which all transactions are executed serially.

set function: A function that produces a single result based on the contents of an entire set of table rows. Also called an *aggregate function.*

SGML (Standard Generalized Markup Language): A standard for how to specify a document markup language or tag set. SGML is not in itself a document language, but a description of how to specify one. HTML is an example of a SGML-based language. XML is another example.

solutions document: A document that responds to the requirements document of a proposed database development project. It tells exactly how the requirements will be met and what the project will cost in terms of time, resources, and money.

SQL: An industry standard data sublanguage, specifically designed to create, manipulate, and control relational databases. SQL:1999 is the latest version of the standard.

SQL, dynamic: A means of building compiled applications in which all data items are not identifiable at compile time.

SQL, embedded: An application structure in which SQL statements are embedded within programs written in a host language.

SQL, interactive: A real-time conversation with a database, using SQL statements.

SQL/DS: A relational database management system marketed by IBM Corporation.

subquery: A query within a query.

table: A relation.

TANSTAAFL: Acronym for "There Ain't No Such Thing As A Free Lunch." In the context of databases, it means that whenever you find a new way of doing something that has an advantage, a hidden disadvantage is probably mixed in there somewhere.

TCP/IP (Transmission Control Protocol/Internet Protocol): The network protocol used by the Internet and by intranets.

teleprocessing system: A powerful central processor connected to multiple dumb terminals.

transaction: A sequence of SQL statements whose effect is not accessible to other transactions until all the statements are executed.

transitive dependency: One attribute of a relation depends on a second attribute, which in turn depends on a third attribute.

translation table: Tool for converting character strings from one character set to another.

trigger: A small piece of code that tells a DBMS what additional actions to perform after certain SQL statements have been executed.

tuple: A group of attributes in a relation that all pertain to the same entity. Same as row and record.

update anomaly: A problem introduced into a database when a table row is updated.

users' model: The users' concept of the physical or conceptual system that they want to model with a database system.

validation rule: A rule that applies a constraint to the values that an attribute of a relation may take on.

value expression: An expression that combines two or more values.

value expression, conditional: A value expression that assigns different values to arguments, based on whether a condition is true.

value expression, datetime: A value expression that deals with DATE, TIME, TIMESTAMP, or INTERVAL data.

value expression, numeric: A value expression that combines numeric values using the addition, subtraction, multiplication, or division operators.

value expression, string: A value expression that combines character strings with the concatenation operator.

value function: A function that performs an operation on a single character string, number, or datetime.

VBScript: A Microsoft scripting language that is a subset of Visual Basic for Applications, with functionality comparable to that of JavaScript.

view: A database component that behaves exactly like a table but has no independent existence of its own.

virtual table: A view.

weak entity: See **entity, weak**.

wizard: A tool provided by software development software packages that automates one of a variety of procedures.

World Wide Web: An aspect of the Internet that has a graphical user interface. The Web is accessed by applications called *Web browsers,* and information is provided to the Web by installations called *Web servers.*

XML: An acronym for eXtensible Markup Language. In contrast to HTML, with XML you can create your own tags, which convey meaning about the objects they contain rather than merely specifying formatting.

Index

Notes

Notes

Notes

Notes

Notes

Notes

Notes

Notes

Notes

Notes

Dummies Books™
Bestsellers on Every Topic!

GENERAL INTEREST TITLES

BUSINESS & PERSONAL FINANCE

Title	Author	ISBN	Price
ccounting For Dummies®	John A. Tracy, CPA	0-7645-5014-4	$19.99 US/$27.99 CAN
usiness Plans For Dummies®	Paul Tiffany, Ph.D. & Steven D. Peterson, Ph.D.	1-56884-868-4	$19.99 US/$27.99 CAN
usiness Writing For Dummies®	Sheryl Lindsell-Roberts	0-7645-5134-5	$16.99 US/$27.99 CAN
onsulting For Dummies®	Bob Nelson & Peter Economy	0-7645-5034-9	$19.99 US/$27.99 CAN
ustomer Service For Dummies®, 2nd Edition	Karen Leland & Keith Bailey	0-7645-5209-0	$19.99 US/$27.99 CAN
ranchising For Dummies®	Dave Thomas & Michael Seid	0-7645-5160-4	$19.99 US/$27.99 CAN
etting Results For Dummies®	Mark H. McCormack	0-7645-5205-8	$19.99 US/$27.99 CAN
ome Buying For Dummies®	Eric Tyson, MBA & Ray Brown	1-56884-385-2	$16.99 US/$24.99 CAN
ouse Selling For Dummies®	Eric Tyson, MBA & Ray Brown	0-7645-5038-1	$16.99 US/$24.99 CAN
uman Resources Kit For Dummies®	Max Messmer	0-7645-5131-0	$19.99 US/$27.99 CAN
vesting For Dummies®, 2nd Edition	Eric Tyson, MBA	0-7645-5162-0	$19.99 US/$27.99 CAN
aw For Dummies®	John Ventura	1-56884-860-9	$19.99 US/$27.99 CAN
eadership For Dummies®	Marshall Loeb & Steven Kindel	0-7645-5176-0	$19.99 US/$27.99 CAN
anaging For Dummies®	Bob Nelson & Peter Economy	1-56884-858-7	$19.99 US/$27.99 CAN
arketing For Dummies®	Alexander Hiam	1-56884-699-1	$19.99 US/$27.99 CAN
utual Funds For Dummies®, 2nd Edition	Eric Tyson, MBA	0-7645-5112-4	$19.99 US/$27.99 CAN
egotiating For Dummies®	Michael C. Donaldson & Mimi Donaldson	1-56884-867-6	$19.99 US/$27.99 CAN
ersonal Finance For Dummies®, 3rd Edition	Eric Tyson, MBA	0-7645-5231-7	$19.99 US/$27.99 CAN
ersonal Finance For Dummies® For Canadians, 2nd Edition	Eric Tyson, MBA & Tony Martin	0-7645-5123-X	$19.99 US/$27.99 CAN
ublic Speaking For Dummies®	Malcolm Kushner	0-7645-5159-0	$16.99 US/$24.99 CAN
ales Closing For Dummies®	Tom Hopkins	0-7645-5063-2	$14.99 US/$21.99 CAN
ales Prospecting For Dummies®	Tom Hopkins	0-7645-5066-7	$14.99 US/$21.99 CAN
elling For Dummies®	Tom Hopkins	1-56884-389-5	$16.99 US/$24.99 CAN
mall Business For Dummies®	Eric Tyson, MBA & Jim Schell	0-7645-5094-2	$19.99 US/$27.99 CAN
mall Business Kit For Dummies®	Richard D. Harroch	0-7645-5093-4	$24.99 US/$34.99 CAN
axes 2001 For Dummies®	Eric Tyson & David J. Silverman	0-7645-5306-2	$15.99 US/$23.99 CAN
ime Management For Dummies®, 2nd Edition	Jeffrey J. Mayer	0-7645-5145-0	$19.99 US/$27.99 CAN
riting Business Letters For Dummies®	Sheryl Lindsell-Roberts	0-7645-5207-4	$16.99 US/$24.99 CAN

TECHNOLOGY TITLES

INTERNET/ONLINE

Title	Author	ISBN	Price
merica Online® For Dummies®, 6th Edition	John Kaufeld	0-7645-0670-6	$19.99 US/$27.99 CAN
aking Online Dummies®	Paul Murphy	0-7645-0458-4	$24.99 US/$34.99 CAN
ay™ For Dummies®, 2nd Edition	Marcia Collier, Roland Woerner, & Stephanie Becker	0-7645-0761-3	$19.99 US/$27.99 CAN
mail For Dummies®, 2nd Edition	John R. Levine, Carol Baroudi, & Arnold Reinhold	0-7645-0131-3	$24.99 US/$34.99 CAN
enealogy Online For Dummies®, 2nd Edition	Matthew L. Helm & April Leah Helm	0-7645-0543-2	$24.99 US/$34.99 CAN
ternet Directory For Dummies®, 3rd Edition	Brad Hill	0-7645-0558-2	$24.99 US/$34.99 CAN
ternet Auctions For Dummies®	Greg Holden	0-7645-0578-9	$24.99 US/$34.99 CAN
ternet Explorer 5.5 For Windows® For Dummies®	Doug Lowe	0-7645-0738-9	$19.99 US/$28.99 CAN
Searching Online For Dummies®, 2nd Edition	Mary Ellen Bates & Reva Basch	0-7645-0546-7	$24.99 US/$34.99 CAN
Searching Online For Dummies®	Pam Dixon	0-7645-0673-0	$24.99 US/$34.99 CAN
esting Online For Dummies®, 3rd Edition	Kathleen Sindell, Ph.D.	0-7645-0725-7	$24.99 US/$34.99 CAN
vel Planning Online For Dummies®, 2nd Edition	Noah Vadnai	0-7645-0438-X	$24.99 US/$34.99 CAN
ernet Searching For Dummies®	Brad Hill	0-7645-0478-9	$24.99 US/$34.99 CAN
oo!® For Dummies®, 2nd Edition	Brad Hill	0-7645-0762-1	$19.99 US/$27.99 CAN
Internet For Dummies®, 7th Edition	John R. Levine, Carol Baroudi, & Arnold Reinhold	0-7645-0674-9	$19.99 US/$27.99 CAN

OPERATING SYSTEMS

Title	Author	ISBN	Price
s For Dummies®, 3rd Edition	Dan Gookin	0-7645-0361-8	$19.99 US/$27.99 CAN
NOME For Linux® For Dummies®	David B. Busch	0-7645-0650-1	$24.99 US/$37.99 CAN
NUX® For Dummies®, 2nd Edition	John Hall, Craig Witherspoon, & Coletta Witherspoon	0-7645-0421-5	$24.99 US/$34.99 CAN
ac® OS 9 For Dummies®	Bob LeVitus	0-7645-0652-8	$19.99 US/$28.99 CAN
ed Hat® Linux® For Dummies®	Jon "maddog" Hall	0-7645-0663-3	$24.99 US/$37.99 CAN
mall Business Windows® 98 For Dummies®	Stephen Nelson	0-7645-0425-8	$24.99 US/$34.99 CAN
NIX® For Dummies®, 4th Edition	John R. Levine & Margaret Levine Young	0-7645-0419-3	$19.99 US/$27.99 CAN
indows® 95 For Dummies®, 2nd Edition	Andy Rathbone	0-7645-0180-1	$19.99 US/$27.99 CAN
indows® 98 For Dummies®	Andy Rathbone	0-7645-0261-1	$19.99 US/$27.99 CAN
indows® 2000 For Dummies®	Andy Rathbone	0-7645-0641-2	$19.99 US/$27.99 CAN
indows® 2000 Server For Dummies®	Ed Tittle	0-7645-0341-3	$24.99 US/$37.99 CAN
indows® ME Millenium Edition For Dummies®	Andy Rathbone	0-7645-0735-4	$19.99 US/$27.99 CAN

Dummies Books™
Bestsellers on Every Topic!

GENERAL INTEREST TITLES

FOOD & BEVERAGE/ENTERTAINING

Bartending For Dummies®	Ray Foley	0-7645-5051-9	$14.99 US/$21.99 CAN
Cooking For Dummies®, 2nd Edition	Bryan Miller & Marie Rama	0-7645-5250-3	$19.99 US/$27.99 CAN
Entertaining For Dummies®	Suzanne Williamson with Linda Smith	0-7645-5027-6	$19.99 US/$27.99 CAN
Gourmet Cooking For Dummies®	Charlie Trotter	0-7645-5029-2	$19.99 US/$27.99 CAN
Grilling For Dummies®	Marie Rama & John Mariani	0-7645-5076-4	$19.99 US/$27.99 CAN
Italian Cooking For Dummies®	Cesare Casella & Jack Bishop	0-7645-5098-5	$19.99 US/$27.99 CAN
Mexican Cooking For Dummies®	Mary Sue Miliken & Susan Feniger	0-7645-5169-8	$19.99 US/$27.99 CAN
Quick & Healthy Cooking For Dummies®	Lynn Fischer	0-7645-5214-7	$19.99 US/$27.99 CAN
Wine For Dummies®, 2nd Edition	Ed McCarthy & Mary Ewing-Mulligan	0-7645-5114-0	$19.99 US/$27.99 CAN
Chinese Cooking For Dummies®	Martin Yan	0-7645-5247-3	$19.99 US/$27.99 CAN
Etiquette For Dummies®	Sue Fox	0-7645-5170-1	$19.99 US/$27.99 CAN

SPORTS

Baseball For Dummies®, 2nd Edition	Joe Morgan with Richard Lally	0-7645-5234-1	$19.99 US/$27.99 CAN
Golf For Dummies®, 2nd Edition	Gary McCord	0-7645-5146-9	$19.99 US/$27.99 CAN
Fly Fishing For Dummies®	Peter Kaminsky	0-7645-5073-X	$19.99 US/$27.99 CAN
Football For Dummies®	Howie Long with John Czarnecki	0-7645-5054-3	$19.99 US/$27.99 CAN
Hockey For Dummies®	John Davidson with John Steinbreder	0-7645-5045-4	$19.99 US/$27.99 CAN
NASCAR For Dummies®	Mark Martin	0-7645-5219-8	$19.99 US/$27.99 CAN
Tennis For Dummies®	Patrick McEnroe with Peter Bodo	0-7645-5087-X	$19.99 US/$27.99 CAN
Soccer For Dummies®	U.S. Soccer Federation & Michael Lewiss	0-7645-5229-5	$19.99 US/$27.99 CAN

HOME & GARDEN

Annuals For Dummies®	Bill Marken & NGA	0-7645-5056-X	$16.99 US/$24.99 CAN
Container Gardening For Dummies®	Bill Marken & NGA	0-7645-5057-8	$16.99 US/$24.99 CAN
Decks & Patios For Dummies®	Robert J. Beckstrom & NGA	0-7645-5075-6	$16.99 US/$24.99 CAN
Flowering Bulbs For Dummies®	Judy Glattstein & NGA	0-7645-5103-5	$16.99 US/$24.99 CAN
Gardening For Dummies®, 2nd Edition	Michael MacCaskey & NGA	0-7645-5130-2	$16.99 US/$24.99 CAN
Herb Gardening For Dummies®	NGA	0-7645-5200-7	$16.99 US/$24.99 CAN
Home Improvement For Dummies®	Gene & Katie Hamilton & the Editors of HouseNet, Inc.	0-7645-5005-5	$19.99 US/$26.99 CAN
Houseplants For Dummies®	Larry Hodgson & NGA	0-7645-5102-7	$16.99 US/$24.99 CAN
Painting and Wallpapering For Dummies®	Gene Hamilton	0-7645-5150-7	$16.99 US/$24.99 CAN
Perennials For Dummies®	Marcia Tatroe & NGA	0-7645-5030-6	$16.99 US/$24.99 CAN
Roses For Dummies®, 2nd Edition	Lance Walheim	0-7645-5202-3	$16.99 US/$24.99 CAN
Trees and Shrubs For Dummies®	Ann Whitman & NGA	0-7645-5203-1	$16.99 US/$24.99 CAN
Vegetable Gardening For Dummies®	Charlie Nardozzi & NGA	0-7645-5129-9	$16.99 US/$24.99 CAN
Home Cooking For Dummies®	Patricia Hart McMillan & Katharine Kaye McMillan	0-7645-5107-8	$19.99 US/$27.99 CAN

TECHNOLOGY TITLES

WEB DESIGN & PUBLISHING

Active Server Pages For Dummies®, 2nd Edition	Bill Hatfield	0-7645-0603-X	$24.99 US/$37.99 CAN
Cold Fusion 4 For Dummies®	Alexis Gutzman	0-7645-0604-8	$24.99 US/$37.99 CAN
Creating Web Pages For Dummies®, 5th Edition	Bud Smith & Arthur Bebak	0-7645-0733-8	$24.99 US/$34.99 CAN
Dreamweaver™ 3 For Dummies®	Janine Warner & Paul Vachier	0-7645-0669-2	$24.99 US/$34.99 CAN
FrontPage® 2000 For Dummies®	Asha Dornfest	0-7645-0423-1	$24.99 US/$34.99 CAN
HTML 4 For Dummies®, 3rd Edition	Ed Tittel & Natanya Dits	0-7645-0572-6	$24.99 US/$34.99 CAN
Java™ For Dummies®, 3rd Edition	Aaron E. Walsh	0-7645-0417-7	$24.99 US/$34.99 CAN
PageMill™ 2 For Dummies®	Deke McClelland & John San Filippo	0-7645-0028-7	$24.99 US/$34.99 CAN
XML™ For Dummies®	Ed Tittel	0-7645-0692-7	$24.99 US/$37.99 CAN
Javascript For Dummies®, 3rd Edition	Emily Vander Veer	0-7645-0633-1	$24.99 US/$37.99 CAN

DESKTOP PUBLISHING GRAPHICS/MULTIMEDIA

Adobe® In Design™ For Dummies®	Deke McClelland	0-7645-0599-8	$19.99 US/$27.99 CAN
CorelDRAW™ 9 For Dummies®	Deke McClelland	0-7645-0523-8	$19.99 US/$27.99 CAN
Desktop Publishing and Design For Dummies®	Roger C. Parker	1-56884-234-1	$19.99 US/$27.99 CAN
Digital Photography For Dummies®, 3rd Edition	Julie Adair King	0-7645-0646-3	$24.99 US/$37.99 CAN
Microsoft® Publisher 98 For Dummies®	Jim McCarter	0-7645-0395-2	$19.99 US/$27.99 CAN
Visio 2000 For Dummies®	Debbie Walkowski	0-7645-0635-8	$19.99 US/$27.99 CAN
Microsoft® Publisher 2000 For Dummies®	Jim McCarter	0-7645-0525-4	$19.99 US/$27.99 CAN
Windows® Movie Maker For Dummies®	Keith Underdahl	0-7645-0749-1	$19.99 US/$27.99 CAN

Dummies Books™
Bestsellers on Every Topic!

GENERAL INTEREST TITLES

EDUCATION & TEST PREPARATION

Title	Author	ISBN	Price
he ACT For Dummies®	Suzee Vlk	1-56884-387-9	$14.99 US/$21.99 CAN
ollege Financial Aid For Dummies®	Dr. Herm Davis & Joyce Lain Kennedy	0-7645-5049-7	$19.99 US/$27.99 CAN
ollege Planning For Dummies®, 2nd Edition	Pat Ordovensky	0-7645-5048-9	$19.99 US/$27.99 CAN
veryday Math For Dummies®	Charles Seiter, Ph.D.	1-56884-248-1	$14.99 US/$21.99 CAN
e GMAT® For Dummies®, 3rd Edition	Suzee Vlk	0-7645-5082-9	$16.99 US/$24.99 CAN
e GRE® For Dummies®, 3rd Edition	Suzee Vlk	0-7645-5083-7	$16.99 US/$24.99 CAN
litics For Dummies®	Ann DeLaney	1-56884-381-X	$19.99 US/$27.99 CAN
e SAT I For Dummies®, 3rd Edition	Suzee Vlk	0-7645-5044-6	$14.99 US/$21.99 CAN

AUTOMOTIVE

Title	Author	ISBN	Price
to Repair For Dummies®	Deanna Sclar	0-7645-5089-6	$19.99 US/$27.99 CAN
ying A Car For Dummies®	Deanna Sclar	0-7645-5091-8	$16.99 US/$24.99 CAN

LIFESTYLE/SELF-HELP

Title	Author	ISBN	Price
ting For Dummies®	Dr. Joy Browne	0-7645-5072-1	$19.99 US/$27.99 CAN
king Marriage Work For Dummies®	Steven Simring, M.D. & Sue Klavans Simring, D.S.W	0-7645-5173-6	$19.99 US/$27.99 CAN
renting For Dummies®	Sandra H. Gookin	1-56884-383-6	$16.99 US/$24.99 CAN
ccess For Dummies®	Zig Ziglar	0-7645-5061-6	$19.99 US/$27.99 CAN
ddings For Dummies®	Marcy Blum & Laura Fisher Kaiser	0-7645-5055-1	$19.99 US/$27.99 CAN

TECHNOLOGY TITLES

SUITES

Title	Author	ISBN	Price
crosoft® Office 2000 For Windows® For Dummies®	Wallace Wang & Roger C. Parker	0-7645-0452-5	$19.99 US/$27.99 CAN
rosoft® Office 2000 For Windows® For Dummies® Quick Reference	Doug Lowe & Bjoern Hartsfvang	0-7645-0453-3	$12.99 US/$17.99 CAN
rosoft® Office 97 For Windows® For Dummies®	Wallace Wang & Roger C. Parker	0-7645-0050-3	$19.99 US/$27.99 CAN
rosoft® Office 97 For Windows® For Dummies® Quick Reference	Doug Lowe	0-7645-0062-7	$12.99 US/$17.99 CAN
rosoft® Office 98 For Macs® For Dummies®	Tom Negrino	0-7645-0229-8	$19.99 US/$27.99 CAN
rosoft® Office X For Macs For Dummies®	Tom Negrino	0-7645-0702-8	$19.95 US/$27.99 CAN

WORD PROCESSING

Title	Author	ISBN	Price
d 2000 For Windows® For Dummies® Quick Reference	Peter Weverka	0-7645-0449-5	$12.99 US/$19.99 CAN
el® WordPerfect® 8 For Windows® For Dummies®	Margaret Levine Young, David Kay & Jordan Young	0-7645-0186-0	$19.99 US/$27.99 CAN
d 2000 For Windows® For Dummies®	Dan Gookin	0-7645-0448-7	$19.99 US/$27.99 CAN
d For Windows® 95 For Dummies®	Dan Gookin	1-56884-932-X	$19.99 US/$27.99 CAN
d 97 For Windows® For Dummies®	Dan Gookin	0-7645-0052-X	$19.99 US/$27.99 CAN
dPerfect® 9 For Windows® For Dummies®	Margaret Levine Young	0-7645-0427-4	$19.99 US/$27.99 CAN
dPerfect® 7 For Windows® 95 For Dummies®	Margaret Levine Young & David Kay	1-56884-949-4	$19.99 US/$27.99 CAN

SPREADSHEET/FINANCE/PROJECT MANAGEMENT

Title	Author	ISBN	Price
l For Windows® 95 For Dummies®	Greg Harvey	1-56884-930-3	$19.99 US/$27.99 CAN
l 2000 For Windows® For Dummies®	Greg Harvey	0-7645-0446-0	$19.99 US/$27.99 CAN
l 2000 For Windows® For Dummies® Quick Reference	John Walkenbach	0-7645-0447-9	$12.99 US/$17.99 CAN
osoft® Money 99 For Dummies®	Peter Weverka	0-7645-0433-9	$19.99 US/$27.99 CAN
osoft® Project 98 For Dummies®	Martin Doucette	0-7645-0321-9	$24.99 US/$34.99 CAN
osoft® Project 2000 For Dummies®	Martin Doucette	0-7645-0517-3	$24.99 US/$37.99 CAN
osoft® Money 2000 For Dummies®	Peter Weverka	0-7645-0579-3	$19.99 US/$27.99 CAN
E Excel 97 For Windows® For Dummies®	Greg Harvey	0-7645-0138-0	$22.99 US/$32.99 CAN
ken® 2000 For Dummies®	Stephen L. Nelson	0-7645-0607-2	$19.99 US/$27.99 CAN
ken® 2001 For Dummies®	Stephen L. Nelson	0-7645-0759-1	$19.99 US/$27.99 CAN
kbooks® 2000 For Dummies®	Stephen L. Nelson	0-7645-0665-x	$19.99 US/$27.99 CAN

Dummies Books™
Bestsellers on Every Topic!

GENERAL INTEREST TITLES

CAREERS

Cover Letters For Dummies®, 2nd Edition	Joyce Lain Kennedy	0-7645-5224-4	$12.99 US/$17.99 CAN
Cool Careers For Dummies®	Marty Nemko, Paul Edwards, & Sarah Edwards	0-7645-5095-0	$16.99 US/$24.99 CAN
Job Hunting For Dummies®, 2nd Edition	Max Messmer	0-7645-5163-9	$19.99 US/$26.99 CAN
Job Interviews For Dummies®, 2nd Edition	Joyce Lain Kennedy	0-7645-5225-2	$12.99 US/$17.99 CAN
Resumes For Dummies®, 2nd Edition	Joyce Lain Kennedy	0-7645-5113-2	$12.99 US/$17.99 CAN

FITNESS

Fitness Walking For Dummies®	Liz Neporent	0-7645-5192-2	$19.99 US/$27.99 CAN
Fitness For Dummies®, 2nd Edition	Suzanne Schlosberg & Liz Neporent	0-7645-5167-1	$19.99 US/$27.99 CAN
Nutrition For Dummies®, 2nd Edition	Carol Ann Rinzler	0-7645-5180-9	$19.99 US/$27.99 CAN
Running For Dummies®	Florence "Flo-Jo" Griffith Joyner & John Hanc	0-7645-5096-9	$19.99 US/$27.99 CAN

FOREIGN LANGUAGE

Spanish For Dummies®	Susana Wald	0-7645-5194-9	$24.99 US/$34.99 CAN
French For Dummies®	Dodi-Kartrin Schmidt & Michelle W. Willams	0-7645-5193-0	$24.99 US/$34.99 CAN

TECHNOLOGY TITLES

DATABASSE

Access 2000 For Windows® For Dummies®	John Kaufeld	0-7645-0444-4	$19.99 US/$27.99 CAN
Access 97 For Windows® For Dummies®	John Kaufeld	0-7645-0048-1	$19.99 US/$27.99 CAN
Access 2000 For Windows For Dummies® Quick Reference	Alison Barrons	0-7645-0445-2	$12.99 US/$17.99 CAN
Approach® 97 For Windows® For Dummies®	Deborah S. Ray & Eric J. Ray	0-7645-0001-5	$19.99 US/$27.99 CAN
Crystal Reports 8 For Dummies®	Douglas J. Wolf	0-7645-0642-0	$24.99 US/$34.99 CAN
Data Warehousing For Dummies®	Alan R. Simon	0-7645-0170-4	$24.99 US/$34.99 CAN
FileMaker® Pro 4 For Dummies®	Tom Maremaa	0-7645-0210-7	$19.99 US/$27.99 CAN

NETWORKING/GROUPWARE

ATM For Dummies®	Cathy Gadecki & Christine Heckart	0-7645-0065-1	$24.99 US/$34.99 CAN
Client/Server Computing For Dummies®, 3rd Edition	Doug Lowe	0-7645-0476-2	$24.99 US/$34.99 CAN
DSL For Dummies®, 2nd Edition	David Angell	0-7645-0715-X	$24.99 US/$35.99 CAN
Lotus Notes® Release 4 For Dummies®	Stephen Londergan & Pat Freeland	1-56884-934-6	$19.99 US/$27.99 CAN
Microsoft® Outlook® 98 For Windows® For Dummies®	Bill Dyszel	0-7645-0393-6	$19.99 US/$28.99 CAN
Microsoft® Outlook® 2000 For Windows® For Dummies®	Bill Dyszel	0-7645-0471-1	$19.99 US/$27.99 CAN
Migrating to Windows® 2000 For Dummies®	Leonard Sterns	0-7645-0459-2	$24.99 US/$37.99 CAN
Networking For Dummies®, 4th Edition	Doug Lowe	0-7645-0498-3	$19.99 US/$27.99 CAN
Networking Home PCs For Dummies®	Kathy Ivens	0-7645-0491-6	$24.99 US/$35.99 CAN
Upgrading & Fixing Networks For Dummies®, 2nd Edition	Bill Camarda	0-7645-0542-4	$29.99 US/$42.99 CAN
TCP/IP For Dummies®, 4th Edition	Candace Leiden & Marshall Wilensky	0-7645-0726-5	$24.99 US/$35.99 CAN
Windows NT® Networking For Dummies®	Ed Tittel, Mary Madden, & Earl Follis	0-7645-0015-5	$24.99 US/$34.99 CAN

PROGRAMMING

Active Server Pages For Dummies®, 2nd Edition	Bill Hatfield	0-7645-0065-1	$24.99 US/$34.99 CAN
Beginning Programming For Dummies®	Wally Wang	0-7645-0596-0	$19.99 US/$29.99 CAN
C++ For Dummies® Quick Reference, 2nd Edition	Namir Shammas	0-7645-0390-1	$14.99 US/$21.99 CAN
Java™ Programming For Dummies®, 3rd Edition	David & Donald Koosis	0-7645-0388-X	$29.99 US/$42.99 CAN
JBuilder™ For Dummies®	Barry A. Burd	0-7645-0567-X	$24.99 US/$34.99 CAN
VBA For Dummies®, 2nd Edition	Steve Cummings	0-7645-0078-3	$24.99 US/$37.99 CAN
Windows® 2000 Programming For Dummies®	Richard Simon	0-7645-0469-X	$24.99 US/$37.99 CAN
XML For Dummies®, 2nd Edition	Ed Tittel	0-7645-0692-7	$24.99 US/$37.99 CAN

IDG BOOKS WORLDWIDE
BOOK REGISTRATION

We want to hear from you!

Visit **http://my2cents.dummies.com** to register this book and tell us how you liked it!

- ✔ Get entered in our monthly prize giveaway.

- ✔ Give us feedback about this book — tell us what you like best, what you like least, or maybe what you'd like to ask the author and us to change!

- ✔ Let us know any other *For Dummies*® topics that interest you.

Your feedback helps us determine what books to publish, tells us what coverage to add as we revise our books, and lets us know whether we're meeting your needs as a *For Dummies* reader. You're our most valuable resource, and what you have to say is important to us!

Not on the Web yet? It's easy to get started with *Dummies 101*®: *The Internet For Windows*® *98* or *The Internet For Dummies*® at local retailers everywhere.

Or let us know what you think by sending us a letter at the following address:

For Dummies Book Registration
Dummies Press
10475 Crosspoint Blvd.
Indianapolis, IN 46256

BESTSELLING
BOOK SERIES